The Life of
Glückel of Hameln

University of Nebraska Press
Lincoln

The Life of
Glückel of Hameln

A MEMOIR

Glückel

*Translated from the original Yiddish
and edited by*
BETH-ZION ABRAHAMS

The Jewish Publication Society
Philadelphia

Manufactured in the United States of America

Library of Congress Cataloging-in-Publication Data

Glueckel, of Hameln, 1646–1724
[Zikhroynes. English]
The life of Glückel of Hameln: a memoir / Glückel; translated from the original Yiddish and edited by Beth-Zion Abrahams.
  p. cm.
Includes index.
ISBN 978-0-8276-0943-3 (pbk.: alk. paper) 1. Glueckel, of Hameln, 1646–1724. 2. Jews—Germany—Biography. 3. Jewish women—Germany—Biography. I. Abrahams, Beth-Zion. II. Title.
DS134.42.G58A3 2012
305.892'40435954—dc23
[B] 2012025405

IN
CHERISHED REMEMBRANCE
OF
MY MOTHER
EVA COHEN-LASK
DAUGHTER OF
HINDA (NEÉ KOVALSKY)
AND ISRAEL MEÏR TAUB

*Her living example taught
me to appreciate the qualities
she shared with
Glückel of Hameln.*

When shall their like rise again?

BETH-ZION ABRAHAMS

INTRODUCTION

GLÜCKEL, daughter of Beila and Leib Pinkerle and wife of Chaim Segal of Hameln, began to write the story of her life in 1689. Her aim, she states, was 'to while away the long and melancholy nights' which tormented her after her husband's death, and to inform her children of their family and the stock from which they came. She could hardly have imagined that her narrative would become a classic of its kind two hundred years afterwards, nor could she have foreseen that her grief at the death of her beloved husband would lead her to give so inimitable an account not only of her own life and immediate circle, but equally of her period. What she provided is unique of its kind. It is a cross-section of Jewish history in the Germany of her time. A history which, beginning with the Roman settlement of the Rhineland considerably more than a thousand years before, assumed a fresh form following the Enlightenment and Emancipation in the decades after her own days, and was brought to its cataclysmic end under Hitler and the Nazis in our own time.

Glückel, who died at the age of seventy-eight on September 19, 1724, ended her narrative with the year 1719. Her tale is told in Jüdisch-Deutsch, the dialect spoken and written in Hebrew characters by the Jews of Central and Eastern Europe in those days. It derived from Middle High German and had more than fifteen per cent of Hebrew to spice and flavour it. It became the forebear of the modern Yiddish, which was the vernacular of East European Jews before the extermination of the Yiddish-speaking communities during the Second World War.

Glückel[1] was born in Hamburg in 1646, two years before the termination of the Thirty Years War, which devastated vast areas of Germany, impoverished many ancient cities and communities and resulted in great suffering and hardship for the German Jews of the time. They lived on a contractual basis, so to say, with rulers of states, duchies and principalities, and in

[1] The name Glückel (pronounced Glickel)—variously spelt Glueckel, Glickel, Glikel, Glikl—is derived from the German noun *das Glück*, denoting luck, good fortune, happiness.

some cases with the free cities, which then helped to make up Germany; and in each community, they were dependent on the grace and good will of the local rulers.

As the Thirty Years War drew to its exhausted end in 1648, a flood of Jewish refugees fled from Poland, escaping from the Cossacks who had risen under their leader Bogdan Chmielnicki, and seeking a haven among their brethren in Germany. From the other side of Europe there was still more than a trickle of Marranos seeping out of the Iberian Peninsula and the Spanish and Portuguese empires. These Marranos, known in their countries of origin as New Christians, were descendants of the Spanish and Portuguese Jews who during the fifteenth century had been forcibly converted to Christianity. They were suspected of adhering to Jewish beliefs and practices in secret—as indeed many did—and were accordingly subjected to the special attentions of the Holy Office of the Inquisition. Those who were able to leave the Spanish and Portuguese territories in the seventeenth century made their way, either directly or via the West Indies, to Amsterdam and Hamburg, where Sephardi communities had long been established. In Hamburg, Sephardi Jews had residential and other privileges in recognition of the exceedingly important part they played in promoting the commercial and overseas trade of the city. (As Glückel herself comments, the Ashkenazi or German-speaking Jewish community, to which she herself belonged, had no right of domicile there.)

In 1654, when she was eight years old, the first Jewish immigrants, also from the West Indies, arrived in New Amsterdam, the later New York; and a year after Rabbi Manasseh ben Israel proceeded from Amsterdam to London in order to canvass for the legal re-admission of the Jews to England, whence they had been expelled in 1290. Though there was no Jewish press at the time, news spread with remarkable speed from one community to another.

Glückel's world differed greatly from our own; and indeed, nothing makes this clearer than her narrative itself. It was a world which knew the horrors and perils of warfare no less than our own. In addition there was the perpetual menace of plague and pestilence, the danger of fire desolating the narrow streets of cities; the travel by wagon or on foot along bad roads, with footpads lurking in wait for the solitary traveller. People tended to rise and to go to bed with the sun, even in the cities. Food supplies were far scantier and less varied than now. In Glückel's childhood tea, coffee and cocoa must still have been virtually if not entirely unknown, though the situation had changed considerably by the end of her life.

All that, however, was part of the external world, which was shared by Jew and Gentile alike. For the Jews as such there were certain other elements which made their life vastly different from that of their neighbours. To begin with, their religious faith taught them, and they believed beyond the shadow of a doubt, that they were in exile and must suffer that exile as their fathers had done before them. Their faith taught them also that the Lord had chosen them from among mankind for His own mysterious reasons, and that as a result certain responsibilities and definite duties were imposed upon them.

They practically all lived within their own Jewries or ghettoes, even when this was not required of them by the law and even when no visible walls cut them off from their surroundings. What was important for them was that in those close quarters they could live their own life to the very utmost within the four ells of the Torah, with none to mock or say them nay. From there they could sally forth for their business dealings with the outer world—and Glückel makes the nature of some of those dealings very clear.

Yet even if the Jews were aware of the social aspects of the outer world, they do not seem to have missed them. Theirs was a rich and full life, albeit they had to accept the fact of exile which had commenced about sixteen hundred years earlier with the destruction of the Temple in Jerusalem but which, they knew by tradition, belief and above all by an inner conviction, was bound to end in Israel's return to the Land of their Fathers. This could come about at any time by the Grace of God or, alternatively, at the End of Days. To sum up, Glückel's politics, if the term may be used, came from the Bible in its traditional Jewish interpretation, from the Jewish Prayer-book and the works of the Sages of Israel throughout the ages. And by these Glückel lived her daily life together with all other Jews, in a present that was to all intents and purposes outside local and world history.

The needs of Jewry were shaped by the harsh and difficult conditions of having to buy rights of domicile and permission to transact business. What the Rhineland rulers had described hundreds of years earlier as the 'sponge policy' towards the Jews was still being followed to a very considerable degree. They were allowed to absorb the money required by the rulers which was then squeezed from them by varying degrees of pressure. Since the Jews of those days were presumably at least as intelligent as their descendants, they were quite aware of this situation but did not waste their time complaining about things that they could not help. This is clearly shown throughout by Glückel, who has no illusions about the position and status of moneyless Jews. It also accounts for the overriding need for money, even as a kind of insurance for future well-being. Children were betrothed and married in their early teens, long before they were capable of providing for their own needs or those of a family. The dowries which play so large a part in Glückel's story were no luxury, but a necessity, a provision for the future and a capital sum for starting business on one's own. While they were still young, such youthful couples lived with one or the other set of parents, learning the facts of daily life from them, until some opportunity arose which enabled them to begin their own independent career.

Glückel herself was twelve years old when she was betrothed, and fourteen when she married Chaim, the son of Joseph Baruch the Levite, known in official documents as Jost Goldschmidt, a wealthy dealer in gems and a worker in precious metals, as his official name denotes. Joseph Baruch lived in Hameln on the river Weser, a small town in Hanover which English readers will remember as the Hamelin town of Robert Browning's *Pied Piper*. Owing to the vicissitudes of the Thirty Years War the one-time Jewish community of the city had been reduced to no more than two families of which her father-in-law's was one.

Whenever Glückel refers to her husband and other Jews of standing it is by the term Reb, the abbreviation of 'Rabbi' and more or less the equivalent of 'Master' in the Elizabethan or Tudor sense. It is also her habit to refer to her husband as Segal, the initials of the Hebrew *Segan Leviyim, i.e.*, superior Temple Levite. In this way she denoted that he and their male children belonged to the tribe of Levi, though not of priestly stock like those bearing the name of Cohen—the Hebrew for priest.

Throughout her life Glückel retained her girlish wonder and enthusiasm at the piety of her father-in-law, together with her admiration for his other qualities. Still, there were only two Jewish families in Hameln, and after a year she began to long for the lively social activities of her native community. So she returned to Hamburg with Chaim, who was a young man starting in business on his own at the time. With him she lived for thirty years, bearing thirteen children, of whom only one died in infancy—an achievement at a time when infant mortality was so high. During the dreadful, grief-laden nights that followed Reb Chaim Segal's death, so poignantly described in Book Five, she began to write down the story of her life.

In all their years together Chaim never transacted any business without first consulting Glückel, who even drew up his business agreements. She herself had received her education in Cheder, the traditional Jewish school; and while it did not take her as far as the Talmud and Rabbinics, the basis of Jewish learning, she was certainly taught Hebrew and the rudiments of other necessary knowledge. Her own capacity for writing in Jewish vernacular is attested by her autobiography, and knowledge of the current and Jüdisch-Deutsch literature is evidenced by her reference to popular works of the period and the way she utilizes some of the current moralistic tales then so popular.

Jews prominent in the Germany of those days are referred to familiarly in these pages. Reb Chaim Segal's early partner, Jost Lieberman, afterwards Court Jew to the Great Elector, stands revealed as a strictly observant Jew who never lost his friendship for Glückel. Again there is her brother-in-law Lipman Cohen, familiar in official German circles as Leffman Behrens, who was held in high regard at the Guelphic Courts together with his sons after him.

Then there were the famous or notorious people outside her own immediate circle. She remembered, too, the sensational effect of Shabbatai Zevi, the false Messiah, whose renown and claims swept like wildfire in 1665 from Asia Minor and the Holy Land to the Jewish communities of Europe. The fervent belief in and conviction of the Messianic Redemption of Israel had indeed been strengthened by the sufferings of Polish Jewry in

1648 and the subsequent years, which were regarded by mystics, Kabbalists and everyday folk as the long-foretold 'birth-pangs of the Messiah'. Jewry was filled with the hope of an imminent return and restoration to the Holy Land. Indeed, following the tidings of this 'Messiah', Glückel's parents-in-law sent two large casks to Hamburg. One was filled with food, the other with linen and clothing; and they were to be kept until the summons came to set triumphant sail from the port of Hamburg to the Holy Land.

Life was insecure throughout. Jewry continued to balance, from Glückel's birth until her death, on the thin edge of permits and business risks on the one hand, withdrawal of permits and official pressures of various kinds, and the fear of recurrent 'Schueler-geleif' (student riots, as the pogroms of the period were known) on the other. Nevertheless the ever-resilient Jewish spirit insisted on asserting itself. Glückel set her trust in God, the enemy was routed or outlived in one way or another; and Glückel's Jüdisch-Deutsch runs on to the next episode, or returns again to a point where she had branched off to describe some incident that had come to mind, or to point a moral and adorn a tale.

She never strives after literary effect. Indeed she probably did not realize that there was such a thing. The story of her life flows on like a stream winding and twisting from place to place, running gaily through smooth and easy times, troubled when sorrow is her portion. Here and there she slips in a tale to stress a moral or impart some lesson to her children; for it must be remembered that she was writing for them. Above all she was a woman and a mother. When her husband Chaim died she still had to provide for eight orphans of tender years, while the other four older children, who already had married, were still in need of parental guidance. From this child there was much joy, from another heavy sorrow, but she watched over him and tended him; and made up her mind that when all the children were suitably married, please God, and she no longer needed to worry about their welfare, she would leave this erring world and go to the Holy Land in order to end her days in piety as was incumbent upon every Jewish woman.

Circumstances were too strong for her, however, and the many claims too urgent. Centuries before career women were dreamed of, Glückel was engaging in business, conducting financial transactions on the Exchange, attending fairs in different parts of the country and even running a stocking factory. But after ten years of widowhood when she was fifty-four years old, she began to feel that she could not rush around seeking business very much longer. Travelling to the winter fairs in bumping springless wagons along rutted tracks was becoming more and more of a strain. Apprehensive of old age, earlier then, when the expectation of life was so many years less than today, she yielded to the persuasion of her children and married again.

Her second husband was Hirsch Levy, president of the Jewish community of Metz and the foremost banker in the whole of Lorraine. She never writes of him with the warmth she uses for her beloved Reb Chaim Segal, who had been her family shepherd, the crown of her life, her beloved, her dearest, most precious friend. Hirsch Levy was a later, carefully considered and calculated, dispassionate choice; while her love for Reb Chaim was indelible, tempered and annealed in the happy formative years of her young womanhood.

But alas! Hirsch Levy lost his money within a year, together with the funds entrusted to him by Glückel and her children. She whose proud boast had been that she owed nobody, neither gentile nor Jew, even as much as the meanest coin, found that her husband could not meet his commitments, and could not pay his creditors because he was bankrupt. She admits quite frankly that she had married him solely because she desired a comfortable old age, and counted on the relationship proving of benefit to her children. His bankruptcy was a bitter blow indeed. In 1712 he died, after she had been married to him for twelve years.

Following the death of her second husband Glückel lived with her daughter and son-in-law, Esther and Moses Krum-Schwab, to whose betrothal she devotes a number of pages. It was in Metz that she ended her days.

In her own fortunes Glückel ran the gamut from riches to near-poverty. Yet any despair she felt was always coloured by the hope of betterment; and while she mourned those dear ones whom she had lost, she accepted their passing as the Will of God, and rejoiced at any good fortune enjoyed by the living. Always she respected and honoured Jewish scholarship and learning; and she lived her own life according to the teachings of the rabbinical sages of blessed memory.

Her narrative is based on her own experience and her own standard of values. True, many of her own kind and acquaintances were playing parts which proved to be of historic significance, yet that aspect of them hardly seems to have concerned her. Her task and her pleasure was to record their doings and sayings as she herself knew of them. It was out of her own personal experience that she wrote, to point the right and proper way for her own children to follow. Though there were great events going forward in her own land and elsewhere, she was concerned with them only in so far as they impinged on her own life and that of her immediate kin.

And so, above all else, Glückel of Hameln's autobiography is an individual and characteristic human story. In writing of herself and hers she not only displays herself as she wished her children to remember her, but also and unconsciously reveals herself to those of a later age. She stands in undress, in her domestic costume, visible in her griefs and afflictions, her joys and happinesses, revealing the lights and shades, the heights and depths; a woman worthy to become, as indeed she did become, an ancestress of many of the outstanding figures in later German Jewry. And in taking leave of Glückel one visualizes her—large and matronly, with wise face and the kindly, tolerant eyes with which experience sometimes endows the aged. The face is framed, maybe, by many chins and several rows of coral, or the seed pearls in which she traded when she was young. Pen in hand she traces her life in her book giving an account of the days of her years so that he who runs may read.

BETH-ZION ABRAHAMS

ACKNOWLEDGMENTS

IN 1896 the great Austrian-Jewish scholar Dr. David Kaufmann (1852–1899) published, in Frankfort-on-Main, the life-story of Glückel of Hameln under the title *Die Memoiren der Glückel von Hameln*. This was a transcription of the Jüdisch-Deutsch which had been copied by Glückel's son Moses, Rabbi of Baiersdorf, from his mother's original manuscript—her 'seven small books'. The publication of this unique life-story, the first written by a Jewish woman, made an immediate impact on the world of Jewish letters. It took its place at once as a classic and became the subject of innumerable studies—sociological, historical, philological, etc. Since its first appearance in print, the autobiography has been translated in whole or in part into Hebrew and modern Yiddish as well as German. The translation presented here is the first English version directly made from the original Jüdisch-Deutsch as transcribed by Kaufmann.

My attention was first called to Glückel's writing by my father Joseph Chaim Cohen-Lask, who loved Jewish letters profoundly. Without his knowledge and scholarly help in the elucidation of the many archaic terms and obsolete words in the text, as well as in tracing the numerous Hebrew references, my Englishing would not have been possible. This is written not merely out of filial regard, but with deep gratitude for his encouragement and active help; and with regret, alas, that he did not live to see this complete translation in print. And joined in this regret I cannot omit—if only in this glancing reference—to mention my husband.

Nor can I fail to mention with deep appreciation the late Dr. Bela Horovitz, whose keen interest in Glückel of Hameln's work, followed by the continued active participation of his wife Mrs. Lotte Horovitz, has brought this publication into being. My gratitude and thanks are also due to my brother Mr. I. M. Lask of Tel Aviv, Mr. and Mrs. H. Lewis, the late Mr. L. N. Cooper, Mr. Jacob Sonntag, Mr. Siegfried Oppenheimer and, by no means least, to that doyen of German-Jewish writers, my friend Mr. Hermann Schwab for their active and always sympathetic interest in the vicissitudes of Glückel of Hameln's saga in English.

B.-Z.A.

LIST OF ILLUSTRATIONS

Grateful acknowledgement is made to Mr. Alfred Rubens, London, and to all museums who have given permission for the reproduction of originals in their collections. Other reproductions are based on material owned by the editor and by the publishers.

BOOK I

IN the year of Creation 5451[1] I begin writing this with an aching heart, as will follow later. May the Lord make us rejoice as often as He has afflicted us and send our Messiah and Redeemer speedily. Amen.

All that the Lord has created, He created for His glory. The world was founded on loving-kindness. We know that the Almighty, blessed be He and blessed be His name, in His goodness and mercy created all things. He is not in need of any of His creations which He in His grace has made in diverse kinds for the use of us sinful mortals. Every created thing is of some use, more than we realize or imagine. King David, on whom be peace, asked, of what use are the fool, the wasp, and the spider in the world? But he found out in good time. First God and then these three saved his life—as is written in the Book of Kings. Anyone who wishes to know can read it in Holy Writ.

It is known that many pious people live sad and lonely lives, suffering hardship and misery in this passing world while, in contrast, rogues enjoy much honour and great comforts. They and theirs have riches while, on the other hand, it fares badly with the righteous and their children. We ponder: How is it that Almighty God, who is just, permits this? But this also, I think, is vanity, for it is impossible to penetrate God's actions and uncover their meaning.

Moses our Teacher, on whom be peace, wanted to find out and asked: *Make me know Thy ways.* But as even he could not attain this, we need not concern ourselves about them. In any case, this world, which is as naught, has been created solely because of the world-to-be. God in his manifold kindness has made the passings of this world to enable us to do good and serve Him well. Also, there is a limit of seventy years in this toilsome world, of preparation for the next; hundreds of thousands of people do not reach even this age. But the world-to-come exists for ever.

Oh how abundant is Thy goodness, which Thou hast laid up for them that fear Thee.[2] Happy is the one who has his reward in the everlasting world-to-come. The sorrows and troubles man suffers

---

[1] 1690–91 of the common era.　　　　[2] Psalm 31: 20.

I

here are temporary and last but a while. And when time has flown, the poor man, as does the rich man also, lays down his life—there is no difference. Furthermore, the poor man, who has suffered so much in his lifetime, dies in peace, for every day was for him a living death, ever hoping that it would fare better with him in the next world. And always thinking that God owed him this as his due. All his consolation lies in the future world: *When shall I come and see the face of the Lord?*

According to my limited understanding, I therefore think that his suffering is not too hard to bear.

But this is not so with the wealthy rogue who all his days has lusted after riches, his good being solely for himself. Nothing restrained him. When his time comes to leave this world and he reflects that, though God has given him everything, he has not used his riches for good as he should have done, woe unto him! How much harder then is his last journey than that of the poor man.

But, my dear children, what need to speak longer on this?

I began writing this, with the help of heaven, after the death of your pious father, to stifle and banish the melancholy thoughts which came to me during many sleepless nights. We are strayed sheep that have lost our faithful shepherd. I have spent many sleepless nights and for fear of falling into a melancholia, I arose in the wakeful hours and spent the time writing this.

I do not intend to write a book of morals, for I am not able to do so. Our wise men have written such books: and we have the Holy Torah,[1] from which we may learn what is useful and what will lead us from this to the future world.

We must hold fast to the Torah. As an example: a ship full of passengers sailed the seas. A passenger on deck leaning towards the waves, fell overboard and began to sink. Seeing this, the captain threw a rope and called to him to hold it tight and he would not drown. We in this world of sin are as if we swim in the sea, not knowing at which moment we may drown. But Almighty God who created us without sin—through the sins of Adam the Evil Spirit overpowers us—also created hosts of angels without any evil inclinations, to do His work. They do good only. Besides these, God created beast and fowl who know

[1] The word Torah is left untranslated. It means variously the Pentateuch, Scriptures, the oral law; also religious truth, study and practice.

nothing of good; and then man in His own image, with sense like the angels, but also with will to commit—God forbid—evil, or do good. But gracious God threw us a rope for our guidance, to which to hold fast and so save ourselves. This is our Holy Torah. Hold tight to it and you will not drown.

Our Holy Torah instructs us so that we shall not drown. How well it would be with us if we did good and were as righteous as the angels. The Torah guides us to the rewards for obeying the Commandments and the punishments for sinning—*therefore choose life* [Deut. 30: 19]. God forbid that we should not serve our Creator but live after the desire of our wicked hearts like the unknowing beasts that have no reward either in this or in the future world. If we do the same, God forbid, then we are worse than the beasts. When an animal falls and dies, it has no account to render to God. But as soon as the poor human being dies he must render his account to his Creator. Therefore well for us that we can prepare our accounts while yet we live: for well we know that we are sinful and evil desires rule us, for *There is not a righteous man upon earth that doeth good and sinneth not* [Eccles. 7: 20]. So, one should follow this path: as soon as he has committed a great or a minor sin, repent immediately and do penance, as our teachers of morals have written; so that the sin may be blotted out of his book of records and a merit be marked in its place. When the sinner lives on, doing naught but evil, and dies in sin, woe! For how will it fare with him in the world-to-come when his book of records is full of sins, and the opposite pages where the balance of repentance and good deeds should be, are blank! Therefore, you sinner, you are in debt. How will you repay your Creator who in very truth warned you?

Why then should I write of the tortures and sorrows that a sinful person must suffer, with what anxiety, bitter tears and suffering as long as he has to pay his debts because of his great sins? Because God is merciful and takes from the sinner his debts in this world if he pays them off singly. If, for instance, he does penance, prays, gives charity and does good deeds singly; thus he can pay off his debts in this world. God does not require that he should take his life through repentance. Everything must be seemly as our Sages write and as stands written in the Torah. And if a man acts thus, he makes clean his record in this world and in this way has no muddled accounts and can come with joy before his Maker. Almighty God is merciful, for, indeed, what difference need it be to Him if a man is righteous or is, God forbid, an evil-doer? Only and only out of His great mercy and loving kindness he Has done this for us, as a *father has mercy on his children.*

We are His children. The Holy One, blessed be He, will show us mercy if only we pray *Father have mercy on His children.* God forbid if the Holy One had no more mercy on us than a human father has for his children! If a man has an evil child he helps and takes trouble over him two, three times but at length grows tired and thrusts the child from him, even though he knows it means his ruin. But we poor children sin against our Heavenly Father all the time, every hour, every minute. But the Heavenly Father through His mercy lets us know when we are be-smirched with sins. And if we call on Him in true repentance He takes us again to His heart, not as does a human father his evil child.

So, my heart-beloved children, do not give up hope, but be penitent, charitable and pray, and God will protect you, for His mercy is great. The Lord God of mercy is long-suffering, as well for the wicked as for the richest who does penance in time. Everyone should try his utmost not to sin, for every sin is a wrong to God. If it is a merit to obey the commandment en-joining us to honour our parents, how much more so should we heed lest we anger our Heavenly Father who created us and our parents? We were created naked and bare. He gave us life, food, drink, clothed us and sees to all our needs with a full hand. Even if one has more and another less in this world, we cannot judge, for many merits He repays in this world and others He rewards in the world-to-come. Be assured that Almighty, Beneficent God misses nothing. If it does not go well with the righteous in this world, in the future world, rest assured, all will bear interest. Then, all the pleasures and riches he, *nebbich*,[1] was denied here, which he saw many wicked men enjoying while the devout had not even bread enough to satisfy himself and which he accepted meekly, even thanking his Maker the while, all will be his. When he stands at length before the Highest Judge he will learn why things go contrarily for the pious yet well for puffed-up haughty ones and the wicked. Then he will learn that

[1] Term of commiseration, in place of *poor thing*; *alas*; *shame!*

piety is right and will praise and thank the All Highest who punishes us for our own good, for we are sinful and bad children whom God would train to be good, obedient children, servants to a gracious Lord and Father. So He punishes us that we may learn to go His way. The good that He has given us we have not deserved and cannot serve Him enough for all that He has done. These are too many for me to write, yet we must remember that everything we have is from Him—free gifts bestowed. And if we are sometimes punished, it is because of our own misdeeds. We must accept all with love—as you will read in the story of the doctor.

I found this story in the book of morals written by the Gaon Abraham, son of Reb Shabbatai Levi. If the Holy One, blessed be He, bestows sorrows and troubles, this portion must be accepted for good.

There was once a clever man, a physician, who was held in high esteem by a certain king. On one occasion he displeased the king, who angrily ordered that he should be cast in prison, castigated and tortured, and irons riveted to his neck and feet. His fine clothes were taken from him and rough, prickly garments given in their place. For food he was given a slice of barley bread and a measure of water daily. The king ordered the keepers of the prison to guard the physician well, listen to his talk and report, every few days, what they heard.

Some time later the keepers came to the king and told him that they had nothing to report as the physician had said nothing. 'We have felt all the while that he is a very wise man,' they added.

After he had been in prison a long time, the king sent for his family. They came before him with great trembling, for they feared that the king had decreed his death. When they appeared before him, he ordered them to visit the physician in prison and talk to him, thinking perhaps their talk would be welcome to him and thus reach his ears.

The kinsfolk went to the prison and saw the physician and began their talk with him. 'O noble friend, we are sad to see you suffer such trials in this prison—in irons, chained by your neck and feet; and instead of the fine food you were wont to have, you eat only a slice of barley bread; instead of the best wine, only a measure of water. O noble friend, whose clothes were of silk and satin, now your garments are of coarse and prickly wool. In spite of this, we are surprised to see your face unchanged, the flesh of your body undiminished and your strength perfect as in your best days. We beg our noble friend to tell us how he can endure all these tortures and yet remain unaffected and his appearance unchanged.'

And on this, he answered, 'My dear friends, when I came in to prison I took seven different kinds of herbs and pounded them well together and made a sort of drink from them. I sip a little of it every day and this is the reason that my face is unchanged, my flesh is not diminished, and that I retain my full strength and am able to withstand all torture. I am well satisfied.'

Upon this his kinsmen said to the physician, 'Sir and friend, we entreat you very much: tell us, what are these herbs which you have made into a drink? In case any one of us has such great misfortunes as you, then we can make ourselves such a drink, and sipping it, save ourselves from tortures and suffering.'

Then said he, 'My dear friends, I will tell you. The first herb is the trust I have in the Holy One, blessed be He and blessed be His Name, who can protect me from all troubles and anxieties, even if they are greater and more than they now are—and also from the hand of the king, for *The heart of the king is in the hand of the Lord* [Prov. 21: 1]. What God wills he must do.

'The second herb is hope and the good advice I give myself: that I take everything for good and accept my pains with love. That is the advice I give myself so that I am not lost in despair.

'The third herb: I know well that I have sinned and because of my sins I have been imprisoned. As this came about for this reason, I am myself guilty. So why should I be impatient? and complain? As is written: *Your iniquities have divided you from your God* [Isaiah 59: 2]. And about this our Sages have also said, no pain comes without sin.

'The fourth herb is as follows: When I *do* become impatient and am in pain because of torture, what can I do? Can I alter it? Things could be even worse. What if the king had decreed that I should die? I should have been dead before my time and then all would indeed be lost. As King Solomon said: *Better a living dog than a dead lion* [Eccles. 9: 4].

'The fifth herb is: that I know that because of my present plight here the Blessed Name will relieve me of all my sins in the next world; and I shall merit the world-to-come as is written: *Happy is the man whom* the Lord correcteth [Job 5: 17]. And so, therefore, I am happy in my pain and with the joy of happiness I do good, for as the Sages say: *All who rejoice in their suffering bring redemption to the world* [Talmud].

'I can suffer more pain than that from iron chains. I could be castigated with sticks and rods, or with things worse than death. I

now eat barley bread. If the king had wished, I could have had
nothing at all to eat; neither barley nor wheaten bread. At present
I get a measure of water. If he had wished, I would have had
nothing to drink. Now my garments are of coarse prickly wool. Had
the king so wished I would have had to go naked winter and summer. And it could have been that my tortures were so unbearable
that *when morning dawned I would wish it night; and when night fell that
it should be day* [Deut. 28: 67]. Therefore I accept troubles without
complaint.

   'The seventh: God's help is in the flick of an eye. *For God is
gracious and compassionate* [Jonah 4: 2], and forgives the wicked.
What God, blessed be His name, gives God can take away and
heal pain and sorrow.

   'So, my friends, I found and used the seven herbs and these have
preserved my face and strength. Let everyone therefore fear God
and accept punishment with willing joy—for suffering is a redemption for his body and merits the eternal world-to-be, in the certainty
that his Maker will reward him with good.'

   Dear children, I must not go into further depths, for then
another ten books would not be enough for me. Read the German 'Brandspiegel' and the 'Leib Tov'. In the books of morals
you will find everything.

   This I beg of my dear children: Have patience. If God sends
you an affliction, accept it meekly and do not cease to pray.
Perhaps He will have mercy. Who knows what is best for us sinful folk? Who knows if it is good to live in great riches and have
much pleasure, enjoying all that the heart desires in this transient world; or if it is better, if the Heavenly Father holds much
from us in this sinful world so that we can have our eyes always
fixed on heaven. Our gracious Father: call on Him with hot and
sincere tears every moment. I am sure that the True and Good
Lord will show mercy and redeem us from this long, sorrowful
exile. Great is His mercy. He is full of graciousness. What He
has promised us, that will come to pass. Only, let us be patient.

   My dear children, be devout and good. Serve the Lord God
with all your heart as well if things go well with you as when,
God forbid, all is not well: *As we have to bless God for good, so also
must we for evil* [Talmud]. If He punishes you, do not be too
grieved. Remember everything comes from the Lord. Should,
God forbid, children and dear friends die, do not grieve too
much, for you did not create them. Almighty God, who created

them, when He desires, takes them again to him. What can the helpless mortal do? He himself must go the same way. If God afflicts you so that you lose money, the Highest who gives, takes: naked were we born and naked must we depart. All the money in the world does not help. So, my dear children, no matter what you may lose, be patient for nothing belongs; it is only lent.

When then should a person grieve? When a day passes in which he has not performed a good deed. And much more shall he grieve if, God forbid, he has sinned. We were created only to serve God and observe His commandments and to hold fast to His Holy Torah: *For that is thy life and the length of thy days* [Deut. 30: 20].

It is the duty of a man to support his wife and children respectably. By *he who is charitable all the time* [Talmud] is meant he who sees to the wants of his wife and children. God, blessed be His name, helps him and if he helps the poor—then it is well with him. Such labour is also a merit, for the great heavenly Father arranged everything with wisdom. A father loves his child; the same the nearest relatives one another. Without this the world could not exist.

Almighty God did all this in His infinite mercy that parents should love their children and help them to do right. And then the children seeing this from their parents, do the same to their children.

For example: There dwelt on the sea shores a bird that had three fledgelings. Once, seeing that a storm was coming and that the sea waves rose over the shore, the old bird said to the young ones, 'If we cannot get to the other side at once we shall be lost.' But the birdlings could not yet fly. So the bird took one little one in his claws and flew with it over the sea. When half-way across, the parent bird said to his young one, 'What troubles I have to stand from you, and now I risk my life for you. When I am old, will you also do good to me and support me?' On which the fledgeling replied: 'My dear beloved father, just take me across the sea. I will do for you in your old age all that you demand of me.'

On this the old bird threw the birdling into the sea so that he was drowned and said, 'So should be done with such a liar as you.' He flew back and returned with the second one. When they reached half-way across he spoke to this one as he had to the first. The little bird promised to do all the good in the world. But the old bird

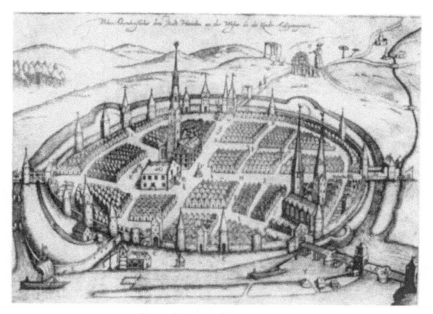

1. *View of Hameln.* Engraving, 1622

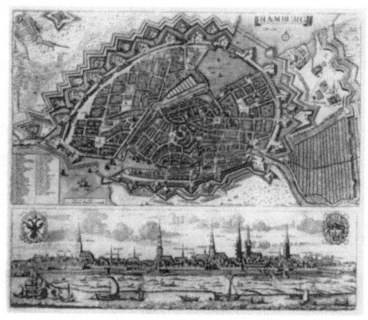

2. *Bird's Eye View of Hamburg.* Engraving by Arnoldus Petersen, 1644

3. *Sounding the Shofar on New Year's Day.* Engraving by Bernard Picart, 1723

4. *Family Scene at Amsterdam during the Feast of Tabernacles.* Engraving by
Bernard Picart, 1723

took this one too and threw him into the sea, saying, 'You also are a liar.'

He flew again to the shore and brought the third birdling. When he came midways he said to him, 'My child, see what hardships I undergo and how I risk my life for your sake. When I am old and cannot move any more, will you be good to me and support me in my old age, as I do you in your youth?'

To which the little bird answered his parent, 'My dear father, all that you say is true, that you take great care of me and my need. I am in duty bound to repay you, if it is possible; but I cannot promise for certain. But this I can promise: when one day I have a birdling of my own, I will do for my young as you have done for me.' On this his father said, 'You speak well and are also clever. I will let you live and take you across the water.'

From this we can see that God gave the unreasoning bird sense to bring up his young; and the difference: how parents toil for their children while they, if they had the trouble with their parents as their parents with them, would soon tire.

To return again to our purpose. People should love one another, for it is said *Thou shalt love thy neighbour* [Lev. 19: 18]. This is a principal point. But we very seldom find in these times that a person loves another with his heart. On the contrary. If one can ruin another he will do so. That parents love their children is no surprise. We find the same among unreasoning creatures who have young and look after them until they are grown and can fend for themselves. And then they are left to themselves. We humans are in this sense better. We seek to support our children till they are grown; not only when they are small but as long as we live.

There are people who say, 'Why should I always worry about my children? Is it not enough that I saw to them when young? Brought them up well? Gave them fine dowries and made good matches for them? Now they can see to themselves.' And really this is the best way, for should parents always be slaves to their children? This is quite right when children are in a good position and all goes well with them. But if, God forbid, things go badly which person with feelings would not bear the burden of his children and friends?

Rachel mourning for her children—*I am the one who has seen affliction*[1]—it is indeed a very great affliction to be childless. To

---

[1] Lamentations 3: 1.

C

my understanding it would have been much easier for Abraham
had the Lord asked him to slay himself than that he should slay
his only son Isaac. For who can witness the doing-away of his
own offspring? Still, Abraham would do this out of his great
love for God.

Even if we had no other example before us, we would know
how to serve God, and not care for what is worldly and passing.
For God, who gave everything, when He desires, can also take
away.

Your prayers should be said with devotion and awe. And at the
time of prayer, do not stand talking with anyone, leaving the
Creator waiting until you have finished. Our Sages have already
said enough of all this and you can read it elsewhere. After praying,
study a page of Torah according to your ability. Do everything with
diligence; and support your wife and children honestly. This is a
great merit. And especially that you should do honest business with
Jew or gentile lest by not so doing, God forbid, you desecrate the Holy
Name. If one has another's money or goods in hand, one must be
more careful than with his own, so that one should not do an
injustice to another.

The first question in the future world will be: have you dealt
honestly? If you have acted as a rogue, stolen so as to gather riches,
God forbid, and after giving your children fine dowries left them
great inheritance—alas! and woe! to those evildoers who enrich
their children and lose their share in the world-to-come. Above all,
they cannot be sure that the stolen money will remain with their
children. If we do admit that they have it, then it is only temporary
and not eternal. Then why should one keep the passing at the
expense of the everlasting? If a sandy hill is dug and the grains taken
away little by little, there is hope that in time the hill will be cleared.
But to lose eternity, God forbid, that is the world-to-come—that is
a terrible consideration and much to be deplored. What are we?
and what is our life if we do not consider this?

We find in the writings about Alexander of Macedon: He heard
that in a certain land there lived men of great wisdom who were
not concerned about the rest of the world; they ate only that which
nature grew and had no drink but water. Among them there was no
envy or hatred. They wore no clothes. Alexander of Macedon,
conqueror of the world, heard much of these people, their mode of
living and their wisdom. He sent messengers to them, that they
should come and do him, their lord and king, honour. If they
refused to do so they would be destroyed. They answered: 'We come

nowhere and never go out of our land. We do not desire silver or gold. We are satisfied with that which God has given us and nature brings forth. If your king will come and kill us if we do not go to him, let him do so. He does not need much bravery for this because we will not withstand him. We do not care for our lives for when we are dead then we will begin to live. Should your king desire to come to us peacefully and learn of our wisdom and observe our customs, we shall be pleased to welcome him.'

The messengers returned to Alexander and told him of all that had passed. The king and his important men journeyed to the land of wise men. There they stayed some days and heard and learned much wisdom. He learnt many things and was well pleased with them and wished to give them many costly presents. But they refused these, saying, 'We do not need money, or gold, or silver. Nature provides us with enough.'

On this king Alexander said, 'Ask of me and I will grant you all that you desire.' They answered with one voice, 'My lord king, give us eternal life.' Said the king, 'How can I grant you this? If I had it to give I would give it to myself.' Answered the wise men, 'Then has the lord king considered in your own mind—for you yourself know all that the king does—with what labour and trouble and how many lands and people you have destroyed—which you can hold for a short time only: to what purpose is all this labour?'

And he knew not how to answer them. Still, he said, 'I have found the world like this and like this I must leave it. The heart of a king cannot be content without war.'

This story I do not write as truth. It may be a heathenish fable. I have written it here to pass my time and to show that there are people in this world who care not for riches, relying always on their Creator. We have, thank God, our books of morals from which we can learn much good.

I write all this not for admonition, but as I have already mentioned, to while away the long wearisome nights, for *She weepeth sore in the night* [Lament. 1: 2]. I have undertaken to write as much as I can remember of my childhood, not because I wish to present myself as a pious woman or pretend I am better than I am. No. My sins are too heavy to bear. I am a sinner. Every day, every hour, every minute, every second—full of sins, and unfortunately am shut out from very few sins. *For these I weep and mine eyes runneth down with water* [Lament. 1: 16]. I would rejoice to do penance and weep for all my sins but the anxieties and sorrow for my orphaned children do not let me do penance as I should like.

I pray that God, my Creator, be gracious to me and lift from me the cares and worries I bear. *In the hid places I weep.* I have no one in whom to put my trust but only God in heaven. We humans do not confide our great troubles to one another. Each person thinks his the greatest. Once a philosopher walking in the street met a friend, who bemoaned the great hardships and worries he suffered. Said the philosopher to his friend, 'Come with me; let us go up on the roof.' They both ascended to the roof. From there they could see all the houses in the town. 'Come hither, my friend,' said the philosopher, 'I will show you all the houses in town. Look at this house—there is trouble and joy. In that house—care and money.' The philosopher showed him that every house had its troubles and worries. 'Well, my friend, take your own burdens and cares and throw them among the houses and in their place take those from one of these houses.' But the friend had observed well what worries there were everywhere and so decided to retain his own burden.

> The world is filled with such pain
> That each his own would retain.

Therefore, put your trust in God. Pray that He should not desert us, nor all Israel—but bring us good tidings soon and send us our Messiah speedily, in our own time. Amen.

END OF MY FIRST BOOK

BOOK II

THAT which I have written and shall write comes from my troubled heart after the death of your father, peace unto him. He was our faithful shepherd. Surely because of our sins God took him to Himself.

While I am yet in good health I shall with God's help, leave all in seven small books. I shall begin with my birth.

It was in the year of Creation 5407 [1646–47], I think, in Hamburg, that my pure, pious mother, with the help of merciful God, brought me into the world. And though our Sages have well said, it were better that man had not been born because man must suffer much, I thank and praise my Creator who has made me according to His will.[1]

[*One page is here missing from the manuscript. The missing page apparently described the household and charity of Glückel's parents.*]

. . . (whoever) came into the house hungry, went out satisfied. He had his daughters taught religious and worldly things. I was born in Hamburg and as my parents and others told me, I was not yet three when Jews were driven thence[2] and went to Altona which then belonged to the King of Denmark, where they enjoyed many privileges. Altona is about a quarter of an hour's distance from Hamburg. Some twenty-five Jewish families lived there at that time and had a synagogue and cemetery.[3] They lived there for a time and through the efforts of prominent men of the Community obtained permits to trade in the town. Each was valid for one month and cost one ducat, and had to be renewed at the end of the month. But the four weeks were always eight because they knew the burgomaster and the officials. Still, it was a very hard life especially for the poor and needy, who risked going without a pass; if they were caught they

---

[1] This quotation is in reality from the morning prayers and is recited by women only as an offset to that by men who say: 'Blessed be He who has not made me a woman.'

[2] On 16 August 1648, the Council of Aldermen issued an order expelling all German Jews (Hochdeutsche Juden) from Hamburg.

[3] The cemetery first used in 1621 was closed in 1872.

were imprisoned. This meant ransoming them and called for much expense and trouble before they were released. In the mornings, as soon as the men came from the synagogue, they went to town, returning to Altona towards evening when the gates were closed. When they passed through the gates their lives were in continual peril from attacks by sailors, soldiers and all sorts of hooligans. Each woman thanked God when her husband returned safely home. Counting those that had come from Hamburg, there were at that time about forty householders. There were then no very wealthy men and each earned his living in an honest way. Chaim Fürst, peace unto him, possessor of 10,000 reichstaler, was the wealthiest; my father, peace unto him, had 8000, and there were others with 6000, some 3000— all lived well and at peace with one another; even people who possessed only 500 taler were content with their portion, not as the wealthy of these days, who are never content. Of them it has been said: No person before he dies receives half his desires.[1] I remember my father as a God-fearing man, without equal. Though he suffered from gout he brought his children to good positions and settled us all comfortably.

When I was about ten there was a war between the Swedes and Danes.[2] I cannot write much of it as I was in *Cheder*[3] all day. The winter that year was the coldest for fifty years and is still known as the Swedish winter. Everything was so frozen that the Swedes were able to come right into Altona. Suddenly, one Sabbath day, the cry arose, 'The Swede is coming!' It was early. We were still in bed. We sprang up, half clad as we were, and rushed into the town seeking help from the Sephardi Jews[4] and partly from the citizens. We were refugees for a short while.

---

[1] Talmud.

[2] Charles Gustav X of Sweden, after defeating Poland, moved against the Danes, with whom the Poles were in alliance. Advancing to attack South Jutland, via Schleswig-Holstein, in the very severe winter of 1657-8, the Swedish army performed the astounding feat of crossing the frozen sea into Zealand. It is this winter to which Glückel refers as the Swedish winter.

[3] *Cheder*, literally chamber or room, and to this day a colloquial term for the old-fashioned Jewish elementary school, in which children are taught the elements of Hebrew and religion. It was only in Germany that Jewish girls and boys attended *Cheder* together.

[4] The Sephardi Jewish community had right of residence in Hamburg. See Introduction.

After a time, through great exertion on his part, and influence, my father received permission to resettle in Hamburg. He was the first German Jew to return. Later the other Jews returned from Altona, apart from those who had been living in Altona before. At that time government taxes were very low. We had no synagogue in Hamburg and no privileges and lived only by the grace of the town council. Still, Jews met together and held services in private rooms. This the town council looked at 'through their fingers'. But when the priests learnt of this they would not allow it and we were driven, like timid sheep, to attend the Altona synagogue. This lasted a long while: we crept back to our little synagogue, had peace for a time, and then were driven away again, and so on, just as it is today.[1] I am afraid that this will last as long as we are in Hamburg and the town council rules. May God be gracious and send our Messiah that we may serve Him with good hearts and once more offer Him prayer in Jerusalem. Amen.

So we lived in Hamburg. My father traded in jewellery and, like a Jew, in anything else which could be profitable. The war between Denmark and Sweden grew fiercer till the King of Sweden was victorious and took everything he could from the King of Denmark and marched on the capital and besieged it. He would have succeeded if the Danish King had not had such good advisers and subjects who gave their blood and lives for him. This was God's reward to him, for he was a just monarch and treated Jews well. Although they lived in Hamburg, every Jewish householder had to pay a tax of 6 reichstaler to the Danish Government. Later the King of Holland came to the aid of the Danes by bringing his ships through the strait and thus ended the war. But though the Swedes and Danes may be friendly and intermarry, they never remain on good terms for long but always peck away at one another.

During this time my sister Hendelé, peace unto her, was betrothed to the son of the learned Rabbi Gumpel of Cleve.[2]

---

[1] Glückel refers to the prohibition of synagogue services for the German Jews. The Hamburg archives testify to the strict scrutiny to which Jewish houses suspected of serving as synagogues were subjected. The Sephardi community, however, were allowed synagogues.

[2] Rabbi Mordecai Gumpel, known officially as Marcus Gompertz, distinguished land rabbi and community representative of the duchy of Cleve,

She received 1800 reichstaler as her dowry, a very large sum in those days and one that no one had until then given in Hamburg. It was the most important match in all Germany, and the whole world wondered at the large dowry. But my father was a man who trusted that God would not forsake him when it came to the turn of his other children. He lived better and was more hospitable than people who had 30,000 reichstaler—and lived thus to his last day.

Now I will write of my sister's wedding. I cannot describe how magnificent everything was and the distinguished company that came with Rabbi Gumpel, nor what a pious saintly man he was. There is none today to compare with him. The poor and needy in particular rejoiced. May his merits stand us in good stead!

My father, as I have already mentioned, was not very wealthy but he had great faith; he owed no one money and brought up his children to be honest. He suffered much ill health and because he was old, he was eager to marry off all his children. He was a widower when he married my mother, having lived fifteen years with his first wife, but they had no children. My dear, devout mother has often told me how much she suffered when she was young, for she was an orphan. Her mother, my grandmother Mattie, whom I knew, was a clever, pious woman whose equal may not be readily found. Her father was Nathan Melrich, a wealthy upstanding man who lived in Detmold and when expelled from there moved with his family to Altona at a time when there were not ten Jews living there.

At that time Altona belonged not to Denmark, as now, but to the Duke of Schomberg, for it was part of the duchy of Pinneberg. When the duke died childless the district fell to the kingdom of Denmark. It was Reb[1] Nathan Spanier[2] who obtained permission for Jews to live in Altona, and there he settled his son-in-law Leib, who came from Hildesheim. Though not rich,

was founder of the Gompertz family. He lived first in Emmerich and later in Cleve, where he died 1664. Part of the Gompertz family settled in London; one of whom, Lewis Gompertz, was an inventor and a founder of the R.S.P.C.A.; his brother Benjamin a well-known actuary, and their brother Isaac a poet.

[1] A respectful mode of address and reference to a Jew.

[2] Nathan Moses Spanier of Stadthagen, died in Altona 1647. He was the representative of the Altona community.

he was an honest man and provided well for the settlement of his children, as was the custom in those days. His wife Esther was a pious, upright woman who understood business well and supported the household. She went regularly to the fairs, taking not too much stock with her, for at that time people were satisfied with little. She spoke well and God gave her favour in the eyes of all who saw her; the aristocratic ladies of Holstein esteemed her very highly. Though they gave their children dowries of only 3 to 400 reichstaler, their sons-in-law were rich men; one was Reb Moses Goldzieher, and another Reb Elia Ballin who was worth 30,000 reichstaler. Their son Reb Moses was a wealthy man to the end of his days, and though Reb Lipman was not so rich, he lived honestly and in a seemly way as did the other children. I write this to show that big dowries are not always the cause of great riches, for even people who have given small ones have had wealthy children.

But to return to my grandfather, Reb Nathan Melrich. When he was driven out of Detmold and came to Altona, he went to the house of Reb Leib Hildesheim, the son-in-law of Nathan Spanier, and took with him all his riches. Reb Leib's wife Esther told me incredible tales of his great wealth: he had boxes full of golden chains and jewels and bags full of pearls so that for more than a hundred miles around there was no one as rich as he. But, unfortunately, this did not last long. A plague—God preserve us—broke out, and my grandfather and several children died of it. My grandmother was left bare and destitute with two unmarried daughters. They fled from the house, just as they were, taking nothing with them. Often did she tell me of the terrible hardships she underwent. They had no bed to sleep on but plain boards and stones, and though she had a married daughter, this daughter could not help her. Her married son Mordecai[1] was well off, but unfortunately he and his wife and child died of the same plague. So my poor grandmother and her daughters underwent severe trials and had to go from house to house until the plague had passed. When she returned to disinfect her house, she found all her best things gone and little left. The very floor-boards had been pulled up by the neighbours and the rooms were bare. What could they

[1] Mordecai, the son of Nathan, and his wife Hannah, both died of the plague towards the end of 1638.

do? My grandmother still possessed some pledges and with these managed to bring up her remaining children, my aunt Ulka and my mother Beila—may she live long! My grandmother scraped and economized and was able to marry my aunt Ulka to Reb Elijah Cohen, the son of Rabbi David Hanau, the great scholar who bore the distinguished title 'Morenu'.[1] He was, I think, land rabbi of Friesland and thence came to Altona to take up the position of rabbi. He gave his son a dowry of 500 reichstaler. But though Reb Elijah was a successful business man, he unfortunately died before he was forty. Had he lived he would have become immensely rich; in his hands dust turned to gold. But fate carried him off.

At that time there were angry quarrels about the wardenship of the synagogue. My father had been *parnass*[2] for many years; and Reb Elijah Cohen, a young man whose wealth grew from day to day, who was also a clever man—was he not the son of the learned Rabbi David Hanau?—was often heard to say aloud, 'Why should I not become warden like my brother-in-law Leib?[3] Am I not as clever? Am I not as rich? Do I not come from as fine a family as he?' But God in His time took him unto Himself.

While he was alive there were many quarrels in the community, and, as is the way of the world, each person belonged to a different party. So, unhappily, many misfortunes befell the community. Firstly, *parnass* Feibelman died; after him, Chaim Fürst, the wealthiest man among them. Then Abraham the *shammus* (verger) lay down and died, but before his death he said, 'I have been summoned to the heavenly *Beth Din*[4] to give evidence.' Zalman, the learned and highly respected son of Chaim Fürst, who was warden, also died,[5] besides many others

[1] A title of honour, bestowed on married men only, and indicative of great learning. Hebrew, literally 'our teacher'.

[2] In Glückel's time the office of *parnass* (president or warden) was a monthly one. Each *parnass* in turn was appointed as overseer of the poor. He was empowered, when in office, to distribute alms to the needy, up to a certain sum. It was the duty of the *parnass* in office to allot the guests, *i.e.*, strangers then in town, to different householders for meals and lodging on sabbaths and holy days.

[3] Gluckel's father, Leib Pinkerle.

[4] See footnote on p. 64.

[5] This was in 1653, according to his tombstone in the Altona cemetery.

whose names I have forgotten. In this way God settled the quarrels among the *parnassim*.

To return to my grandmother Mattie. When she settled Ulka she found herself with nothing left to support her eleven-year-old orphan, my mother. They went to live with her daughter Glück, the wife of Jacob Ree. Though he was not a man of riches, Reb Jacob Ree was very honest. He gave his children dowries of from 400 to 500 reichstaler and made fine matches for them with young men of good families. After a time differences arose because the orphan grandchildren visited her often, so that my grandmother left this daughter and went to live with Ulka. She and my mother, who knew how to make pointed gold and silver lace, supported themselves. My mother found favour in the eyes of the Hamburg dealers; they gave her gold and silver to work and for the first transaction Jacob Ree stood as surety. When the dealers saw that she was honest and prompt in her work, they trusted her, so that in time she was able to take in girls and teach them the trade. She and her mother lived from this, and clothed themselves neatly and cleanly. But besides this they had little, and at times no more than a crust of bread all day. Still they did not complain but trusted God not to forsake them—and my mother has the same trust today. I wish I had such a nature; God does not bestow the same gifts on everyone.

My father, as I have already mentioned, had a former wife, Reize by name, an honest, capable housewife who kept a large house. Though she bore my father no children, she had by her first husband, a daughter who had no one to compare with her for beauty and accomplishments. She knew French perfectly, the knowledge of which was of great service to my father on one occasion. My father had a pledge for 500 reichstaler from a certain landreeve. When the time for repayment was due he came, accompanied by two others, to redeem it. My father, not suspecting anything underhand, left them and went upstairs to bring the pledge. His stepdaughter sat playing the spinet, to amuse the men while they waited. She overheard them speaking softly behind her, 'When the Jew returns with the pledge, we'll snatch it from him and run away with it.' They said this in French, not suspecting that the young girl understood a word. When my father returned, with the pledge, she sang out loudly in Hebrew, 'Take heed! No pledge! Today here, to-morrow fled!' This was all she could say in her haste. But my father understood and said to the reeve, 'Where is the money?' He replied, 'Give me the pledge first.' My father answered, 'I must have the money first.' Then one of the men cried to the others, 'We are betrayed! The hussy understands French!' and they ran out of the house, shouting threats as they went. Next day, the chief reeve came alone, and giving my father capital and interest for the loan, said, 'It has paid you well to have your daughter taught French', and with these words went on his way.

He brought her up as his own child and married her to the son of Kalman Aurich, a fine match. She died in her first childbirth. A few days after her death she appeared, in a dream, to her husband, robbed and stripped of her shrouds. She was dug up and found to be without her cerements. The women quickly got together to sew her others. As they sat sewing, a servant rushed into the room, crying, 'For God's sake! hurry with your sewing! Don't you see that the corpse is sitting among you?' But the women saw nothing. When they were finished they clothed the corpse and since that time she has not appeared again to the living, but remained resting in peace.

When my parents married, they took my grandmother Mattie to live with them and set her at the head of the table, which position of honour was hers for the rest of her days. My father treated her with the greatest respect, as if she was his own mother. The underwear which she gave my mother on her marriage, my mother, with the knowledge and approval of my father, returned to her for her own use. She was as well treated as if she was in her own home. For seventeen years she lived with them, comforted and honoured. God grant that we and our children enjoy the fruits of these merits!

It was about this time that people fled from Vilna to Hamburg[1] and an epidemic broke out and there was no *hekdesh*[2] or

---

[1] The anti-Polish rising of the Cossacks under Bogden Chmelnicki in 1648, affected numerous Jewish communities in Poland; thousands of Jews were slaughtered, and whole settlements annihilated. Glückel's mention of Polish Jewish refugees appearing in Hamburg is an interesting contemporary proof of the wide effect of the outbreaks—and of the plight of the Jewish refugees.

[2] *Hekdesh*, a sort of workhouse in charge of a superintendent where des-

any other place for sick people. There were in our attic ten sick people for whom my father cared. Several of these died. My sister Elka was also ill at the time. My revered grandmother tended all the sick and saw to their wants, they lacked nothing. Though my parents were not pleased at the risks she ran, they could not restrain her. Three or four times a day she would climb to the garret to tend the sick, till at last she, too, caught the sickness and after ten days in bed, in good repute, at the age of seventy-four, she died. She was as robust as a woman of forty.

On her death-bed she made her confession and praised and thanked my father for all that he had done for her. Every week she had received from my parents either half a reichstaler or two marks for pocket-money, and my father never once went to a fair without bringing her back some present. All this she saved and did business in small loans. When she lay dying, she said to my father: 'My son, I am going the way of all flesh. I have lived so long in your house and you have treated me as if I was your own mother. Not only did you serve me with the best food and clothe me well, but you have also given me money. I kept nothing of it for myself but saved it and lent it out on small loans. I have about 200 reichstaler. Whom does this money belong to more than my beloved son-in-law? It is all his. But if he desires to renounce it, let him give it to my two poor orphan grandchildren, of my son Mordecai. I leave it to him to do as he thinks fit.'

Reb Judah and Reb Anschel, all her children and sons-in-law were present. My father answered her, 'My dear mother, be at ease. God grant that you remain with us a long while yet, and that you yourself will divide the money as you wish. I renounce it with all my heart and, God granting, will give you another 100 reichstaler so that you may earn more and do with it as you yourself desire.'

When my grandmother heard these words she rejoiced and was happy and blessed him and my mother and their children with all the blessings of the world; and praised him before all the people present. The next day she fell asleep, gently and peacefully, and was buried with due honour. May her merits

titute people slept. Every large Jewish community supported a *hekdesh* for the use of wandering Jewish beggars and refugees.

stand in good stead for her children and children's children. Amen.

To return again to my father, and how he married off my sister Hendelé, peace unto her. But why should I write at such length? I wanted to show how my mother was left an orphan. How she put her trust in God who rewarded her in such a manner as the following story shows. For it shows that if things do not go well with all the children, still, thank God, most of them have bread. Therefore, whoever puts all his trust in Him, the All Highest will never desert: *Blessed is the man that trusteth in the Lord and whose hope the Lord is* [Jeremiah 17: 7].

This is a pleasant story to comfort the bereaved and sorrowful heart. A man should never despair of God's help, even as the pious man of whom I shall tell, for though poverty and sorrow befell him, he suffered patiently without wavering in his faith. And God, on His part, stood graciously by him and helped him, as you will read.

There was once a pious man. He had a pious wife and two sons. He also had a little money on which he lived, so that he did no business but devoted the whole of his time to study. Nevertheless he wished to earn a little by the work of his hands so that his family should be secured against reliance on strangers. But fortune was not with him and he, poor man, fell into debt and could not pay. None would even be surety for him, with the result that his creditors brought him before the judge, and the judge decided that he must go to prison. And so it happened.

His wife wept bitterly for she did not know how she would support herself and her two little ones, particularly as she now had to provide her husband with food while in prison. And as she lamented and wept, an old man came to her and asked her why she cried so bitterly. Seeing what a respectable, fine-looking old man he was, she told him all her troubles. And the old man said, 'Cease weeping; God will help you. Because your husband studies Torah He will not desert you, for He does not desert a Talmid Chocham;[1] if He does not help him in his youth, He helps him in old age. Even more, I know that you will suffer much and, together with your husband, pass through much storm and stress, yet if you are patient, God will reward it all with good.' Thus he comforted her and advised her to become a washerwoman; people would pay her for washing their shirts. 'In this way,' he concluded, 'you will support your husband and children—if you are not shamefaced and approach all and sundry for work.'

[1] A wise and clever man, one well versed in the Torah and Talmud.

So counselled by the old man, she was quieted and thanked him warmly, promising to obey his every word. Then the old man departed and she saw him no more.

She went home, prepared some food for her husband and cheered him, telling him not to be impatient, but to continue his Talmud study even in his dire condition, while she would work day and night to support the family. And in that dark cell the pious prisoner and his wife wept bitterly imploring the mercy of Heaven on their little ones.

The woman was the first to recover. She dried her eyes and said, 'My dear husband, our cries and wails will not give us and our children bread: I will go and see what work God sends me, that I may support you and the children.' So saying she went home to sleep a trustful sleep with full faith in the morrow.

The following morning, while the children yet slept, she arose and went into the town, from house to house, to ask for washing.

The town was situated by the shore of the sea. Every day she went with her children to the sea and washed clothes, spreading them out on the sands to dry.

It happened once that as she was washing, a ship sailed by and the captain approaching close to the land, saw the woman and marvelled at her beauty. And when the woman enquired the cause of his staring, he answered, 'My dear woman, I pity you. Tell me, how much do you get for washing a shirt?' 'For a man's shirt,' she replied, 'I get two groschen, but I must wash it quite clean.' Then he said, 'I would gladly give you four groschen, if you washed my shirt clean.' 'I will wash it willingly,' she returned.

She took the shirt, washed it clean and spread it to dry on the grass, while the captain waited on the boat for her to finish.

He watched her washing and drying the shirt and her neat folding. The boat was a little distance from the shore. As the captain could not get in close enough to the shore, he threw her the money, wrapped in paper, saying, 'Reach me my shirt into the boat.' But he caught her hand and pulled her into the boat and rowed off quickly. She cried aloud from the boat, but to no purpose. Soon she was out at sea and her cries were no longer heard.

When the children saw and heard their mother no more they ran to their father, who was still in prison, and told him what had occurred. The poor man lifted up his voice and cried aloud, 'God, my God! Why have You forsaken me in such loneliness? I have now no one to help me while I am in prison.' Weeping, he fell asleep and dreamed that he was in a great wilderness and wild beasts surrounded him. They stood over him eager to devour him. He

trembled and looked about him at the desolation. Then he saw a
shepherd and flock approach. When the wild beasts saw the herd
they left him and followed the cattle. He ran away and reached a
castle which stood on a river full of boats. He entered the castle,
where he was enthroned and rejoiced greatly together with his
shipmates. Then he awoke and remembered the dream and said to
himself. 'Surely the dream shows that my troubles will pass away,
and God will help me by the aid of sailors, because through them I
have been abused.'

About this time the king of the town died and his son succeeded
him. The young king remitted the taxes of the land for three years
in order to earn himself a good name. He also freed the prisoners.
And so it came to pass that our pious man, too, was freed.

Once out of prison there was again the need of earning a living.
He and his two sons went to and fro in the market to procure
whatever work they could to buy bread. Once looking towards the
port he saw a ship about to leave for the East Indies, so he said to
his sons, 'Come now. Your mother was taken away in a ship, so
we shall go away in a ship. Perhaps we shall find her, and God
will bring us together again.'

Straightway he went to the captain and told him all that had
happened to him, and asked him to take him and his children on
board, for he was poor and had no money for bread. The captain
had pity on him and took him and his children on board and gave
them food and drink and a place to lay their heads.

When they were in mid-ocean, God let loose a great storm-wind
and the ship was smashed to atoms. The sailors, the cargo and
everything on board were lost—all except the Talmid Chocham,
his sons, and the captain who had sustained them. They each had
seized hold of a spar; our pious friend and the captain on separate
fragments, and the two children together on a single piece of wreck-
age. The sea carried them away to different lands.

The Talmid Chocham was thrown on a great wilderness in a
place where savages lived. Here the king's daughter, who had charge
of the sheep and cattle, saw him. She was naked and very hairy
and wore fig-leaves to cover her shame. Perceiving him, she approached him and made it clear that she loved him and would be
his wife. Out of great fear he pretended love, and showed by signs
that he would take her.

The other savages saw this and they whistled and all the savages
came leaping from their caves in the hills where they lived. They
ran up to him, eager to drink his blood and eat his flesh. Even the
king was there. The Talmid Chocham was so scared that he could

5. *The Passover Meal.* Engraving by Bernard Picart, 1723

6. *Yom Kippur (The Day of Atonement) as observed by German Jews.* Engraving by Bernard Picart, 1723

Purgatio Vaforum ante Pafcha. 250.

Luces Sabbathinæ. 275.

8. *Cleansing the Passover Utensils.* Engraving. Utrecht, 1682

7. *Lighting the Sabbath Lamp.* Engraving. Utrecht, 1682

scarce breathe. When the king's daughter saw his terror she showed
him that there was no cause for fear, and arose and went to the king
and begged him that he should let the man live, as she wanted him
for her husband. He assented and the pious man was once again
preserved. And so the Talmid Chocham lay with her that night
and she was his wife and he was her husband. Nevertheless when he
thought of his own beautiful wife and her miserable plight, and that
nothing could be altered, he bore everything with fortitude, for he
protested that God would help him to reach his dear wife and
children.

Very soon the princess was big with child, and in time she bore
him a savage child, a boy.

For two full years he lived with them and tended the cattle in the
wilderness; eating the flesh of the wild ass and dwelling in a cave
in the hillside with his wife. They were now both overgrown with
hair and he looked as savage as she.

One day he stood on a small hill not far from the sea, thinking
of all that had happened to him; the loss of his wife and children
and—heaviest of all—how he now lived among uncivilized people.
Who knew but that when his savage wife had tired of him her tribe
would devour his flesh and crush his bones for marrow, and he
would not be laid to rest among Jews. 'Is it not better', he mused,
'that I should run from this hill into the sea and drown myself, as
my children were drowned?' (He did not know that the sea had
cast them upon dry land.) Then he would meet them in the future
world. He confessed his sins before God, with hot bitter tears.
When he had made an end of confessing, he began to run towards
the sea, to destroy himself. But a voice called to him by name, and
said, 'O doubting one! Why should you mistrust and thus destroy
your soul? Go back to the hill on which you stood and dig and you
will find a chest of gold and precious stones—a great and wonderful fortune. You will drag the box to the sea and remain standing
there a while. Then a ship full of civilized people, bound for An-
tioch, will sail by. Shout to them to take you with them to save
you and the chest in their ship. In the end you will become a king,
things will go well and you will see the end of your sufferings and
the beginning of your happiness.'

When he heard this he returned to the hill, and digging where the
voice had bid him, he found the chest of gold and precious stones.
Quickly he dragged it to the edge of the sea and lifting up his eyes
he saw a ship sailing near. He cried in a loud voice imploring to be
taken aboard as he was a civilized person despite his hairy un-
clothed body. The sailors heard him and drew near to the shore,

D

where he told them all that had happened, and they took him and his chest quickly on board ship.

Just as he was about to step on board, his savage wife, who had heard his shouts, came running up, their child on her arm. Seeing him in the ship, she called to him to take her with him. But he mocked at her, shouting, 'What have I to do with wild animals? I have a better wife than you,' and such like.

When she saw that he would return to her no more, anger arose in her. She took the savage child by his feet and tearing him in two, threw one half into the ship and in her rage began to gnaw away at the other half with her teeth. The Talmid Chocham sailed away.

After some time he came to an islet in the sea where he landed. He opened his chest and lo! it was filled to the top with gold and priceless precious stones. He paid the captain his passage with pleasure, and had his chest carried to an inn. As he lay on his straw bed that night, he said to himself, 'If I could buy this island from the king, I would build a castle, and a town, I would then have a regular income and not be afraid that my money might be stolen.'

Early next morning he went to the king, bought the island and several miles of seaboard and built a castle and town. In time the land became settled and prosperous. The people elected him their duke, and he reigned over all. Still he often thought of his wife and children and their tragic loss. At length he thought that as his wife had been stolen by a sailor, and all ships had to pass his seaboard, every ship should register with him before passing, on pain of complete confiscation. This was proclaimed and confirmed as a regular law.

Owners of all registered ships partook of his hospitality. Time passed and still he had heard nothing of his family. One *Pesach* (Passover), as the Talmid Chocham sat at table, in a happy mood, his page announced the arrival of a well-known and wealthy shipowner who begged that he be not kept waiting long. The Talmid Chocham said, 'Today is a holyday, and I may not ask him the nature of his cargo. He must wait till the holyday is over. Meanwhile let him come and pass the time with me.'

When he arrived, he received him and left him sitting. But the captain asked not to be detained, and that his ship be allowed to proceed. But to no purpose. He was constrained to remain and eat. The Talmid Chocham asked whence he came and whether he had a wife and children.

The captain told him the country of his origin and said he had two wives—one at home with whom he had had three children.

'Her I keep as a housewife. The other is delicate and no good at housework, but she is highly cultured and delicately nurtured. I have her always with me so that she can superintend the affairs of the ship. She collects the money from the passengers and enters it in a book. She manages everything. And all the time, I have never known her!'

Hereupon the Talmid Chocham said, 'Tell me, my dear captain, tell me though, why have you never lain with her?' To this the captain replied, 'The woman once had a husband who was a very clever man. She learnt a riddle from him. And she declares that whosoever solves this riddle shall be her husband—"for he shall be my late husband's equal in cleverness, and him will I wed." She would rather kill herself than allow any other man to come near her. For she says: "It is not meet for a clown to ride on a king's horse!" '

Then said the Talmid Chocham, 'Dear captain, tell me the riddle.'

The captain answered, 'The woman tells how a bird without wings flies from heaven to earth and settles on a little tree.

> From side to side it shakes the tree
> Though we the bird no longer see.
> It gladdens the tree with beautiful flowers,
> And draws to its branches wonder-powers.
> Till sudden the tree is sere and bare,
> And the bird flies crying up in the air.
> O tree! who robbed the strength from thee?
> 'Twas I. Thy strength came all from me.

That, my king, is her riddle and it is impossible for me to solve it.'

When the Talmid Chocham heard the riddle he was very agitated, for he knew that it was indeed his riddle and that the woman was his wife. The captain, seeing his agitation, said to him, 'Sir, why are you upset?' He answered, 'I am overcome because of the rare and clever riddle. I would like to hear it from the woman herself. Perhaps you have forgotten or added to it. I wish to hear her tell it, and maybe I shall find the answer.'

The Talmid Chocham sent his messenger for her. The fellow ran quickly and said to her, 'Get ready. You must come with me to the duke, to eat and drink.'

The heart of the good woman beat furiously when she heard this, for she could not fathom why she should be wanted, and feared that she might fall from a lesser misfortune into a greater one. But what could the poor woman do, but go where she was led? So she

dressed herself and adorned herself with jewels as one about to
enter the presence of a king.

When she came into the castle and the king was informed of her
he said, 'Let her be admitted.' She was brought in and a chair
was placed for her beside the captain.

The Talmid Chocham received her. They did not at first recognize each other, for both faces and modes of dress had changed out
of all recognition. All ate and drank and were jolly, but the Talmid
Chocham sat as one lost in deep thought. The captain asked, 'Sir,
why are you not happy? Why are you lost in heavy thought? Are
you sorry that we eat and drink too much? We can stop, thank you
nicely, and go our way.'

But he answered, 'No. You are my very welcome guests. I am
worried about the riddle, for I should like to hear it from the woman
herself.'

Then the captain asked her to tell the riddle to the duke, and she
told him, in the words I have already given. And the duke wondered greatly and said, 'Woman, from whom did you get this
riddle?'

'Sir,' she answered, 'I had a devout husband, a great Jewish
rabbi. He often told me stories and riddles. It is his riddle and no
one knows the answer to it.'

'If someone gives you the right answer,' he asked, 'will you acknowledge it truthfully?' And she replied, 'Sir, there is no one who
can give the right answer but my husband.'

'Then I am the one who can solve the riddle!' the Talmid
Chocham answered. 'The bird that flies from heaven to earth is
the soul which settles as on a tree, for the body of a person is likened
to a tree that grows fresh, green and full of branches in its youth—
youth which is likened to a pleasure-ground. The bird sways and
shakes the tree—that is the soul—which regulates the limbs; but
no one sees the bird, for the soul is hidden away in the body. So
the tree draws to itself all strength till it dries up and withers—such
is the man who not content with his own, yet wishes to draw everything he sees to himself, and so ends up in losing his own. That
which he acquired through sin, destroys also that which he acquired
righteously. Then speedily man dies and leaves all behind, and the
bird—that is the soul—flies into the air, and mourns for the body,
saying, "While you yet lived nothing was too good for you. You
would not rest or sleep until you had acquired a fortune. But now
that you are dead you leave everything behind you. You die, and
what profited it either of us? But if you had practised charity with
your wealth we should both have benefited." This,' he concluded, 'is

the meaning of the riddle. Acknowledge the truth of it and I shall take you again to me.'

She lifted her eyes and looked long at him. Then she recognized him and knew him as her husband. She sprang to her feet and fell on his neck, and together they wept in a long embrace. And they rejoiced greatly and made a great feast.

The captain, in great fear, fell to his knees and prayed for his life. The Talmid Chocham said, 'Because you have not lain with my wife I will spare your life. But because you have taken that which was not yours, I will take that which is yours.' So the captain left his wealth with the Talmid Chocham, and went out, happy to be granted his life.

They remained living in the island, leading a life of great piety, enjoying their peace and wealth in each other's company. Often they told one another all that had happened. Nevertheless they were both sad about their children whom they thought had been drowned.

Some time later it was so hot that it was impossible to sleep at night. So stifling was it that all the sailors in the port left their ships and went on land to while away the evening. Among those were also the two lost sons, unaware of the nearness of their parents.

To make the night pass the more speedily they said to one another, 'Let us tell riddles to while away the night.' Everyone was pleased and it was arranged that ten gulden should be given to the solver of the riddle; but if no one guessed the answer, the money would be given to the one who had set the riddle. It was readily agreed that the two boys were to give their riddle first, as they were considered cleverer than the rest.

So the boys began: 'We see an exceptionally beautiful girl. But she is blind. She shows a beautifully graceful body, but it is not in being. She rises early each morning, but none sees her all day. In the evening she comes again, clad in costly jewels, such jewels that never were created. With closed eyes we see her; with open eyes she vanishes. That is the riddle, solve it if you can.'

The whole company was silent wondering at the strange riddle, but none could essay its solution.

Among them sat an old merchant, who wished to force some foolish meaning on the assemblage as the correct answer, but the boys would not have it. A discussion followed, and eventually a long noisy wrangle broke out, lasting till dawn. Nevertheless none knew who had really won the ten gulden. At this the captain suggested that they should go to the castle and let the duke choose the winner. They agreed and went to the duke, who said, 'What brings you here so early?'

But when the duke heard the riddle, he was overcome with emotion. He looked at the boys and recognized them, as they were still young and had not changed much. He, however, concealed his feelings and said to them 'How do you know that the merchant's answer is not the right one?'

'Sir,' they replied, 'our father was a very learned man and he composed the riddle and the answer, so that none but our father or we can give the right answer.'

'Then,' said the duke, 'if I give you the right answer, am I your father?'

'If anyone gives us the true solution,' they answered, 'he must indeed be our father, because only he told us the riddle, and we have told it to no one.'

'If you will listen to me,' returned the Duke, 'I may give you the right answer. According to my understanding, the beautiful maiden is the youth of young men. They think of naught all day except of beautiful damsels. At night, too, in dreams, they see beautiful girls, but not with their eyes because the dark nights show them in dreams, but when the eyes are open they are not to be seen; that is why the beautiful maiden is blind. In the morning the dreams vanish once again, but when night comes she shows herself again in pretty jewels—uncreated gems not present in this world, things seen only in dreams. This is the solution: if you acknowledge it, I will declare you my children.'

The lads wondered at this reply. And suddenly they recognized their father. And in a moment their father and mother sprang from their seats and embraced and kissed their sons and they lifted up their voices and wept together, and all saw that they were their children.

The king made a great feast for his subjects and they all rejoiced together, for his children were now noble. And he taught his children the moral of all that had befallen them, and exhorted them to remain for ever devout in the service of God. And He would always help them. 'If God deals adversely with a person,' he said, 'his friends are silent and vanish and do not help or counsel him. They go away from him and say he is good for nothing, and he is left alone.

> And when the Lord would do one ill,
> Then are all one's best friends still,
> None will help him pursue the foe.
> All turn away, and wish him woe.
> So he remains in his despair.
> Of thousand friends no one is there.

But when the Lord's good-will is come,
Then are his greatest foes struck dumb.'

The sailors saw and heard all the wonders that had taken place
and many became Jews. And in that port a fine new Jewish community was established.

Thus we learn that we must be patient and accept everything in a
good spirit. And if we cannot give to the poor, one should at least
comfort them, for God remembers for good and protects from evil.

So God remembering His own for good,
Will guard His own from every ill;
And end our weary exile, and fulfil
His ancient promise to rejoice His band
Once more in our Holy Land.
Oh, with what longing do I write,
That God in mercy will give His own respite!
And when we are as pious as we should be,
He will show us all that we should see.

This story I found in a book written by a certain worthy man
from Prague.

But to return to my purpose and write once again of my
father, the remembrance of the righteous for a blessing. If I
wrote a hundred sheets they would not suffice. He, peace unto
him, always aimed at marrying his children into respected
families and therefore did more than he was really in a position
to do.

As I have already mentioned in my first book, my father was
parnass for a long period and during his time of office everything
went well with the community and in truth everyone *sat under
his vine and fig tree*. The community owed not even a pfennig. I
remember the great quarrels when I was very young, the opposition by evil men to my father and his colleagues. Two obtained permission from the government to be the king's repre-
sentatives. As they are now dead and have already been judged
in the Supreme Court, I do not wish to mention their names
though members of the community know who they were. God
spoilt the counsel of the wicked. With God's help the leaders
quelled the rebellion and then went to Copenhagen to see the
King. The King was a righteous man who loved justice; he
settled matters peaceably and the rascals were humbled. This

did not cost much money, for the *parnass* and the members jealously guarded the community, like the apple of their eye, against debt. If a few hundred reichstalers were lacking, the leaders would advance the money and take it back by easy instalments. My God! when I begin to reflect on those days and compare them with the present, they were happy times, though people did not have half of what they have now. God increase— not diminish—their fortunes. In their days and our days may Judah and Israel be redeemed.

Before I was twelve years old I was betrothed and the betrothal lasted two years. My wedding was celebrated in Hameln. My parents, accompanied by a party of twenty people, drove there with me. At that time there were no post-wagons on this route. We had to hire wagons from the peasants to take us as far as Hanover. When we reached that town we wrote to Hameln for carriages to be sent to us. My mother imagined it a town like Hamburg, and that, at the very least, a carriage would be sent for the bride and her parents. On the third day three or four farm-wagons arrived, drawn by such old horses that looked as if they should themselves have been given a lift in the wagons. My mother was greatly offended but as she could not change it, entrusting ourselves to the God of Israel, we seated ourselves in the carts and arrived in Hameln.

In the evening we had a great feast. My parents-in-law were good honest people, and my father-in-law, Reb Joseph,[1] of blessed memory, had few to equal him. At the feast he toasted my mother with a large glass of wine. She was still offended that no carriage had been sent to meet us. My father-in-law noticed her ill-humour and being a lovable and witty man set out to humour her: 'Harken, my dear *machtanista*.[2] I beg you not to be offended,' he said. 'Hameln is not Hamburg, and being plain country folk we have no carriages. I will tell you what happened to me when I journeyed to my own wedding. My

---

[1] Joseph Hameln is mentioned in an official document as 'Jost' or 'Jobst Goldschmidt', and that 'he is surrounded by such pomp that it can scarcely be told'.

[2] A term, for which there is no English equivalent, applied to the mothers of bride and bridegroom, denoting relationship through marriage to the parents of the bridal pair. The male parent is a *mechutan*, the plural being *machtonim*.

father, Samuel Stuttgart,[1] was *parnass* of the whole of Hesse. I
was betrothed to Freudchen, Nathan Spanier's daughter. I
received 2000 reichstaler as dowry and my father promised me
1500 reichstaler—at that time a large dowry. When the time
for the wedding drew near my father hired a messenger by the
name of Fish. My father placed the whole dowry on his back,
to be carried to Stadthagen, where my sainted father-in-law
lived. I and the messenger Fish went on foot. At that time Leib
Hildesheimer—whom I have mentioned in my first book—a
son-in-law of Nathan Spanier, was also in Stadthagen. When
I neared the town the cry went up that the bridegroom was
not far off. Reb Leib, who came of a prominent Hildesheim
family, drove out with a party to meet me. As I came near he
saw that I and Fish were on foot, and he turned and hurried
back to my bride with the news that her bridegroom was
coming, riding on a fish! But now, I can ride fine horses, as
you see, so I beg of you not to be impatient.' So the ill-humour
was dissolved in joyous laughter and friendship, and the
marriage was celebrated with hearty good cheer.

After my wedding my parents returned home and left me, a
child not yet fourteen, in a strange town, among strangers. I
was not unhappy but even had much joy because my parents-
in-law were respectable, devout people and looked after me
better than I deserved. How shall I write of the righteousness
of my father-in-law? He was an honourable man. He was like
one of God's angels!

Everyone knows the difference between Hameln and Hamburg. I, a young child brought up in luxury, was taken from
parents, friends, and everyone I knew, from a town like Hamburg to a village where only two Jewish families lived. And
Hameln is a dull, shabby place. But this did not make me
unhappy because of my joy in my father-in-law's piety. Every
morning he rose at three and wrapped in talith [prayer shawl],
he sat in the room next to my chamber studying and chanting
Talmud in the usual sing-song.[2] Then I forgot Hamburg. What

---

[1] Samuel Stuttgart, who lived in the town of Witzenhausen, Hesse, was
Jewish government representative of the whole of the electorate of Hesse,
being elected to the office by his fellow Jews. His was a civil office as opposed
to the land rabbis, who dealt with religious matters only.

[2] An invariable accompaniment to Talmudic study.

a holy man he was! May his merits benefit us! And may he persuade God to send no further ills; and that we may not sin, or come to shame.

It was also a pleasure to know his children. When his eldest son Moses, a fine young man, left for his own marriage he was accompanied by the learned Rabbi Moses and a servant known as 'Shot Jacob'. He had his dowry with him. When they neared Bremervorde they were attacked by thieves, robbed of all they had and all three were left dangerously wounded. They were brought into the town and doctors and barber-surgeons were quickly summoned. The doctors said that the bridegroom and Rabbi Moses would live but that the servant was mortally wounded. After two days Jacob was alive and the other two had died. Because of this he received the name of 'Shot Jacob'. One can imagine the weeping and pain of the bereaved parents. All efforts to find the murderers were in vain and the murders remained unavenged. May God revenge their blood!

I knew the other son. He was as full of Torah as a pomegranate of seeds. He was exceptionally clever, well learned in Talmud, who spoke very little, though when he did speak, every breath was full of wisdom. When very young he was sent to Poland[1] to study, and because of his learning soon acquired great fame. He became the bridegroom of the daughter of Reb Chaim Boas of Posen. He continued studying after his marriage and was famed far and wide as a great scholar. When war with Chmelnicki[2] broke out, Poland was in great upheaval and he and his wife and daughter fled barefooted and almost naked to the house of my father-in-law. The birth of this daughter was a miracle. For seventeen years his wife was barren. When his mother-in-law fell ill and was about to die, she summoned her daughter, this Abraham's wife, and said to her, 'My dear daughter, I am in God's hands and will soon die. If I have one merit before God, I shall beg that you should bear children.' And after her death my sister-in-law Sulka became pregnant and in due time gave birth to a daughter whom she named Sarah, after her mother. Seven years later she bore a son, Samuel. Much can be written of this same Rabbi Abraham

---

[1] Talmud study in Glückel's day was in its finest bloom in Poland. The sons of well-to-do German Jewish families were sent there to study.

[2] See footnote on p. 20.

Hameln; how my father-in-law settled him in Hanover where
he was quite rich; how he was tricked by his partners into
returning to Hameln; how the partners did not keep their
word and through this he and his family were ruined. May God
pardon them.

Next came a daughter, Yenta. When she was very young she
was betrothed to the son of Reb Sussman Gans, who lived in
Minden-on-the-Weser. He at that time was reputed to be
worth 100,000 taler. It was while my father-in-law and Sussman Gans were drinking that the match was settled, but the
following day, when Sussman Gans was sober, he regretted the
arrangement. But my father-in-law being an important person,
and as what had been agreed upon could not be altered, things
remained as they were. The betrothed pair being still very
young, the bridegroom was sent to study in Poland. Shortly
after, Sussman Gans died and nothing came of his vast wealth.
His wife married again, a man of the name of Feibusch. After
some years the bridegroom returned from Poland and instead
of several thousands had only a few hundred taler. My father-
in-law wished to break off the match, but my mother-in-law
would not allow an orphan to be so shamed. So the young
couple married and lived for a time in Minden. Now it happened that to celebrate the marriage of their son, Feibusch and
his wife gave a large party on the Friday evening before the
wedding. On the table was displayed expensive cutlery which
Solomon Gans recognized as having belonged to his father from
whom he had inherited so little. He went into the office and
took a box full of bonds for he felt he had a right to them.
But how can I dwell at length on this? Twenty sheets of paper
would not suffice to write of all that happened. Enough to say
that on the following day Feibusch missed the box of documents and straightway suspected his stepson. Quarrels began
and my father-in-law was dragged into them. It cost Feibusch
and my father-in-law more than 2000 reichstaler. It was a
matter of life and death! It lasted several years, each summoned
the other before the courts. At one time Feibusch had my
father-in-law put into prison, at another my father-in-law had
Feibusch imprisoned. It continued until both had only a little
money left. Nevertheless, my father-in-law was in a better
position. In the end, people intervened and rabbis were

summoned from Frankfurt-on-Main to settle the matter. They came, stayed a long while, but settled nothing, though they took great sums back with them! With this money one of the rabbis furnished a fine study, ornamented with a picture of a goose, surrounded by three or four rabbis in black, clerical garb, plucking its feathers.[1]

After this, my father-in-law took Solomon Gans and Yenta from Minden and settled them in Hanover, where he obtained permission for them and their children to reside. It was a large town and Solomon Gans was happy there. He became very rich, but his joy was short—he died young, in his best years. His wife, who was a capable young woman, remained a widow for some years and did not wish to marry again. But Reb Lipman[2] had the luck that Solomon Gans had had to yield and he married my sister-in-law Yenta. At that time he was not so wealthy as he is now. The great Lord, Who has everything in His power, raises up and brings low.

My father-in-law spent many hundreds and spared no trouble to settle his children in Hanover, thinking that by doing so he would secure his children and children's children for ever. But for whom did the good man work and weary himself in the end? For strangers! As it is written: *They will leave their wealth to others*. What more can I add? for everything happens as the dear Lord desires.

The third son was the learned Rabbi Samuel. Like Abraham he studied Talmud in Poland and married the daughter of the renowned Rabbi Shalom of Lemberg. He too had settled in Poland and at the time of the war had fled and came away with nothing. For some time he and his family had to be supported by my father-in-law. Later, he became rabbi of Hildesheim. It is impossible to do justice to his piety and holiness; he predicted to a second the time of his own death, as all Hildesheim knows.

The fourth child was Rabbi Isaac of blessed memory, whom

---

[1] Presumably in jocular reference to one of the litigants Gans whose name signifies 'goose'.

[2] Lipman Cohen, better known as Leffman Behrens, court factor and agent of Ernst August of Hanover and Duke Rudolf August of Brunswick. He frequented the Leipzig Fairs and was held in high favour in the Guelph courts.

I did not know. He lived in Frankfurt-on-Main. Of his purity of soul and learning I leave those that knew him to tell; there was indeed no one like him. He was not fifty when he died, wealthy and honoured. Day and night he studied, fulfilling the verse: *Thou shalt meditate Torah day and night.*

The fifth child was Esther, peace be to her. It is not possible to write enough of her gentleness, her womanly virtues, and of her patient suffering borne uncomplainingly till her pure soul breathed its last. There is much to tell of her, but silence must suffice. It is enough that the whole world knows how virtuous she was.

Reb Leib Bonn was the sixth child, a highly respected man who, though not a great scholar, was well educated. He was the community representative of the Cologne district and lived at Bonn. He died young, wealthy and honoured.

The seventh child was a daughter, Hannah, who may be compared with her namesake of the Bible. She was pious, respectable and died young leaving no fortune behind.

Your dear, devoted father was the eighth child. I shall not say much about him here; you will find it all in its place.

My dear children, I write this of the family lest today or tomorrow your children or grandchildren may not know about their family. I have put it briefly, anxious only that they should know from whom they are descended.

To return. I lived in Hameln for a year after my marriage. We did little business because Hameln is a small town and no place for business. We had dealings with the small farmers and lent money on pledges. But my husband, of blessed memory, was not content with this and from the hour of our marriage had it in mind to settle in Hamburg. As the Talmud says, *Wheresoever a man desires to go, there he is led.* The Lord lead us well. If only the crown of our head had remained with us! The Lord has given and the Lord has taken away; what cannot be changed must be endured.

At the end of the first year of married life, my husband would not stay any longer in Hameln. Though my parents-in-law wanted us to stay and remain with them in their house, he refused. So, with their consent we moved to Hamburg. We were both very young, children who understood little or nothing of business as carried on in Hamburg. But God Who led

my husband from his father's house and birthplace always stood
faithfully by him.

When we reached Hamburg my father, of blessed memory,
undertook to give us *Kest*[1] for two years. My husband, being a
stranger to the city, looked about, to see what he could do. At
that time the jewellery trade was not so well developed as now.
The citizens and gentile bridegrooms wore little or no jewellery
and it was the fashion to wear chains of pure gold and only give
presents made of gold. There was less profit to be made out of
gold than out of precious stones. My husband's first business
was trading in gold. He ran about all day from house to house
buying up gold, which he sold either to the smelters or to the
merchants who sold it again to the betrothed young men. This
brought good profit, and though he was busy running about on
business all day, he never once missed learning the appointed
Talmud lesson for the day. And until he went on long journeys
he fasted every Monday and Thursday.[2] He suffered much
because of this and though still young, fell seriously ill and had
to submit to much doctoring. He never spared himself, but
suffered much for the sake of his wife and children. There is
much to write of him; he was such a loving and faithful husband and father. His like will not be found. All his days he
refused any prominent position in the community, laughing at
people when he saw what store they set by these things. In
short: he was a pattern of a pious Jew, as were also his father
and brothers. I know that even great rabbis do not pray with
such devotion as he did. When he, peace on him, was in his
room praying, and anyone came to sell him something, even
the greatest bargain, neither I nor anyone of the household
dared disturb him to tell him of it. Because of this he once
neglected a deal and lost a profit of several hundreds. But he
did not mind this, for he served his God with zeal, and He
rewarded him doubly and trebly, as it is said, *Trust in the Lord
and the Lord will be your trust.*

Such modesty and patience as he possessed, even under

---

[1] *Kest*, an undertaking to board and clothe the bridal pair for a stated
period, was usually included in the betrothal contract and formed part of
the dowry. Owing to the young age at which marriages were contracted, this
was a necessity of the time.

[2] A minor religious observance of the pious.

sufferings through friends or strangers, is not to be found. When I often, in my human weakness, would complain, he would laugh at me and say, 'You are foolish. I trust in God and do not heed people's words.' May his merits stand us in good stead both in this and the other world!

About the time we came to Hamburg I became pregnant, and my mother, long may she live, was in the same condition. Though I was still a child to whom such unaccustomed things came hard, I was happy when the All Highest presented me with a beautiful, healthy baby. My mother expected her child about the same time, but was pleased that I had had mine first and that she could attend me and the child the first few days. Eight days later she also gave birth to a daughter, so there was no envy or reproach between us. We lay in one room, beside each other, and had no peace from the people who came running to see the wonder of mother and daughter lying in childbed together.

To lengthen this book a little and while away more time, I shall write of a pretty incident. It was winter time and my mother and I lay together in a small room. My father's family was large and the room was crowded, but both parents and children suffered the discomfort quite patiently. I left childbed eight days before my mother, and to make the room less crowded returned to my own chamber. As I was still so young, my mother would not let me take my baby to my room at night. So, the baby was left in her room, where she and also her maid slept. My mother told me not to worry; if the baby cried she would send the maid with it for me to suckle it and later return the babe to its cradle. With this arrangement I was well satisfied.

For several nights all went well: usually, as I lay in bed, about midnight, the maid would bring the baby to be fed. One morning, about three o'clock, I awoke with a start and cried to my husband, 'What can be the matter? the maid has not yet brought the baby!' He replied, 'Baby must be still sleeping.' This did not satisfy me. I ran to my mother's room to see what had happened to the babe. I went straight to the cradle: it was empty! Though I was very alarmed I was afraid to shout for fear my mother would awake and suffer a fright. I went over to the maid and began to shake her, hoping to rouse her quietly.

But she was in a deep sleep. I had to shout before I could rouse her from her torpor. I asked her, 'Where is my baby?' The girl answered, speaking out of her sleep, and did not know what she was saying. My mother—long may she live—woke up. She too cried to the maid, 'Where is Glückel's baby?' But she was still so sleepy that she could not give a clear reply. Then I said to my mother, 'Mumma, perhaps you have my baby in bed with you?' She answered, 'No! I have *mine* in bed with me,' and held it close to her as though someone was trying to snatch the baby away. I bethought me to go to the other cradle, and there lay her baby, fast asleep! I said, 'Mumma, give me *my* baby, *yours* is in the cradle.' But she would not believe me, so I had to fetch a light and take her baby to her, so that she could see for herself before she returned my own to me. The whole household had been awakened and alarmed, but soon the consternation turned to laughter, and they said we would really have needed King Solomon soon.

Though the arrangement was intended for two years, because it was so crowded at home, we only lived one year with my parents. My husband refused to remain longer and would not take a pfennig of the money offered him in place of the second year's *Kest*. We found a nice house, 50 reichstalers rent a year, and with *mazal tov*,[1] together with our maid and one manservant, we moved into our own house. If God had not struck us such a severe blow and so soon taken the crown of my head, I do not think that there would have been a more loving couple than we in the whole world. But we must bear all patiently.

So, while still very young, we went to live in our own house. Though we were economical, we had everything necessary for the upkeep of a fine house. Abraham Kantor of Hildesheim was our first servant; he looked after our children. He left us after some years and did business on his own. He married a widow who died soon after the wedding. Then he married again, a young girl from Amsterdam, and they settled in Hamburg. We lent him money to go to Copenhagen to do business. In short, people say he is now worth more than 10,000 reichstaler.

When my daughter Zipporah was two years old, I was again brought to my bed, with my son Nathan. My husband's happiness cannot be described; nor the wonderful party to celebrate

[1] Hebrew for good-luck, good fortune, a term of felicitation.

Tuguriola. 177

Matrimonium Judaicum. Pag. 13.

9. *Scene from the Feast of Tabernacles.* Engraving. Utrecht, 1682

10. *A Jewish Marriage Ceremony.* Engraving. Utrecht, 1682

ברוולופט

יר דר נב'א זאנגט מן נאפרוש
וש ליגט אן דער כלה רעם
ההמט קין כל ת ח יל' ער
ח מן הז' גטרייפט) מונ'
זמ מונ'אלט ברכת אירוסין.
ן ענג גלמו לו מיר.דר בתולה
ה דען טעם וייס אן חמול.
זינר אלמנה מין מיררן כלי
ן ברכת אירוסין מוז מיז זמ
וג' דער כלה דר נאך גיבט
רב מול' דר רב רופט ערים
זוה פריוטהאין · אן טמר
ד רו מין סטיין המט · דען
אין ווערט זין לו ע' וו ורם
ני לאיש ר'ת אבן לא יש וון
יר דם טלית פום קמחל מונ'אן ליחט דר נאך רים כתובה · מן נעמט
ט ברכת אירוסין מונ' ברכת נישואין מויל מין גלמו · אן זמ רים אלות
ברכת אירוסין גיאמלט זמנג דר ער ז אמר מי אן ברכת נישואין גולט האט

11. *A Jewish Wedding*, from a Book of Minhagim. Woodcut, 1692

the *Bris Milah*.[1] May God grant that I live to see such joy of my children, for now my only comfort is in them.

Here I end my second book and beg all who read this to be indulgent to my follies, for this is written in sorrow and heart-ache. Praised be God who has given me strength to bear adversity. Now with the help of the All Highest I will begin my third book.

[1] Circumcision.

E

BOOK III

WHO can write and who can tell of the wonders that happen
to mortals? I was about twenty-five years old at the time of
which I write. My husband was very energetic in business and
I, too, helped. It is not to praise myself that I mention that he
took advice from no one but me, and did nothing until we had
talked it over together.

At this time a young man, Mordecai, from Hanover—may
the Lord avenge his blood—who worked for my brother-in-
law Lipman, came to Hamburg and was our guest. We took a
liking to him and engaged him to travel for us in such places
where business could be done. He was a native of Poland and
knew the language well. We sent him to Danzig to buy seed
pearls,[1] for we had heard that there were several parcels to be
bought there, and seed pearls were then the most important
article in the jewellery trade. We gave him a credit note for a
few hundred reichstaler and instructed him how to buy the
pearls. Had we sent jewellery to Danzig to be sold there and
bought in return, we should have made handsomer profits, but
we were so deep in the pearl business that we did not think of
this.

Mordecai went to Danzig, bought the pearls and sent them
on to us. He bought well and we made a good profit. But he
was a young man, and desiring to marry did not wish to remain
in Danzig. He therefore returned to Hamburg, became engaged to the daughter of Tall Nathan and the marriage was
fixed for six months later.

My husband wished him to return to Danzig until his wedding. As if decreed from heaven, he refused. He said, 'It is less
than six months to my wedding day. Before I go there and
return the time will have gone. I will go instead to Germany
to buy wine.' My husband then said, 'How do you come to
buy wine? I want nothing to do with that business.' And Mordecai answered, 'Then I'll buy it on my own account.'

My husband did not approve, and tried to dissuade him,
first in a friendly and then an angry way, from this business,

[1] These small pearls are sold, not singly, but by the ounce. The profit is
made by picking and sorting, and selling according to size.

42

but it was of no avail. He remained quite firm and no one
could move him. My husband sent for his future father-in-law
to get him to use his influence to dissuade him from the ill-fated
journey, but to no effect. It was just as though the good man
had to go to make room for others. If God had prolonged his
life, perhaps Judah Berlin and Issacher Cohen would never
have come to their wealth, as I will relate later.

Thus Mordecai set out on his journey carrying with him
about 600 reichstaler. This money he handed to my brother-in-
law Reb Lipman, when he reached Hanover, to be forwarded
to those places where he bought wine. Thence he had to go to
Hildesheim. Mordecai was a stingy man who grudged the
money that taking the post would have cost him. He made the
distance from Hanover to Hildesheim, three miles, on foot.
When he was about 2000 feet[1] distant from the latter place, he
came face to face with a poacher, who said to him, 'Jew, give
me money for a drink, otherwise I will shoot you!' Mordecai
laughed at him, for he knew that the highway between Hanover and Hildesheim is safer than that between Hamburg and
Altona. The poacher addressed him again, 'You Jew carcase!
Why do you think so long? Say yes or no!' and took his gun
and shot him in the head. Mordecai fell dead immediately.

This road was rarely deserted for as long as a quarter of an
hour, but on this occasion, unfortunately, it just happened that
no one passed. Thus the upstanding, noble and honest young
man met an early end and instead of celebrating his marriage,
he had to creep into dark earth, though so innocent. My God!
When I remind myself of this, my hair stands on end. He was
a truly good, God-fearing man, and had his life been spared, he
would have done great things and it would have been better for us.
God knows how pained we were over his death, and how much
sorrow we suffered, as will be revealed later. He had not lain
long wallowing in his young blood when people coming from
Hildesheim found him in this miserable plight. He was recognized immediately, for he was well-known in that district. The
grief is indescribable! But what did it help? We received letters
from Hanover and Hildesheim, for people knew that he was our
partner and thought he had had much of our money with him.
All that he had was a few reichstaler for immediate needs. I can

[1] The Sabbath walking distance, permitted by Rabbinical law.

remember how upset my husband and I were when the news reached us, for at that time I was pregnant with my daughter Mattie, peace unto her. We could have done much business with him—but what has come to pass cannot be changed, especially death. Though efforts were made in Hildesheim and Hanover to find the murderer, he was never discovered. May his name be blotted out! and may the Lord avenge the guiltless blood, with the rest of the holy and pious martyrs.

We were left without anyone to help us in our business. A short time after, the wealthy Reb Judah Berlin,[1] then a very young man, was brought by Jacob Oberkirchen, the matchmaker, as a possible suitor for Pinches Harburg's daughter. Nothing, however, came of this match, through whose fault I cannot say. Judah, who was related to us on my husband's side—he was a cousin to my brother-in-law, Lipman—remained with us as our guest for a short time. He pleased us in every way; he was well read, understood business very well, and was, besides, very intelligent. One day, my husband said to me, 'Glückelchen, what do you say to our engaging the youth and sending him to Danzig for us? He seems to be a very sharp fellow.' 'I have already thought the same,' I replied. 'We must have someone.'

We spoke to him and he was very pleased to travel for us. Before eight days passed he was on his way to Danzig. All that he had of his own was amber to the value of 20–30 reichstaler, which he left with my husband to sell or hold for him. See, my dear children, if God wishes to help anyone, He makes much out of little, for from this small capital, which really amounted to next to nothing, He brought Judah to great riches, and today he is a great man.

Reb Judah was in Danzig some time and did good business, buying up seed pearls. He did not strive much after deals, for we did not enjoy such big credits in Hamburg as we do now, we were still young and had no great fortunes. Still, we supplied him with letters of credit and promissory notes so that he was

[1] Later, the well-known Court Jew, Jost Liebman, son of Elieser Liebman of Göttingen, who through his second marriage with the widow of Israel Aron, factor of the Great Elector (1670), succeeded him in the Elector's favour and later in that of his son, Frederick I of Prussia: the composer Meyerbeer and the poet Michael Beer are among his descendants.

not short of money. He was in Danzig about two years. On his return my husband went over the accounts with him and gave him 800 reichstaler as his share of the profits. With this he moved to Hanover, intending to marry and settle there.

During this time I was brought to bed with my daughter Mattie; she was a beautiful child. And also, about this time, people began to talk of Sabbatai Zevi,[1] but *woe unto us, for we have sinned*, for we did not live to see that which we had heard and hoped to see. When I remember the penance done by young and old—it is indescribable, though it is well enough known in the whole world. O Lord of the Universe, at that time we hoped that you, O merciful God, would have mercy on your people Israel and redeem us from our exile. We were like a woman in travail, a woman on the labour-stool who, after great labour and sore pains, expects to rejoice in the birth of a child, but finds it is nothing but wind. This, my great God and King, happened to us. All your servants and children did much penance, recited many prayers, gave away much in charity, throughout the world. For two or three years your people Israel sat on the labour-stool—but nothing came save wind. We did not merit to see the longed-for child, but because of our sins, we were left neither here nor there—but in the middle. Your people hope daily, that you in your infinite mercy will redeem them yet and that the Messiah will come—if it be your divine will to redeem your people Israel.

The joy, when letters arrived, is not to be described. Most of the letters were received by the Portuguese. They took them to their synagogue and read them aloud there. The Germans, young and old, went into the Portuguese synagogue to hear

[1] The advent of Sabbatai Zevi and his rise to pseudo-messiahship in the years 1665–7 provided a romantic and colourful interval in the life of the Jewries in most parts of the world. In many countries Jews were wrought up to a fervour of faith which made them ready to believe that redemption was at hand and that the sons of Israel were now to prepare for the second exodus. In many communities whole families liquidated their possessions and waited only for the trumpet of Messiah before setting forth on their journey to the Holy Land. There is no doubt that Glückel's sidelight is by no means an exaggeration, but an interesting personal picture of the effect of the messianic delusion upon her immediate surroundings. The excitement spread also to the non-Jews. The Fifth Monarchy literature of Puritan England was not unconnected. In Pepys's diary reference is made to these Jewish messianic expectations.

them. The young Portuguese on these occasions all wore their best clothes and each tied a broad green silk ribbon round his waist—this was Sabbatai Zevi's colour. So all, 'with kettle-drums and round dance' went with joy 'like the festival of the house, of the pouring of the water', to hear the letters read. Many people sold home, hearth and everything they possessed, awaiting redemption.

My father-in-law, peace unto him, who lived in Hameln, moved from there, leaving things standing in the house, just as they were, and went to Hildesheim. He sent us here, to Hamburg, two big barrels of linenware, in them were all kinds of food—peas, smoked meat, all sorts of dried fruits—that could keep without going bad. The good man thought they would leave from Hamburg for the Holy Land. These barrels were more than a year in my house. At last, fearing that the meat and other things would get spoilt, he wrote that we should open the barrels and take out all the food, so that the linen underneath should not spoil. They remained here for three more years, my father-in-law always expecting to need them at a moment's notice for his journey.

But this did not suit the Almighty. We knew well that He had promised us that if we were devout and pious from the bottom of our hearts, He would have mercy on us, if only we obeyed His word: *Love your neighbour as yourself*. But the jealousy, the needless hate that is among us! No good can come of it. That which you have promised, dear Lord, will be graciously fulfilled. If it is delayed because of our sins, when the right time comes we shall surely have it. For this we pray and hope, great God, that we will rejoice in a perfect redemption. I shall end this matter and begin anew.

As I have related, about this time I was in childbed with my daughter Mattie. It began to be whispered that the Plague[1]— not upon us!—had broken out in the gentile quarter. Three or four Jewish houses were afterwards infected and the people living in them died, so that the houses remained unoccupied. It was a time of trouble and desolation. May God shield us from the way in which the dead were treated. Most of the Jewish householders moved to Altona. They had with them pledges to the value of several thousand reichstaler, small ones from 10

[1] This was July 1664.

taler to larger sums of 100 taler. Nevertheless, in dealing with pledges one must be as careful of one worth only a schilling as of one worth 20 taler. We had no peace from the gentiles in the town who rushed to redeem their pledges. Though we knew that they were infected, we had to let them redeem their pledges. We knew that even if we moved to Altona they would follow us there, so we decided to move to Hameln, where my father-in-law lived. We left Hamburg the day after *Yom Kippur*[1] and arrived in Hanover the day before the Feast of the Tabernacles.[2] Here we were the guests of Abraham Hameln, my brother-in-law, who was then living in that town. The festival being so near, we were not allowed to continue our journey. With us were my daughter Zipporah, then four years old, my two-year-old son Nathan, and Mattie, peace unto her, a baby of eight weeks.

My brother-in-law, Leib Hanover,[3] invited us to stay with him for the first days of the festival; the synagogue was in his house. My husband was there praying on the first day, and I was in my room downstairs dressing Zipporah.

I must write here of an incident that happened while he was still alive. There are many troubles of which I cannot tell, particularly now, for to whom can I tell them? We have no one in whom to confide save God, our father in heaven; may He be our help, and to His people Israel, and make us rejoice even as He has afflicted us. When my husband was alive trouble did not miss us, bringing up our children and other worries. Some things may be told, but others must not be mentioned. My beloved companion would allay all my worries and comfort me, so that somehow they passed easily. But now, who is my comforter? and who listens to my heavy thoughts now, and lightens my sad heart as kindly and easily as he? Half an hour before his pure soul left his body, when my mother fell on his bed weeping and lamenting and asked, 'My beloved son-in-law, have you any request that I may carry out for you?' he said, 'My dear mother, I have nothing to ask or say—only comfort my afflicted Glückelchen'. After this he did not wish to say more, as

[1] The Day of Atonement: the chief fast in the Jewish Calendar.
[2] The Feast of Tabernacles is celebrated after the Day of Atonement and lasts a week. The journey to Hanover took five days.
[3] He was married to Esther, the sister of Chaim Hameln.

I will relate later on. Who is now my comforter? Before whom shall I pour out my bitter lot, and whither shall I turn? At present I am overwhelmed in a sea of sorrows and despondent thoughts.

There were many incidents like the following—great trouble which the merciful God removed from us. To start where I left off: I noticed, when dressing Zipporah, that the child recoiled when I touched her. 'What ails you, Zipporah, my dear?' I asked. 'Mumma, dear,' the child answered, 'it hurts me very much under my arm.' I examined her and saw that there was a boil under her arm. My husband, too, had had such a boil and cured it with a small plaster applied by a barber-surgeon in Hanover. I said to my servant who was with me, 'Go to my husband—he is upstairs in the synagogue—and ask him which barber he went to and where he lives. You will then take the child there and have a plaster applied.' I had no bad forebodings.

The maid went into the synagogue, obtained the address from my husband and had to return through the room where the women sat, for one had to pass there to reach the men's section. My sisters-in-law Yenta, Sulka and Esther, who were seated there, asked the maid, 'What were you doing in the men's synagogue?' Quite innocently, having no suspicion of trouble, the maid answered, 'Our child has a boil under her arm. I asked my master which barber it was that had healed his boil, so that I could take the child to him.'

The women were cowards in such matters and were greatly alarmed, particularly as we had come from Hamburg. They put their heads together and conferred. There was seated among them an old Polish woman, a visitor, who heard what they said and noticed their terror. She said to them. 'Do not be frightened; nothing will happen. I have had about twenty years' dealings with such things. If you like, I will go down and examine the little girl and let you know at once if—God forbid!—it is dangerous, and what you should then do.' My sisters-in-law answered, 'Yes. For mercy's sake, go straightway and see whether there is any danger.'

I knew nothing, then, of this talk. The old Polish woman came down and said, 'Where is the little girl?' 'Why?' I asked. 'I am a healer,' she answered. 'I will give her something which

will make her better at once.' Not suspecting any ill, I led the
child to her. She examined her, rushed away and up to the
women crying, 'Flee from here! All who can, fly and run! For
our great sins we have the *true* plague in the house. The little
girl has the pestilence!' Well, you can imagine the wailing and
confusion among the women, especially among such a timorous
crowd. Men and women rushed from the synagogue during the
most solemn prayers of the holy festival and quickly thrust the
maid and the child out of the house. You can conceive our feelings. I wept and cried aloud, 'For God's sake, people, what are
you doing? Nothing is the matter with the child, she is quite
healthy, God be praised. She had a sore head before we left
Hamburg, I anointed it and the fluid from the head has,
doubtless, led to this boil. If, God forbid, one has the plague the
signs are different. See how freely my child is running about
the street and eating a roll.'

Nothing helped. They said, 'If it comes to the knowledge of
his highness, our duke, that anyone has this in his residential
city, desolation will befall us.' The old woman stood in front
of me saying that she would give her neck if the child had not
something catching. What could we do? I begged: 'For mercy's
sake, let me remain with my child. Where she is, I want to be.
Let me out to her.' This also they would not allow. In short,
my brothers-in-law, Reb Lipman, Reb Leib and Reb Abraham and their womenfolk held counsel where to lodge the
maid and child and keep the whole thing secret from the
authorities; great troubles would befall the Jews if, God forbid, the Duke heard of the matter.

They decided to dress the maid and child in old, torn clothes
and send them to a small village not a Sabbath's journey from
Hanover. This village was called Peinholz [Pinewood]. There
they were to lodge with some peasants and say that as the Jews
in Hanover were celebrating their festival, they would not
receive them, for they already had as many poor people as they
could accommodate. They would pay for their keep and were
sure that food and drink would be sent to them from Hanover,
so that they would not suffer hunger during the festival.

There was an old Polish Jew staying in Hanover, a guest of
the community. We hired him, and the old Polish woman whom
I have already mentioned, to stay with the child until we saw

how things turned out. Neither would move from the place until they received 30 taler, because they insisted that they were putting themselves into dire peril. My three brothers-in-law again held counsel and with them the teacher of Hanover, a great scholar. They discussed whether it was permissible according to the Torah to desecrate the holy festival by giving the money the Poles demanded. They decided that it was, as it was a question of danger to life.

So we were compelled to send our dear child from us on this festival and to persuade ourselves that—God forbid!—there was something really the matter with her. Every father and mother can imagine our feelings. My husband, of blessed memory, stood weeping in one corner of the room and I in the other, imploring God's mercy. It was surely because of my husband's piety that God heard him. I do not think that our father Abraham was heavier of heart than ours then. Our father Abraham, out of obedience and love of God, did his duty, so his sorrow was mixed with joy. But this befell us in a strange place and troubled our hearts sorely. We could do nothing but suffer patiently. As we must praise the Lord God for good, so also must we for the bad.

My maid put her clothes on inside out, dressed the child in old, tattered rags and tied up the clothes into bundles which she carried like the beggar-women. So, my good maid, my child, the old man and woman, set off for the hamlet. The Priest's benediction, which we sent after them, and the hundreds of tears we shed may easily be imagined. Nevertheless, the child was jolly and carefree, as a child is who does not understand. But we ourselves, in Hanover, wept and implored God and spent the holy day in great grief.

They reached the small village and found lodgings in a peasant's house, for they had money with them, and as long as one has money, use can be made of it. The peasant said, 'To-day is your festival: why are you not among Jews?' They answered as they had been told: that there were enough poor Jews in Hanover by the time they had arrived and that they had not been allowed to enter; however, they expected the community would send them out food.

When we returned again to the synagogue, prayers had ended. At that time Judah Berlin, still a bachelor, was in

Hanover. Also Michael, a young man from Poland who taught the children and later took a wife from Hildesheim and is now living there in great wealth and highly respected as the *parnass*. The same Reb Michael was a kind of household servant, as was then the practice in Germany when a young man was brought from Poland to teach young children. Coming out of the synagogue Reb Leib invited us to the feast, for as I have already mentioned, he had invited us to be his guests. My husband of blessed memory said to him, 'Before we eat I must first take my child and the others some food. It is *Yom Tov*.'[1] 'Yes, certainly,' answered the others. 'You are right. None of us will eat before those outside have had something.'

The village was as near Hanover as Altona to Hamburg. When the food was brought they argued as to who was to take it to the village. Reb Judah said, 'I will take it.' Reb Michael answered, 'I will go with you.' In the end my husband, who loved the child well, too, went with them. But the Hanoverians did not trust him not to go near the child. My brother-in-law Lipman joined them, and all went off together with the food.

Meanwhile, the child and the others, being very hungry, went in the fields, to await the arrival of the food. When the little one espied her father she was full of joy and, like a child, wanted to run up to him. On seeing this, Reb Lipman shouted that the child must be kept back and that the old man should approach to take the food. My husband had to be held fast as though by a rope, for he strained from the grasping hands to reach our child. They both wept; for he saw her hale and well, yet could not approach her. The food and drinks were placed on the grass and after the maid and company took it, the others went away. This lasted until the eighth day of the Tabernacles.

The old man and woman had plaster and salve with them, which they applied to the boil. It was soon quite nicely healed and the child sprang about the fields like a young doe.

We said to the Hanoverians, 'What will be the outcome of your folly? You can see that the child is quite healthy and well, and that there is no danger. Let her in again.'

Once more they held counsel together and decided that the child and her companions were not to return before *Simchat*

[1] Literally good day—the term for religious festivals.

Torah.[1] We had to be content with this. On the day of the festival Reb Michael brought back the child and the others. Oh, the great joy of my husband and myself! We wept for joy. Yes, the eye wept but the heart was glad. Everyone wanted to eat the child, she was so lovely, without an equal. For a long time after she was called the maid of Peinholz.

So, my dear children, this sad event passed happily and the end was full of joy. We cannot praise and thank the Highest enough for His goodness and mercy to me, His unworthy servant, even if I should write ten books they would not suffice.

I will hold my peace about the great hardships I underwent through my children's sufferings. I would have given half my health for their sakes. But God in a second helped so graciously that I did not know where the sufferings remained. Years I worried and was troubled about the health of a child, and of a sudden God restored to us a strong and healthy child. Therefore we must ever thank and praise the Lord for His great mercy. We poor, sinful people should accept our fate with love, thanking God for everything comes from Him, God gives and God takes away—blessed be His Name.

Here is a pleasant story to show what happened to an empress and how patiently she bore adversity and all that befell her. Charlemagne was a mighty emperor as one may read in German books. He had no wife. It was resolved at a council which he held one day that he and Irena Empress of the Orient who likewise had no spouse, should wed. He sent an embassy to the Empress to ask her hand in marriage so that in this way the East and Germany would be united in amity. He sent grand ambassadors to Constantinople for this purpose and alliance.

The Empress was neither in favour nor against this suit, and said, 'I will give you an answer in a few days.' The ambassadors were well pleased with these words expecting a favourable outcome which they would convey, with this treasure, to their emperor. They expected joyful celebrations in Constantinople and right royal receptions, and so waited in happy expectation of her final answer.

But, my God! what a change occurred in a few days to the Empress! In place of the settlement of the marriage plans which they awaited, they were forced to witness a tragic change—the Empress Irena was driven from her royal throne and her govern-

[1] Festival of the Rejoicing of the Law, celebrated immediately after that of Tabernacles.

ment was overthrown. Then a great lord, Nicoporas by name, who claimed to be the emperor and had a large following, got the royal servants on his side and in great haste had himself crowned emperor.

Before the coronation he, in person, spoke to the Empress out of his false heart, first excusing himself diffusively, declaring that all that had taken place had been against his will. It would have been more to his liking to have remained in his former low state and serve her as a loyal subject. But as the courtiers and nobles of the land wanted to relieve her from the yoke of the heavy cares of the State and governing the nation, so that she could live in peace and quiet, they had chosen him to take her place. This they had decided. He bowed to their will and so took on the high office. He hoped that she would refrain from all interference and reveal to him the secrets of State and all its treasures. He promised his friendship; that she would lack nothing and that no harm would befall her.

Hereupon the Empress Irena answered him in a friendly manner, 'Dear Nicoporas, the All Highest who reigns over all, acts according to His will: giving the kingdom to whom He will, setting up and casting down kings as He chooses. He set me on the throne and sustained me till now, but because of my sins and misdeeds, He has taken away my rule. Yet, I must praise His Name and as a true noble lady say with patient Job, *The Lord has taken, praised be His Name*. If power came justly to you, you will give account to God. That which has befallen me has happened often before. I know I had the means to prevent such events as happen to those who do as you have done, but because of my tender heart, I am the cause of what has happened, and have helped towards it. Now it is impossible for me to alter the position. Therefore, I entreat you, spare me and let me spend the rest of my life peacefully in the palace which I have built.'

Nicoporas promised to grant her behests and give her what she desired, but only if she would reveal the whereabouts of the whole royal treasure, hiding nothing from him.

When she had done this and disclosed the treasures, in the very presence of the Emperor Charlemagne's ambassadors, he sent her to the lonely Isle of Lesbos, where, after much hardship, she died the following year.

To know what befell such a mighty empress and how patiently she bore all, is to learn that everyone should accept sufferings with patience, as I have already written.

We had a happy festival and rejoiced that God had brought us out of sorrow. We remained in Hanover till the beginning of

Marcheshvan,[1] after which we all left for Hameln. We intended to stay there until all was well again in Hamburg. We
had no rest where we were, for we did a great deal of business
and had an agent in Poland who was called Green Moses. We
received letters from him to say that he had bought 600 Lot[2]
of seed pearls and had arrived with them in Hamburg. From
there he wrote again to say that he had brought the pearls with
him and my husband should leave forthwith for Hamburg. My
husband did not leave immediately but remained another fourteen days in Hameln, for things were still very bad in the
former place and his parents would not suffer him to endanger
his life by going there, and would not even allow us to receive
letters from there. When a letter did come, we had to fumigate
it two or three times, and immediately after we had read it,
we threw it into the river.

Once, as we sat chatting together, Green Moses came suddenly into the room. It was mid-winter and he had a cowl
drawn over his head. We recognized him immediately, and
signed to him to go out; no one else had seen him, for we were
alone in the room. Had my parents-in-law known that anyone
from Hamburg had come to see us, they would have driven
him and us away.

In truth, it was dangerous, in case the authorities got to
know; it was perilous, a matter of death, if anyone from Hamburg was taken in. All travellers were thoroughly examined
before they were allowed to enter the city gates. We asked
Green Moses, 'How did you manage to get here?' He answered,
'I said I was the clerk to the official of Hachen'—a village not
far from Hameln. What were we to do? He was already here
and had the pearls with him. We could not hide him, for our
parents were sure to find out. We decided that we would have
to tell them, and even if they did not like it, it could not be
altered.

But Green Moses did not wish us to say anything; he only
wanted my husband to return to Hamburg with him and sell
the pearls, so that he could go away and buy more goods. What
was my husband to do? There was much money tied up in the

---

[1] October/November.

[2] A Lot equals half an ounce. Seed pearls were sold by the two Lots or
ounce.

pearls and it does not pay to keep such goods a long while, for the profits are not large; when they lie a long time, the interest eats up the profit. He therefore resolved to return with Green Moses, to sell the pearls and look round and see whether I and the children could return to our little nest. Though I lacked nothing, I was used to Hamburg and we had our business there, and I was tired of being away from home.

So, my husband returned to Hamburg with his pearls, worth 6000 reichstaler banco,[1] and went with them to the merchants trading with Moscow. Altogether he went to six merchants, but no one made him a good offer; the profit was too small. This was in the month of Shevat.[2] The bill which he had had discounted to enable us to buy the pearls had to be met. As ships bound for Moscow leave Hamburg in the month of Ab,[3] it is best to sell in the month of Tammuz.[4]

Because of the low bids he had received, my husband pawned the pearls for 6000 reichstaler. He thought he would get better prices in Tammuz. But he was wide of the mark! Letters arrived from Muscovy with tidings that a great war was raging.[5] The merchants lost all inclination to buy pearls. My husband had to sell at 4000 reichstaler, less than he had been offered, besides having to pay six months' interest. See, therefore, the first buyer is always the best and a dealer must know his own mind at once—yes or no.

My husband enquired how things were in Hamburg. Everyone told him that all was quiet. He sent me as travelling companion a Jew of the name of Jacob. Though he was an honest man, he had one fault—a fondness for drink, a failing over which he had no control. My good Jacob went to Hanover where he stayed, idling. From thence he wrote that I and my children should come and together we would take the post to Hamburg. I wrote straightway to Hildesheim, to Abraham Kantor, who had once worked for us, that he should come to Hameln and travel with us to Hamburg. We rode to Hanover and there found our Shot Jacob. He went on Friday to the deputy postmaster, who was his sworn pot-brother, and hired the post for us. We remained for the Sabbath in Hanover. The

---

[1] Cash.   [2] January/February.   [3] July/August.   [4] June/July.
[5] Warfare between Poland and Russia was frequent under the first Romanoff Tsar.

weather was very bad and I had three little ones with me. All day Saturday my brother-in-law Lipman and his wife Yenta spoke with Jacob and begged him to take good care of me and the children and look after us well, and not to drink as was his custom. He promised them by hand and mouth, not to get drunk but only to drink that which he needed. But how he kept his word you will see.

Early Sunday I, the three children, the maid, the man-servant, and our guide Jacob, left Hanover. The deputy post-master, too, journeyed with us. As I have already mentioned, he was Jacob's pot-brother. Jacob helped us into the wagon and saw to everything; he and the deputy walked together beside our vehicle. I thought they would wait until we had passed through the gate and then seat themselves in the wagon. When we had left the gates behind us, I told Jacob that he and the deputy should take their seats so that we should not be held up and arrive too late at the inn. But Jacob answered, 'You ride on in God's name. I and the deputy must go to the village, as he has to speak with someone there. We will walk as quickly as you ride, and will soon be with you again.' I did not know the secret reason for this. The village lay quite close to Hanover and was called Langenhagen. It was a mile in length and throughout the land there was no better 'Broyan'[1] than in that village. So, my good helper Jacob and the post-deputy remained the whole day and a good part of the night, drinking in Langenhagen. I knew nothing of this at the time. We rode on our way; every second I looked behind to see whether Jacob was coming, but whoever came into view, it was not Jacob. We rode until we came to a pass, two miles from Hanover, where we had to pay toll. The postillion said to me, 'We must pay toll here.' I paid the toll and asked the postillion to ride on, so that we should reach the inn in time. The weather was bad, not fit to send dogs out in. It was about Purim[2] time, with dismal dripping rain and snow which froze as it fell on us. The children, poor things,

---

[1] A wheaten beer of sweet, spiced flavour, named after its supposed inventor Kurd Broyan, a brewer who lived near Hanover.

[2] This feast, preceded, by Orthodox Jews, by a fast, is in commemoration of the downfall of Haman and the triumph of the Jewish queen Esther and her uncle Mordecai, as related in the book of Esther. It usually falls either in February or in March.

12. *Purim Players.* Engraving by Johan van den Avele.
17th Century

13. *The Purim Feast.* Engraving. Nürnberg, 1734

14. *A Jewish Wedding Procession.* Engraving. Nürnberg, *ca.* 1700

15. *A Jewish Wedding Ceremony.* Engraving. Nürnberg, 1734

suffered greatly—I also. I again begged the postillion to drive
on. 'You can see', I cried, 'what the weather is like—and here
we are without shelter, under the open sky.' He answered, 'I
must not leave here till the deputy postmaster comes; he
ordered me to wait here till he and Jacob arrive.' What was I
to do?

We sat there another two hours, until the tollman came and
had pity on us. He let us step out of our coach and took us into
his warm room, where the children were thoroughly warmed.
After we had spent an hour there, I said to the tollman, 'I beg
you, sir, make the postillion ride on, so that I and my little
children may get to the inn before night. You can see how bad
the weather is and know how terrible the way is by day. How
much worse will it be in the dark of the night! If—God forbid!—the wagon were to turn over we would break our necks
immediately.'

On this, the tollman told the postillion to ride on straightway. The postillion replied, 'If I ride on, the post-deputy will
break my neck and I shall not get a pfennig of my wages.' But
the tollman was a good, honest man; he urged him to drive on.
'When the two drunken knaves arrive,' he said, 'let each hire
a horse and follow after you; you will stay overnight at the inn.'

What was the poor postillion to do? He had no choice but to
ride on with us. It was really awful weather, but we arrived at
the inn in good time, and there found a fine, warm room where
we were nicely received. Though the place was packed with
drivers and travellers so that the room was crowded, everyone
showed kindness and sympathy for the children, who had not a
dry thread on them. I hung up their little frocks to dry and
soon they were themselves again. We had good food with us and
in the inn there was good beer. So, after our dreary, laborious
journey we were revived with good fare and drink; and sat up
till late at night expecting the two pot-brothers to arrive. But
no one came, so I had straw spread on the floor and I and my
little ones lay down to rest.

I could not fall asleep, but lay still, thanking God that the
children at least were sleeping. About midnight I heard a fearful scream in the room: the post-deputy, quite drunk, had
entered, and with a drawn sword had fallen on the postillion
to kill him for driving on by himself. The postillion answered as

F

well as he could. The innkeeper came in, tried to calm the drunkard, and at length succeeded in quietening him. I sat, poor me, in my little corner, quiet as a mouse, for he was drunk and mad and I was in terror, for I did not see Jacob with him. A little while later the deputy postmaster sat down to eat and I saw that his fury had died down. So I went up to him and said, 'Herr Petersen, where have you left my Jacob?' 'Where should I have left him?' he answered. 'He could not go any farther, so remained by a hedge near some water; he may already be drowned.' This frightened me very much: I did not know what to do; he was a human being, and a Jew, and I was alone. I begged the innkeeper to send two peasants to look for him and bring him back.

The two peasants rode away. Half an hour from the village they found my good Jacob, lying as one killed, worn out by his journey and drunkenness. The good overcoat and little money he had had with him, were all gone. The peasants put him on a horse and brought him to the inn. Though I was very angry with him, still I thanked God when I saw him again. It cost me more than 6 reichstaler. I gave him something to eat, and my fine servant, who was to look after me and my children, I had to serve! Well, day dawned, the drivers brought out the wagon, ready once more to set out. I, the children, the maid and servant seated ourselves. I told Jacob to get up behind and not behave as he had done before. He answered, 'No, I only want to go back and see if anything has been left behind in the room.' I thought he meant this, but my fine Jacob went again into the inn and began drinking anew. I sent the drivers in to tell them to come out, since we had been delayed enough by the bad weather. The drivers, too, began to shout that their horses would be ruined standing idly about in such weather. But nothing helped—the post-deputy was master and the drivers had to wait. So, once more, we sat waiting two hours and did not set out before both were quite drunk, and at length took their seats in the wagon.

What more shall I write of this journey? The same thing happened at all the inns. But God helped us to Harburg, which is a mile distant from Hamburg, where my husband and father met us. Our joy is easily imagined. We went by water to Hamburg and I thanked God that I found all our friends well. Very few Jewish houses had been attacked by the plague while I was away. But the trouble was not yet over, for here and there it flickered. Among the Jews everything was well and remained well. May God continue to protect us, and redeem us from all our troubles.

So, we were once more back in our dear Hamburg, after an absence of half a year. We reckoned that we lost during the time, in pearls and interest, more than 1200 reichstaler. Still, we were thankful that we had been saved, for we did not care too much for money. 'Give me the person and the wealth take unto thee.' God again vouchsafed these to us.

After this, the people who had moved to Altona because of the pest, singly, one after the other, came back to the town, and once more attended to business. During the time of the plague little business had been done, as a Hamburger could not go anywhere.

Shortly after, my husband went to the Leipzig Fair and there fell very ill. At that time things were very dangerous for Jews in Leipzig. If a Jew—God forbid!—died there, it would have cost him all he had. Reb Judah Berlin was also at the fair, at this time; he was very good to my husband and tended him well. When he got better, he spoke to him, as one good friend to another, and told my husband that as he was not a strong man he should not undertake such difficult journeys, but should go into partnership with him. He was a young man, he could travel all over the world and earn enough for both to live royally. My husband answered him, 'I can give you no answer here in Leipzig; I am not quite well yet and dare not remain longer because I am afraid I may—God forbid!—get worse. I will hire a wagon and go home. As it is now pay week, there is little to do at the Fair. Why not come with me, free of charge, on the wagon? When we are, if God wills, at home, we can talk it over. And, besides, my Glückelchen will then be present and will be able to give her good advice.' For my dear husband did nothing without my knowledge.

At this time Reb Judah was already married.[1] My husband had induced his brother, the learned Rabbi Samuel of Hildesheim, to give him his daughter as wife, together with a dowry

[1] To Malka, daughter of Rabbi Samuel Hameln of Hildesheim, and resided in Hildesheim.

of 500 reichstaler. They both arrived here from Leipzig and though my husband had not recovered his full strength, he was not ill enough to lie in bed. It was eight days before he was quite well. During this time Judah pleaded with me to persuade my husband to go into partnership with him. I could not bear the thought of my husband travelling again, for if—God forbid!—anything had happened to him in Leipzig, he would have lost his life and fortune.

In truth I never cared for him to go on these long journeys and suffered much agony in case he should fall ill, just as had happened in Leipzig. Once, before this, he had come home in the middle of a Fair. I knew nothing and was looking out of the door when I saw him come riding up—my fright can easily be imagined. And besides this, there were other things of which I cannot write. Who can write of all that happens?

Once when my husband had gone to the winter fair at Leipzig, about New Year's time, he journeyed back with other Jews and was to be here on a certain day. But they did not arrive on the day expected. The woman letter-carrier brought me letters from Frankfurt and told me that in the king's post-office they had received terrible news: two wagons, full of Jews and Christians, on the way over the Elbe in a ferry-boat to the customs office were all drowned; the ice was moving so strongly that the flat-bottomed boat was smashed to pieces. Then, my God, as though my soul flew out, I began to cry and call out and lament. Then Green Moses, whom I have already described, came into the room, and finding me in such a state asked me what had happened. I told him and begged him, 'For the sake of His Name, take a horse, quick, and ride to the *Zollen pieker*[1] and see what has happened.' Although Green Moses and others tried to comfort me, I could not be comforted. So Green Moses rode off. I ran to a man who had horses for hire and he sent his servant straightway on a horse by another road to the same place. When I reached home again I found my dear husband sitting in the room, warming himself and drying his wet clothes, for the weather was frightful. All that the letter-carrier had told me was quite untrue.

---

[1] *Zollen pieker*, a toll-house. This was an old fortified house dating from the thirteenth century where toll was collected from the merchandise proceeding across the Elbe from Hamburg and Lübeck.

I write of this to show what worries and frights I underwent with every journey, and I longed to see things were so arranged that my husband could remain at home. For this reason I was not averse to the partnership with Reb Judah.

So, once more, Reb Judah spoke with us and made the best propositions. I said to him, 'What you say is good and right, but you see our big household and the large responsibilities we have. Our expenses are more than 1000 reichstaler a year, apart from the interest we have to pay, and other expenses. I do not see where this money is to come from.' Reb Judah replied, 'Are you worried about that? If I do not bring in at least 1000 reichstaler banco a year, you will have the right to cancel the partnership.' He promised this and more than is possible for me to write.

I spoke with my husband and told him what Reb Judah and I had discussed, and how he had praised his business abilities. On this my husband said to me, 'My dear child, talk is very easy. I have heavy expenses; I do not see how they can be met by partnership with Reb Judah.' Said I to my husband, 'We can try it for one year. I will draft a short agreement and see how it suits you.'

That night I sat up alone and drafted an agreement. Reb Judah insisted that we should not worry but trust the business to him, for he knew all ways and means and everything would be all right. I said, 'How can we give over all our business to you?' To which he replied, 'I know well that you have jewels worth many thousands; these you will not throw away. We will arrange that you sell or exchange these jewels as best you can or will.' This was the first point. The second was that the partnership should last ten years and every year account should be taken. If the partnership did not show 2000 reichstaler profit yearly, my husband had the right to cancel it. Without this condition we would not consider the business. When the partnership ceased, everything would be sold and each get his money back. Thirdly, my husband should go to Amsterdam once or twice to show Reb Judah where and how to buy; and the latter should hold the goods and sell them. Fourthly, my husband should put in at the beginning of the business 5000 or 6000 reichstaler and Judah 2000; all our goods and jewels we had we could sell or exchange.

On these conditions a precise agreement was drawn up, and each point well guarded. Reb Judah then left for Hildesheim, saying he would get together the cash he had undertaken to put into the business; two or three weeks after they were to go together to Amsterdam. My husband prepared for this journey and remitted his money to Amsterdam. Nothing was missing but that Reb Judah should arrive with his money. He came at the appointed time and brought with him a bill for 500 reichstaler. We said to him, 'What is this? There is supposed to be 2000,' to which he replied, 'I have left my wife gold to sell and she will remit the rest from Hildesheim to Amsterdam.'

We were satisfied with this. Together, in the name of the God of Israel, they left quite happily for Amsterdam. There my husband began to buy up small things, as was then the custom. At every post he asked Judah, 'Have you received your bills?' He always answered, 'They should be here; I expect them at any moment.' But nothing came of it: nothing arrived. What was my husband to do? Reb Judah gave him hope and spoke a great deal and my husband put his money with Reb Judah's 500 reichstaler, and bought stock—as one can very quickly in Ansterdam. After this they returned—my husband home, and Reb Judah to Hildesheim, taking with him the stock that my husband had bought. He travelled here and there to sell and trade just as he wished.

When my husband returned home, he spoke to me, grumbling at the partnership, saying that I had persuaded him into it. Reb Judah had not kept to the agreement from the very beginning; what would it be like at the end? One could—God forbid!—drop dead over such business. I coaxed him out of his fears as best I could. I said to him—as in truth it was—'Judah is a young man. How much did he receive as dowry? Only 500 taler. He had 800 or 900 of his own, which he had earned from us—that was two years ago. It is impossible for him to get 2000. Let yourself imagine that he has nothing and we are sending him, as before, to travel, and trusting him with several thousands, as we have often done. If God will grant luck, He can do so with little as well as much money.' What could my husband do? Whether he liked it or not, we were involved—and a man in a bath has to get wet.

Some time passed; Reb Judah earned a little and wrote to us from time to time, but *a handful cannot satisfy a lion.*

In short, the year soon ended and we were neither of us satisfied, for we saw that enough had not been earned to support one household, let alone two. At length, after a year of partnership my husband went to Hildesheim to settle the account. He spoke to Judah as one brother to another, 'You can see that neither of us can afford to go on with this partnership. According to the agreement we must make at least 2000 reichstaler profit; we have not made even 1000.' Reb Judah himself saw they could not go on with it. In a friendly way the partnership was dissolved. My husband wrote two bills, one for himself and one for Judah, which they both signed, as is customary. There remained in Judah's hands a few thousand talers' worth of rings and jewellery which he was to sell and then send the money on to my husband. They also fixed a time when this payment should be made.

The time arrived, but no payment was made. We wrote to Judah, in a polite way, to remind him what he had signed; the time had already gone, would he please remit the money to Hamburg? He replied, equally politely, that he had not yet sold all the goods; he would shortly send us a bill.

After this another year passed. We could get nothing from Judah, so my husband sent once again to Hildesheim, expecting to get his money. Instead of this he learnt something new. After Judah had led my husband on for some days, he said to him, 'I won't give you anything and I would be more pleased if I had twice as much of yours. Our business according to the agreement should have lasted ten years, instead of which it lasted one year. I claim many thousands from you, and what you possess is mine. You cannot pay me off with all that you have.'

My husband was very alarmed and cried, 'Reb Judah, what are you saying? Is this the thanks I get for the good I did you? You came to me denuded and bare, and after a short while you got through me 900 reichstaler in ready cash. I have trusted you with many thousands. I have shown you all the places I knew, where business could be done, since I thought you an honest and respectable man. I persuaded my brother Rabbi Samuel to give you his daughter for wife. In spite of all this, from the very beginning you broke our agreement; instead of putting in 2000 reichstaler, you put in only 500. Besides, there was a clause in our agreement that if there was not a profit of 2000 reichstaler, the partnership was at an end. So in friendliness we freed ourselves of all obligations. What do you want now? I beg of you, don't give people the chance of talking about us. We are still relatives; we can still, if God wills, do business again together,' and other words to the same effect. But nothing changed my fine Judah, he remained of his own opinion.

As happens in these affairs, there was much talk and wrangling. People intervened. They made it their business that each should take an arbitrator and go before the Hildesheim *Beth Din*.[1] The time was fixed for four months later and my husband had to agree to this, *who can contend with him that is stronger? As is* known, he is the stronger who holds the goods.

My husband returned home with these new tidings. We were both very upset, for we knew how honestly and justly we had dealt with him and the good we had done him—may God reward us for it. My husband grumbled at me because I had persuaded him to the partnership, but God knows, I did it for the best, in the hope that he would not need to undertake any more difficult journeys. I had no thought that things would turn out so and certainly never expected such treatment from Judah, for I held him to be an honest man. He still had in hand a large sum of our money, which did not please us. I asked my husband why he had agreed to a trial in Hildesheim; he should have insisted on it in some neutral place. He answered quite crossly, 'If you'd been there, would you have done better? He has my goods in his possession, so I have to agree to what he wants.' In short our little dispute came to an end. We had to put our trust in God, Who had before now helped us out of business worries, to help us out of this.

We were young people, just beginning to stand on our own feet, doing good business—now such an unexpected complication had set in!

From what I have written, you see that my husband had the note dissolving the partnership, but perhaps Judah suspected that he had dealings at the time of the partnership which were

[1] Rabbinical court of law, sits to administer justice according to the Jewish code of law. Civil as well as religious matters are judged by the court.

not revealed to him, but of this I am not certain. Maybe the following incident was tinder to the fire. When my husband arrived home from Hildesheim, at the time of the dissolution of of the partnership, he met a Frenchman who dealt in all sorts of merchandise. My husband exchanged goods with him and did good business. But, as is the custom among Jews, if one earns 100 taler, people make thousands out of it. So the cry arose that we had made a fortune. This happening just after the partnership was ended must have come to the ears of Judah. He may have believed the stories that were told to him, or perhaps persuaded himself to believe them.

Whether Judah dissolved the partnership with his whole heart, or regretted the dissolution, or again, perhaps did not wish to let the money out of his hands—God knows. We had never seen any wrong in him and certainly never expected that he would refuse to give up what was ours. *Man looketh on the outward appearance, but the Lord looketh on the heart.*[1] Perhaps he persuaded himself he was in the right and persisted in this, for *man finds no fault with himself* [Talmud]. It was thus harder and more bitter for us, for we knew the whole truth; how straightforwardly we had dealt with him—and now to be paid back in this way! But what God does, He does for good.

The time of the Frankfurt Fair arrived. As usual, my husband attended it, staying at the house of his brother Isaac Hameln. He related to him all that had happened, and asked him to find an upright Talmud scholar as he had to be in Hildesheim by a certain date and must bring an arbitrator with him. My brother-in-law said to him, on the spot, 'You are lost if you go to law with him in his own community.' 'What could I do?' answered my husband, 'I couldn't help it,' and showed him all the papers and told him everything. 'Yes, brother,' said Isaac, 'you are quite right. If you have impartial judges and the trial is in a neutral place, you may win.' To which my husband replied, 'It is too late to change anything. Let it be as God wills. I want to be finished with it. Get me a good arbitrator.' After thinking a while, my brother-in-law said, 'I have someone for you, a young man, upright and honest—Rabbi Asher. He is dayan[2] of our congregation. He will be just right for you.'

[1] Samuel 16: 7.   [2] One of three ecclesiastical judges at the *Beth Din*.

So, my husband saw Rabbi Asher, told him everything and showed him all the papers. 'Do not worry,' said Rabbi Asher. 'You have right with you. I will go with you when the fair is over.' During this time, too, my husband asked his brother whether he could recommend him an honest young man to take into our business. To make it short—he recommended Issachar Cohen, who, unfortunately, was the real Herod of my whole family; of him I shall write later, in the right place, when I come to it.

Straight from the fair my husband and his arbitrator went to Hildesheim. How shall I write at full length of the trial? One hundred pages would not suffice to tell of all that happened. Our arbitrator could do nothing, he was one against two. Rabbi Asher would not agree to a judgement contrary to the Torah. He knew that if he did not agree to their decision, they could imprison him, or at least threaten him with imprisonment. Well, my good Rabbi Asher left Hildesheim secretly. However, before he left, he wrote a great responsum, in my husband's favour. Nothing helped. The chief of the *Beth Din* of Hildesheim and a *parnass*, whose names I do not wish to reveal as they are both in everlasting truth, stood by Judah, limb and life. They wanted my husband to compromise, a thing very hard for him. He would not agree to this and the case nearly came to the gentile courts. My father-in-law, of blessed memory, who then lived in Hildesheim, begged, with tears in his eyes, 'My dear son, you can see quite well what is happening here. I beg of you, for God's sake, not to let this go any further; be patient and make as good a compromise as you can. His Blessed Name will reward you better for it.' Indeed, this happened, as will follow.

What was to be done? As Judah had my husband's goods in his possession and it was hard to get them from him, my husband was compelled to agree. The compromise may easily be imagined. We did not have twice the amount of our expenses out of it. I do not blame Judah so much as those who helped him, for no man sees his own faults. All is long since over. We have all forgiven him and those who helped him and bear no ill-will against Judah, who thought he was in the right and persisted against us. Perhaps, if it happened now, he would act differently. It really hurt my husband very much, but who could help him? *He who weeps over what is past, indulges in useless prayer* [Talmud].

But the dear Lord saw our innocence. Ere four weeks had passed, through a good deal, we earned almost all that we had lost. After this, my husband lived in unity and trust with Judah Berlin and later, in its place, I will tell with what honour I was received by Judah and his wife when I was in Berlin. He always did business with my children, and we had no cause to grumble at him. If the first business had gone through well, there would never have been anything between us. It was Issachar's good fortune that we severed with Judah, for then the former's luck began to bloom.

Although, perhaps, the whole affair with Judah was not worth writing, as also my whole book, I write to drive away miserable sad thoughts when they come to plague me. From it we may see that all human things change with time. *God makes ladders, one He lowers and another He raises on high* [Talmud]. When Judah first came to us he really had nothing; today he cannot be bought out for 100,000 reichstaler banco. He now carries on such a big business and stands in such high esteem with the Prince Elect—God exalt his radiance—that I believe that if God does not set His face against him, when he dies he will be the wealthiest man in all Germany.

We helped many and—before God—all those with whom we had business dealings became rich as kings, but mostly without acknowledgement, as is the way of the world. On the contrary, many to whom we did good repaid our children with evil. But Almighty God is right and we sinful people cannot say, even once, what is good or bad for us. A person often thinks when adversity hits him, that it is bad for him. But what he thinks bad, may be for his good. Had the honest, upright Mordecai—God revenge his death!—remained alive, perhaps many would not then have got into such a pickle. He himself would assuredly have been a great man. After him we had Green Moses; though we did not do much business through him, still, as I have already mentioned, we did get some nice parcels of seed pearls. He journeyed to distant places and left his wife and children here. We had to support them, though we did not know if his profits would come to as much as the cost of keeping them. Of this the Bible says, *Cast thy bread upon the waters, for*

thou shalt find it after many days. In short, though we did not have
much profit, we parted amicably from one another. We would
have been longer together if he had not moved away from
Hamburg and settled in Schottland,[1] near Danzig. He did not
change for the worse, for things went well with him.

Abraham Kantor, of Copenhagen, whom I have also mentioned, as a young lad was in service with us and conducted
himself honestly and well. We later sent him several times to
Copenhagen, where he became rich, and moved there his wife
and children. After this, there was no partnership between us.
It is said that he has a good business and is now worth 15,000
reichstaler and gives his children dowries of thousands. I could
write of all that we did for him, but who acknowledges good?
Ah, we humans are ungrateful creatures.

My nephew Mordecai Cohen, a young man, and Leib
Bischere went into partnership with my husband. He sent them
to England with letters of credit and money. They were unable
to complete their journey as war broke out and they could not
proceed. However, they made good money in Amsterdam.
Since then, my nephew has travelled in Holland and Brabant
and done good business. That first journey was his beginning
in trade and wealth.

I have already written of the now wealthy Judah and how
through heavenly aid he came to great riches.

To my brother-in-law Elia,[2] a young man of no experience
in business, my husband gave big credits and finally he sent
him to Amsterdam with credit to the value of 20,000 reichstaler.

Many of the people of this place who are now the foundation
props of the community, would have thanked God if we had
given them credit. I can name many, but what does it help me?
Nothing avails. For where is the good that you, honest, upright
Reb Chaim Hameln, did in the world, who helped everyone
willingly and did them favours? Often with profit and often with
loss. Many times, though he knew that he would gain nothing,
he did it, without any hope of reward, exercising true charity,

---

[1] A suburb of Danzig, founded by Scottish sailors and named after their
native land. Here Jews were to be found residing before they had received
rights of residence in Danzig.

[2] Elia Ries, of Berlin, son of the head of the Vienna community Model
Ries, was wedded to Glückel's sister Mattie.

for it was as though done to a dead man. And now your dear, devout children are the very same; they would sooner die than do anyone harm. But those to whom we did good do not remember and do not care to know my children, who losing their pious father so young are like sheep without a shepherd. They could help them a little. May God have mercy on them, they do the reverse. I wish I had no bad from them, as I have had no good. They defrauded my children of thousands and caused my Mordecai to lose his money among common people. The president of the council and the whole court decided that it was an honest transaction, and that he did not need to return any of the merchant's goods, which he had bought in a regular way. But they gave him no rest. He lost money and was forced to come to a settlement with them. From this sprung his misfortune. His and my feelings about it—may God take them as atonement for our sins! My son was so pressed. May God avenge him according to their deeds. I cannot blame the man I have in mind because I do not know his thoughts. Man judges according to his eyes, but God by the heart. But I know this well: my children were young and needed a little credit, as is usual in business. They wanted some bills discounted. The merchants took them from them and told them to come after Börse[1] hours. The same merchant, I think, asked a Jew of whom he thought highly, for his opinion. When, after Börse-time, my children went again to the merchant expecting to receive cash for the bills, which bore good endorsements, he returned them. This was why they often did not know where to turn for help.

Thou great and only God, I beg from the bottom of my heart for pardon: perhaps the man did what he did in all sincerity and I do him injustice in my thoughts. Everything must be commended to God and we must always bear in mind that this frivolous world passes soon.

Thou, O Lord, know how I pass my days in sorrow and anxiety. I was a woman held in high esteem by her devout husband, and was to him like the apple of his eye. But with his death my honour and wealth went. For him I have to lament and mourn all my days and years. I know well that in my

[1] Stock market and meeting-place of money-brokers and merchants for the transaction of business.

weakness I do wrong to pass my time in such loneliness and mournfulness. Far better were it if I fell on my knees every day and gave thanks and praised the Lord for the great kindness He shows me, who am unworthy. I still sit at my own table, eat what I desire, rest in my bed at night, still have a schilling to spend—as long as the Lord wills. And I have my dear children. If at times it does not go well with this one or with that one, still, we live and know our Creator. There are many people in this world, better, more pious, more righteous and more truthful than I who yet have much less than I; not enough even for one meal. Some I know personally, exceedingly devout people.

How can I praise and thank the Creator enough for all the goodness he shows us without our repaying Him, as I have already asked? If only we poor sinners would recognize God's great mercy. He made us out of a clod of clay in His awesome and holy name—for which we must serve him with all our heart.

See, my dear children, what a person does to obtain the favour of a monarch who is himself no more than flesh and blood, here today and tomorrow in his grave. Who knows how long he will live, or how long the receiver of his favours will live, or even what he will receive from an earthly king. He can raise him to riches—but this is only temporary, not for ever. He can have all in his power—till the day of his death—but it is naught. When bitter death comes all is forgotten; and his riches and honour are less than nothing! *There is no ruler on the day of death* [Eccles 8: 8]. Even though man knows all this, still he strives to serve the earthly king well and to obtain the temporal reward. How much more then should man consider day and night how best to serve the Holy One, blessed be He, the King of kings who lives for ever and ever! From Him proceeds all the good we enjoy from earthly kings, in whose hearts He gives it to do good according to His will for *the heart of the king is in the hand of God* [Proverbs 21: 1]. Also, the gifts of an earthly monarch are as naught compared with those which the blessed Lord gives to those who fear Him. It is eternity that has no measure, aim or passing.

So, my heart-beloved children, be comforted and patient in your trials and serve God the Almighty with all your heart, as well when things are contrary as when they are well, and know that He does not burden His servants with more than they can bear. I pray to God to give me strength when things go contrary.

Now, I shall with God's help begin again from where I left off.

My daughter Mattie, peace unto her, was in her third year, and a more beautiful and clever child was nowhere to be seen. Not only did we love her, but everyone who saw her and heard her speak, was delighted with her. But the dear Lord loved her more. When she entered her third year, her hands and feet suddenly swelled. Although we had many doctors and much medicine it suited Him to take her to Himself after four weeks of great suffering, and left as our portion heartache and suffering. My husband and I mourned indescribably and I feared greatly that I had sinned against the Almighty by mourning too much, not heeding the story of Reb Jochanan, as will follow. I forgot that there were greater punishments, as I was to find out later. We were both so grieved that we were ill for some time.

I was pregnant with my daughter Hannah and soon after was brought to bed. Because of my great sorrow over my child of blessed memory, about whom I would not be comforted, I was dangerously ill and the physicians doubted my recovery and wished to resort to the last, most desperate of remedies. Not thinking I could understand what they were saying, they discussed it with my family. I told my husband and mother that I would not take the medicine that had been mentioned. This they told the physicians, and though the latter tried their best to persuade me to take it, it was of no use, and I said to them, 'You may say what you like; I take nothing more. If God will help me, He can do so without the medicine. If it is another decision of the Great Lord, what can medicine help?' I begged my husband to dismiss the physicians and pay them off; this he did. And the Blessed Name gave me strength, and five weeks after my confinement I went to the synagogue, although still somewhat weak. Daily I improved, and at length dismissed my nurse and wet-nurse and myself saw to all that was necessary for my household. And at last I had to submit and forget my beloved child, as is the decree of God, *I am forgotten as a dead one to the heart.*[1]

It may be learnt in the following story of what happened to a pious man that it is necessary to be patient when ill befalls one's

[1] Psalm 31: 13.

children or fortune and not give way to immoderate grief. If one is devout and thinks, 'Why, dear Lord, do you afflict me so bitterly? I do not know what are my sins that you punish me so,' he should ask that the full measure of trouble may not come. Accept everything as a just decree and say, 'Blessed be the True Judge,' for whatever the Almighty does, He does justly. Who can say, 'What doest Thou?' for we must understand that all God's doings are for our good. Who knows if it is not better for a man when he—God forbid!—suffers the loss of children, money or other such things, more than if all goes well. The Lord is merciful—and who can stand before judgement in the future world?

What more can I write about this? As I have said many times already: our Sages have written about everything. Reb Jochanan, on whom be peace, a great Tanna,[1] lost nine sons in his own lifetime. He was left with but one son, a child of three. It happened once that a servant, washing clothes, placed a vessel of water to boil on the fire. This soon seethed and boiled over. Now, near the fire on the bench on which the washing was placed, sat the child. He, being curious, got up to see what was doing in the vessel. But the form was not standing straight, and as he stood up it tipped in the air and the child fell into the pan of boiling water. He cried out loud.

Startled, everyone rushed to the pan. The father tried to snatch his son from the water, but only a finger of the child's hand remained in his, for he was already seethed in the boiling water. He, the father, banged his head against the wall, then rushed out to the Bet Hamidrash[2] crying to his pupils, 'Mourn my vanished star! This bone is all that is left of my tenth child whom I brought up, a sacrifice to God.' And from that time he carried, hanging from his neck, the child's bone as a remembrance. Whenever a stranger, a scholar, came to visit him, he would show him in all humility this bone—just as though he was showing his son.

Well, my dear children, if this could come to pass to Rabbi Jochanan, peace unto him, what may not happen to anyone else? Rabbi Jochanan was learned in the Talmud, in the Bible, Mishna, Gemara and the commentaries. He could conjure up angels and demons, and was a great Kabalist and knew what the stars foretell. He understood the swaying of the trees, and their boughs—yet despite all this such misfortune befell him! He took it all for good and was devout and god-fearing all his days.

[1] One of the great sages in the Talmud.

[2] Literally house of instruction, where after *cheder* Jewish youths received instruction in Talmud and kindred subjects.

16. *Jewish Wedding Celebrations*. Engraving. Nürnberg, 1734

17. *Simchat-Thora (The Rejoicing of the Law)*. Engraving. Nürnberg, 1734

18. *Jewish Divorce*. Engraving. Nürnberg, 1734

19. *Circumcision in a Dutch-Jewish Home*. Painting by R. de Hooghe, 1665

Therefore, my heart's children, though I know well that some are pressed by the loss of money and even the loss of children, what does sorrow and lamenting help? We ruin our health, shortening our life, and cannot serve the Almighty with a heavy heart, for the Shechinah cannot dwell in a sad body. When the Prophets wished the Shechinah to inspire them, they had all kinds of musical instruments played to them so that the body should be glad—as may be read in our books. When your father lived, I, your mother, lost a child of three to whom none could be compared, as I have already written. I was not so understanding as King David. When his first child by Bathsheba was ill, he recited many prayers—and gave away much in charity—and did all he could for it. When the child died, the servants were fearful of breaking the news to him because of his great grief over the child's illness. The king understood from their silence that the child had died, and asked them. As no one answered him he knew for certain that his child was dead. He rose from his ashes and asked for water and ordered food and drink. The servants wondered at this and said, 'While the child lived you did not rest by day or night, but sat on ashes; but now that the child is dead. you have accepted the decree and said, "Blessed be the true judge. The Lord has given and the Lord has taken away—blessed be the name of the Lord for ever and ever." And now you order food and drink!'

And the king answered his servants, 'While the soul was still in the child's body, I did all I could for his recovery—called aloud, wept, did penance, prayed, gave charity, and thought that perhaps God would show mercy. But nothing helped, and the Holy One, blessed be He, took away His pledge. Of what use is weeping now? My son cannot return to us; but we shall go to him.'

See, therefore, how the saintly David acted. From this we may learn and take as an example.

We were sinful in sorrowing so much. After this, as long as my husband and I suffered any loss or misfortune, trembling and fearing that we had lost everything, God always assisted us most graciously.

God, the great and living, will yet again have mercy on us and redeem us from exile so that we may serve as befits Him—and that all nations may acknowledge and know that we are His beloved people. And, Almighty God, you are our Father: have mercy on us as a father on his children. You are our master and we are your menservants and maidservants. We will not refrain from praying

G

that the gracious Lord show mercy to His servants; I, your maid-servant, supplicate as a maid to her mistress. Our eyes and heart are set on you.

Here I end my third book and with heaven's help begin my fourth book.

BOOK IV

MY daughter Hannah grew up a very beautiful child, of whom I shall, perhaps, have more to say later. At this time an East Indiaman laden with rough diamonds fell into the hands of the King of Denmark and lay at Glückstadt. Every sailor had diamonds. So all the sons of Israel went to Glückstadt to buy, making good profits. Two Jews got to know that a Norwegian citizen had a big parcel of these diamonds and held evil counsel with one another; he was a baker, I think, who had paid very little for the parcel. The two unclean fellows plotted together to get to the house where the diamonds were. They went to Norway and picked acquaintance with the baker, became very friendly and were invited by him to stay at his house. They remained on the most cordial terms until they found out where he kept his treasure. It was all they wanted to know; they took everything and early next morning they left the house and hired a boat, thinking themselves quite successful in their evil deeds.

But God would not suffer this. When the citizen awoke, early in the morning, and asked after his two guests, the servant told him that they had left earlier in the morning. The host was suspicious, for one who has a treasure is always ill at ease. He went to the chest where his treasure was kept and found it empty. Straightway, he suspected both his guests of the robbery, and ran quickly to the shore to ask the boatmen whether they had seen two sons of Israel sail away? on which they replied, 'Yes, one of the boatmen rowed them off about an hour ago.'

He immediately hired a boat with four rowers and followed on; very soon he sighted the thieves' boat, and when they saw that they were pursued, they threw the entire treasure into the sea. The citizen eventually captured them and compelled them to return with him. They cried out loudly, 'Bethink you what you do! We are honest men. You will not find anything, for we have nothing of yours and you insult us. We shall know how to bring it home to you.' They denied everything. But it is written in our Ten Commandments *Thou shalt not steal*. Therefore, the Holy One did not help them. They were brought back and stripped naked; their clothes were searched, but nothing

75

availed. Then they were tortured until they confessed. Both
were condemned to the gallows. One of the thieves at once
accepted the Christian faith. The other, who until then had
been a pious son of devout parents—he came from Wandsbek—
would not change his religion and so sanctified the Holy Name.
I knew him and his parents well and always held him to be an
honest man. The other man must have misled him, for he was
known as an evil-doer and therefore had such an end. The
other, who was hanged, attained the future world in one hour.
For the sake of his family's honour, I shall not mention his
name; but his story is well known in Hamburg. The Lord will
surely reward the sanctification of His Name, for he could have
been freed, as was his companion, by renouncing his faith. But
he fulfilled the Commandment, *Thou shalt love the Lord thy God
with all thy soul*. His death was an atonement for his sins. One
should learn from this not to allow wicked impulse to lead one
astray after miserable money. . . .[1]

But to start anew. I was brought to bed with my son Mordecai Segal. May God grant that his old age may be as lucky
as was his youth. But what does it help? God has already
decided what is to be.

I have already written in my third book of the Redemption
which we hoped to see in our own days, and mentioned that my
father-in-law sent us two casks, intending to take them with
him when he went to the Land of Israel together with all the
other Jews. When he saw that nothing came to pass, he gave
up his house in Hameln and together with my mother-in-law
moved to Hildesheim, which, only five miles from Hameln,
had a fine, devout community.

After they had lived there a short time, my husband, who
loved and honoured his parents, implored me thus: 'My
Glückelchen, let us go to Hildesheim to visit my parents: it is
now twelve years since you have seen them.' This pleased me.
We took our maid, our manservant and three children and
journeyed to Hildesheim. At that time I was still nursing my
son Mordecai, who was not a year old. The name of the youth
with us was Samuel, a good-looking fellow known as 'Fine
Samuel', for we had had another servant whom the children
had called 'Fat Samuel'.

[1] Here follow five pages of really wearisome repetitious moralizing.

So we arrived at Hildesheim. My parents-in-law, of blessed memory, were happy to see us, for my husband was their youngest child and everything, thank God, was going well with us. We took with us what we thought were handsome gifts, and suitable for Hildesheim. After three weeks spent happily together, we returned home joyous and well. My father-in-law made us a present of a tankard worth about 20 reichstaler; it was as precious to us as if worth a hundred. My father-in-law was then a wealthy man, worth about 20,000 reichstaler, and had already married off all his children. Though the journey had cost us more than 150 reichstaler, we nevertheless rejoiced over our small tankard, not eager like modern children to skin their parents, without asking whether they are in a position to spend much.

My parents-in-law lived about five years in Hildesheim and their stay cost them about 10,000 reichstaler, for though they did not keep a big house their expenses were heavy. The good folk saw that it was aimless to live in Hildesheim, so they moved to Hanover, where they lived in the house of my brother-in-law, the wealthy Reb Lipman, till they died in ripe old age, leaving behind them a good name. Of this I shall write more.

At that time we were doing good business. When my eldest child, my daughter Zipporah, was nearly twelve years of age, Reb Leib, the son of Reb Ansel of Amsterdam, broached a match with Kossman, son of Reb Elia Cleve's[1] son. My husband, of blessed memory, left six weeks earlier than usual on his half-yearly visit to Amsterdam and wrote to the matchmaker to meet him there, to see what was to be done.

A war was in progress about this time[2] and Elia Cleve and his family were forced to move from Cleve to Amsterdam. On my husband's arrival in that town rumour spread that he was about to ally himself by marriage with Elia Cleve. This was on post day when people read their letters on the Börse. Many would not believe it and there was much wagering, for Elia Cleve was a very rich man, worth 100,000 or more reichstaler. My husband was then still quite a young man, just beginning

[1] Kossman Gompertz was the grandson of Rabbi Mordecai Gumpel. (See footnote, p. 15.)
[2] When Louis XIV invaded Holland in 1672 the Great Elector was allied with Holland.

to get on nicely in business, and there was a houseful of little ones—God protect them. What God proposes must indeed come to pass, however much people may dislike it. Is it not proclaimed in heaven forty days before birth that this man's son shall wed that man's daughter?

So it came to pass that my husband joined himself through marriage with the wealthy Reb Elia Cleve, our daughter's dowry being settled at 2000 reichstaler in Dutch money. The date of the wedding was fixed for eighteen months later, in Cleve, my husband to pay 100 reichstaler towards the wedding expenses.

When the time of the wedding drew near we left—with *mazal tov*—for Cleve—my husband, I with a babe at my breast, the bride Zipporah, Rabbi Meyer of the Klaus,[1] who is now rabbi of Friedberg, our manservant Fine Samuel, and a maid, quite a handsome retinue. In company with Mordecai Cohen, Meyer Ilius and Aaron Todelche, we went from Altona by boat. I cannot describe the jollity and merriment of our journey. In joy and happiness we arrived in Amsterdam three weeks before the wedding. We stayed with Reb Leib Hamburger, whom I have already mentioned, and spent more than twelve ducats every week. We did not mind this, as during this very time my husband, of blessed memory, had done some business and earned more than half the dowry.

Fourteen days before the wedding, with drums and dancing, a company of more than two *minyanim*,[2] we travelled to Cleve and were there received with great honour. Reb Elia Cleve's house was really like a king's palace, handsomely furnished in every way; like the mansion of a noble. We had no rest all day from the eminent and distinguished visitors who came to see the bride. In truth my daughter was really beautiful and had no equal. There was great excitement in preparation for the wedding.

At that time Prince Frederick[3] was in Cleve. The senior prince, the Elector, was alive, and Frederick was yet a lad, not more than thirteen. Soon after the Elector died and Frederick

[1] Klaus, a religious foundation which maintained several scholars who lived exclusively for the study of the Talmud and delivered regular lectures thereon.

[2] *Minyan*, a quorum for religious worship consisting of ten men.

[3] Later Elector of Brandenburg; in 1701 King Frederick I of Prussia.

became Elector in his place. Prince Maurice[1] and his court, too, were there. They had made it known that they wished to be present at the wedding. Suitable preparations were made by Reb Elia Cleve for such distinguished guests.

On the wedding day, immediately after the marriage ceremony, there was a collation of all kinds of the finest sweetmeats, foreign wines and out-of-season fruits. One can well imagine all the excitement! How all the thoughts of Elia Cleve and his family were taken up with the reception and accommodation of his distinguished visitors! There was not time even to produce and count the dowry, as is the custom at such times. So we put *our* dowry and Elia put *his* into a bag and sealed it, to be counted after the wedding.

When we stood all together under the *chuppah*[2] with the bride and bridegroom, we found that in the great excitement the *Ketuba*[3] had not been drawn up! What was to be done? All the distinguished guests and the young prince stood about waiting to see the ceremony under the canopy. Rabbi Meyer advised that the bridegroom should appoint a surety who would undertake that the *Ketuba* would be written out immediately after the ceremony. In the meantime, we were to continue with the marriage. And so it was, the rabbi reading the *Ketuba* in set form from a book.

After the ceremony all the guests were led into a great hall, the walls of which were lined with gilded leather. A long table crowded with regal delicacies stood in the centre, and each guest was served in order of rank. My son Mordecai was then about five years old; there was no more beautiful child in the whole world and we had dressed him becomingly and neatly. The courtiers nearly swallowed him for very admiration, especially the prince, who held his hand the whole time. After the royal visitors and other guests had consumed the confects and drunk well the wine, the table was cleared and removed. Masked dancers entered and presented different poses quite nicely and suitably to the entertainment. They ended with the Dance of the Dead.[4] It was all very splendidly done.

[1] Prince of Nassau.
[2] Canopy, under which Jewish marriages are performed.
[3] Marriage contract.
[4] Dances of the Dead came into fashion about the year 1400. These productions symbolized in various forms the power of death over life.

Among the guests there were also many distinguished Portuguese Jews, one of whom was a jeweller of the name of Mocatta. He had with him a beautiful little gold watch set in diamonds, worth 500 reichstaler. Reb Elia asked Mocatta for this little watch, as he desired to make a present of it to the young Prince. But a good friend standing close by said to him, 'Why do this? To give such an expensive present to the young Prince? If he were the Elector it would be worth while.' But as I have already mentioned, the Elector died not long after and the young Prince succeeded him and is still Elector. Thereafter, whenever Reb Elia Cleve saw the friend who dissuaded him from giving the present, he would throw it up at him angrily. And in truth, if he had given the present, the Prince would never have forgotten it, for great people never forget such things. Well, cry for what has gone!

The young Prince, Prince Maurice, and all the courtiers enjoyed themselves and left well satisfied. For a hundred years no Jew had had such high honour. Thus the wedding day ended in joy and gladness.

After the wedding, I rode to Emmerich, to visit the grave of my sister Hendelé, peace unto her. My grief and heartache is known only to God. The pity that one so young and exceptional must chew the black earth! She was not yet twenty-five when she died, leaving behind a son and a daughter. But what helps? We must be content with God's will. Unhappily, the son, a fine young man who studied well, died young and unmarried, mourned alike by friends and family.

The following Sunday, we left on our return journey and travelled to Amsterdam, going by the way we had come, as it is written, *And he went on his journeys* [Genesis 13: 3]. There we remained about fourteen days, my husband doing a little business. Thence we had to go to Delfzyl, to reach which we had to cross the part of the sea known as Dollart, a trial for the strongest person if they are not used to a ship's buffetings by the swift currents. On board we left our household in the large cabin which was crowded with people, while I and my husband hired a small one for ourselves so that we might be on our own. There was a small opening in the wall that could be kept open or closed, through which things could be handed out into the larger cabin. There were two bunks in our little cabin. My

husband said to me, 'Glückelchen, lie down on this bunk and I
will cover you well, but take care to lie still and not move, so
that the sea will not affect you.' I had never before crossed
the Dollart, but he had been over often and was quite used
to it.

I did as I was told and lay still. The maid and my baby were
in the large cabin. The weather was bad and the wind contrary. The ship rolled from side to side; all the passengers were
dead sick and—with pardon—vomited. Truly there is no worse
illness in the world than sea-sickness. I do not believe the death
throes are worse. As long as I lay still, I felt nothing. But my
maid who had the baby with her was already sick and could
not move, The baby, too, poor thing, did not feel well, for he
soon began to howl and shriek. The maid could not move, so
she let him cry on. But I, as a mother, pitying her own child,
could not bear it and had to get up from my bunk.

I took the child in to me through the aperture between the
cabins, and laid him to my breast. But, my God! I became as
ill as though in the throes of death. I really thought my end was
near and began to recite the death confession as best I could
and as much of it as I knew by heart. My husband, who lay
quietly on his bunk, knew that this was no fatal illness and that
it would pass as soon as we set foot on dry land. As I prayed, my
devotions fixed on God, I noticed that my husband lay laughing! I heard his laughter and thought to myself, 'Here I lie in
death's throes, and he lies there and laughs!' Though I was
very angry, I was in no state for a quarrel: I had not the
strength to utter a word. I was terribly sick for another half-
hour, till we reached land and left the ship. There our sickness
passed, God be praised.

Night had fallen when we reached Delfzyl and we could not
get into any inn or Jewish house. The weather was very bad
and we had given up hope and were fully resigned to remaining all night in the street. The following day was the fast before
the New Year, and we had not eaten a morsel of food on the
ship the whole day. Apart from this we were quite exhausted
from the bout of sea-sickness. The prospect of lying on the
street all night, without food or drink, was none too cheering.

At length my husband came to the house of a Jew whose
brother's wife was the daughter of Chaim Fürst of Hamburg,

and entreated him, 'Take us in for the night so that we and our children may be under cover at least.' The master of the house answered straightway, 'Enter, in God's name. My house is open to you. I can give you a good bed, but I have no food, for it is now late at night and my wife is away in Emden.' My husband returned happy that we had found quarters for the night and led us to the house. The Jew kept apologizing for having no food or drink in the house. We, however, still had a little bread with us which we gave to our children. I thanked God when I got into bed—it was a fine bed and more welcome than any food or drink would have been. We arose early the next morning, the eve of the New Year, and journeyed on to Emden.

At Emden we were the guests of Abraham Stadthagen, who was a close relative of my husband's—his father, Reb Moses Kran, of Stadthagen, was an uncle. We remained over the New Year and had so enjoyable a holiday that we forgot Dollart completely. The same Abraham Stadthagen was a most praiseworthy man. He not only received us with all the honour in the world, but at the same time entertained six billet strangers[1] who had seats at the same table and ate and drank the same food and drink as we. And I may add that I have never seen the like at any other wealthy man's board.

After the New Year we left Emden, expecting to reach home in time for *Yom Kippur*. We arrived quite early in Wittmund and hired a boat to take us to Hamburg. One day's journey from there one comes to Wangeroog, where all the vessels cast anchor, pay toll and ship fresh supplies. On reaching Wangeroog the toll-collector said to us, 'Where are you people going?' 'We go to Hamburg,' my husband replied. Hearing this the tollman said, 'Take heed: you cannot go, the sea is full of pirate ships. They rob everything they can lay their hands on.'

It was near *Yom Kippur* and we had paid the captain of the ship 10 taler for our passage. Nevertheless, we had to return to Wittmund and so lost our passage money. We spent the fast there, the guests of Breinelé, a cousin of my husband. There we

[1] It was customary for poor students and wandering scholars to be provided with chits by the different Jewish communities, which householders honoured by providing the holders with board and, in some cases, lodgings.

held counsel as to how best to proceed; because of the pirates we could not go by water, while all routes by land were crowded with soldiers.

The widow Breinelé, a clever, devout woman, was from Hamburg, the daughter of Leib Altona. She was always on good terms with my husband and did all she could to help us. At length it was decided that after *Yom Kippur* we should return home overland. My husband had to go to Aurich, to secure a safe conduct from General Buditz, who had been in the service of many kings and dukes and was popular with all. More than that, Meyer Aurich could obtain for us from General Buditz a brave officer as escort. Before *Yom Kippur* my husband went to Aurich and returned just when we were about to start our last meal before the fast. He had accomplished what he wished and was accompanied by a brave, honest corporal, who was with us till we reached Hamburg.

Immediately after *Yom Kippur* we hired a wagon to take us to Altenburg. There we had to pay nearly as much as the horse and wagon together were worth, for everyone feared for his horses. As is easily understood, my husband was very worried and despondent. I had to take off my fine travelling clothes and put on old rags. Rabbi Meyer, whom I have already mentioned, was with us, and he said to my husband, 'My Reb Chaim, why are you so low-spirited? And why do you clothe your wife so hideously?' To which my husband answered, 'God knows I am not concerned about myself, nor do I worry about the money I carry. I fear for the womenfolk only, my wife and the maid.' 'For that you need have no worry,' replied Rabbi Meyer, in an easy way. 'Joking apart, Reb Chaim, you are mistaken in your wife. You do not need to dress her in such abominable garments: in any case no one will trouble to look at her.' This ill-timed jest hurt my husband very much and he was very cross with Rabbi Meyer.

We left Wittmund at midnight. Breinelé and all the people [*i.e.*, Jews] accompanied us a good way out of the town and sent their blessings after us. We reached Altenburg in peace. I still hope to write of our sufferings in Bremervorde and other places. Our trusty corporal, our safe-conduct, and God more than all, helped us here. In Altenburg the whole place swarmed with soldiers and the wagon in which we had come from

Wittmund would go no farther for all the money in the world.
My husband had to run about, trying to get another vehicle,
and finally obtained one in a village two miles away. It cost
him much money.

We left Altenburg and reached a village where we spent the
evening, and there wished to hire another wagon to take us
farther on our way. We sat round the fire with the innkeeper
and the villagers, taking snuff. While talking of this and that
district a peasant entered and began to tell of the Herzog of
Hanover and said, 'My lord has also sent 12,000 men into
Holland.' My husband was glad to hear this and to learn that
he was on Hanoverian soil, for the Luneberg dukes kept their
land purged of evil, and a soldier dared not harm even a
chicken.

My husband asked how far we were from Hanover and the
peasant answered eight miles. Together they calculated that if
we left the following day we should reach Hanover in good
time for *Succot*—the Feast of Tabernacles. My husband
straightway hired a wagon and we rode away the very same
night; he was happy that it would be possible for us to show
respect to his parents by spending the festival with them.

After all our hardships and sufferings, our worries and trials,
it was with great joy that we reached Hanover. My father-in-
law came out to meet us. We saw him before we reached the
town, like an angel, like the prophet Elijah, a staff in his hand,
his snow-white beard reaching to his girdle, and glowing red
cheeks. If one wanted to paint a handsome old man, one could
not paint anyone handsomer. Our pleasure at the sight of him
and our enjoyment of the festival are indescribable.

Although my parents-in-law wished us to remain with them
till after the next festival, our circumstances would not allow us.
We gave them our reasons, and after Tabernacles we departed
for Hamburg, leaving in peace and joy and rode away. I saw
them no more. God grant when I am called away from this
world of sin that I may be with them in the Garden of Eden.

We wished to pay the corporal well and send him on his way,
but he begged us to take him to Hamburg, as he had heard so
much of that town and had not yet seen it. As he had behaved
himself so well we could not refuse him, so took him with us.
We arrived there in peace, on the eve of the second day and

thanks to God found our family in good health. The journey from home, until our return, cost us more than 400 reichstaler. This did not worry us much, for our business was going well. So, once more, after great hardship, we were again home.

I will now tell of a man of the name of Moses, who lived for a time in Helmstadt, which is, I think, about five miles from Hildesheim, a university town and hence a bad place for Jews. Reb Moses Helmstadt was driven out from there, moved to Pommern and settled in Stettin. There he managed to obtain some very good letters of protection and the monopoly to supply the mint in Stettin with metal, and fix the value of the mark. The government appointed its own superintendent over the mint. Reb Moses Helmstadt did not have enough money of his own to carry out this big undertaking by himself. He therefore wrote to my husband, sent him a safe-conduct and asked whether he would go into business with him and supply him with silver; for this he would have a share in the mint and in all the jewels that were bought and sold.

Stettin was an important place and no Jews had lived there for perhaps more than a hundred years. However, many travelled there and bought up bargains in pearls and other precious stones which were to be had there. There was also a trade in selling precious stones. My husband calculated that in the third-taler coin cast in Stettin there was good profit to be made. If one had 100,000 such *drittels*[1] they could be changed for Luneburger and Brandenburg *drittels*. He therefore replied that if Moses would be honest and respectable he would go into partnership with him. Before he had settled in Stettin, he had lived some years in Berlin, and there owed much money. This we did not know at the time, unfortunately. We did know that he was not a wealthy man, but considered that as he lived in such an important town and enjoyed remarkable privileges, the whole land was open to him, and that he and ten others could grow very rich. It was our great loss that we heard only later that he was so deeply in debt—as will follow.

We sent our son Nathan Segal, who was then about fifteen years old, to Stettin to see how things were, and began to send big parcels of silver. This was soon made up into coin and we were sent Stettiner *drittels*, which we could sell immediately on

[1] A *drittel*—third of a reichstaler.

the Börse. There was fine profit in this—about two in the hundred, sometimes more and sometimes less, according to the rate of exchange. We also received various parcels of pearls and from these, also, good profits were made, so that we were quite satisfied.

About a year before this, I was brought to bed with my daughter Esther. Many matches were proposed for my son Nathan, among them one with the orphan of the wealthy Reb Elia Ballin. Also, with the daughter of Reb Samuel Oppenheimer.[1] This was almost arranged, but it was evidently not fated. We had gone so far as to arrange that the dowries should be deposited in Frankfurt with my brother-in-law Reb Isaac Segal. We always had deposited with Isaac jewellery worth several thousands. Reb Samuel sent on his dowry there. It was winter-time and the district was flooded, so that the money was fourteen days late in arriving. In the meantime, the matchmakers pressed that we should agree to the match with Elia Ballin's orphan daughter. My husband thought to himself, 'I have not received any letter from my brother Isaac, to say that he has received the money as arranged. I daresay Reb Samuel Oppenheimer has changed his mind. If we do not bind ourselves with Elia Ballin's daughter we shall find ourselves between two stools—in the mire!'

So, we resolved upon the match with the orphan. Her mother undertook to give her 4000 reichstaler cash, besides the trousseau, and we gave our son 2400 cash. The *Knass*[2] was deposited with *mazal tov*!

Eight days later we received a letter from my brother-in-law Isaac that the money had arrived and that my husband should forthwith give him power to act as proxy for him. But it was too late! My husband wrote to Isaac excusing himself: he had thought that as more than fourteen days after the allotted time had passed, Samuel Oppenheimer had changed his mind. And as this new party was equally eligible, he could not withdraw. He hoped Samuel Oppenheimer would find a fine match for

[1] Samuel Oppenheimer of Heidelberg was the first Jew to return to Vienna after the Jews had been expelled in 1670. He was court banker and a large army contractor. He was the means of the return of other Jewish families to Vienna.

[2] Half the dowry was forfeited if the betrothal was terminated.

his daughter and wished him much joy. But, my God! what an angry letter came from my brother-in-law in return! The rage he revealed in this letter—I must not write of it. What is passed cannot be changed. We were quite satisfied with our match; it was in fact a princely one. The deceased Reb Elia Ballin was an honourable man with a splendid reputation among Jews and gentiles; for several years he had been *parnass* of our community and 4000 reichstaler in cash was a fine dowry! If God —blessed be His Name—had given the young pair good fortune, they might have been as wealthy as Reb Samuel Oppenheimer himself, who from day to day rose higher. But the Lord shares His gifts, showing favour to those whom He loves. We cannot understand or explain this, but instead must thank the Creator for everything.

On his betrothal we recalled Nathan home so that he could make a present to his bride. This he did at the fine feast to celebrate the engagement. The commencement was full of joy on both sides. Fourteen days after my son returned to Stettin.

We were still in business with Reb Moses Helmstadt. But he was false, and dishonest hearts have no rest when they have money in hand, whether their own or someone else's. If only they have it in hand they write it down as their own, as we— God have mercy—found out.

The first misfortune was when he tried to trick the government inspector or cashier, saying that he had made a mistake of 1000 reichstaler. The cashier denied this, and to prove himself in the right, Reb Moses Helmstadt went to law, before the Tribunal in Stettin. This cost much money. He was a proud, fat, well-fed, stuck-up, wicked man! He always had 10,000– 12,000 reichstaler in hand and never gave a thought that this was not his, and that he must return it to the person who had credited it to him, as an honest man always has in mind. But his thoughts went no further than to enjoy himself with money while he had it in his hand. He had a fine carriage driven by two of the best horses in Stettin, two or three men and maid servants, and lived like a prince. The profits, though, were not so large. Also, as I have mentioned, he was heavily in debt in Berlin, and had to move away because of his debts and quarrels. And this blown-out fool had honest Chaim Hameln's money in hand! He could not control himself any longer. Perhaps he thought, 'I must show my enemies in Berlin what a great man I have become.'

He took his carriage drawn by four horses and 2000–3000 reichstaler in *drittels* and left for Berlin. To mislead us, he wrote that he there wanted to change the *drittels* for ducats which he would send on to us, as there was a difference of one per cent if the latter were sent instead of the former, by post. This was well and good. But when my good Moses Helmstadt arrived in Berlin, he began to jingle his money—an animal and money will not be hid. His creditors, Jews and non-Jews, learnt of his arrival and had my good Reb Moses arrested. In short, he could not be released and let out of the town until he had paid 1800 reichstaler—with it the money of good Reb Chaim Hameln was gone. Moses returned to Stettin but sent no ducats for *drittels* to Chaim Hameln. At the same time, he still had more than 12,000 reichstaler cash of ours in hand. After a time we received 2000 reichstaler in *drittels* and a request for more silver so that the mint should not stand idle. Though my son was not satisfied with the business, he could not write to tell us this because all his letters were opened. At length, through merchants, he sent a message that my husband should come to Stettin. At that time Reb Issachar Cohen had arrived there from Kurland. Though I ought to have written the whole story about Reb Issachar earlier, for he was with us more than ten years, I shall save it till later and write separately of him— it makes no difference if I mention him now or later.

My husband said to Reb Issachar Cohen, 'You must come to Stettin with me, to see how things are.' They went together, to go over the account with Reb Moses Helmstadt, but he put them off from day to day and gave my husband bills on Hamburg, and some pearls and gold. My husband, at length, would wait no longer, and Reb Moses had to show how the account stood. From this it was clear that 5500 reichstaler was short. One can well imagine how upset my husband was over this. Reb Moses said to him, 'Listen, brother. I can see that this account upsets you, for which I cannot blame you. I did wrong in spending your money. Do not worry. I will give you bills so that within eighteen months your money will be paid back. Come with me to my little synagogue.'

They went up to the little synagogue which was in his house.

20. *Seven Turns round the Coffin.* Engraving by Bernard Picart, 1723

21. *A Jewish Cemetery.* Painting by Jacob van Ruisdael (1628/29–1682)

22. *The Two Great Synagogues of the German-Jewish Community in Amsterdam.*
Contemporary Etching

23. *The Spanish and Portuguese Synagogue of Amsterdam.* Engraving, 18th Century

From the Ark Reb Moses took the Scroll of the Law into his arms and swore by all the holy letters, and more, which I must not mention in vain, that he would meet the bills in time. He had the money, but it was tied up. When he was paid, he would see that my husband was satisfied. And more such words, not worth putting on paper. This did not please my husband, and Reb Issachar Cohen was so furious that he wanted to force my husband to go to law, but he did not want to bring an action before the Tribunal of Stettin, for Sweden is a bad land.[1] My husband returned sorrowfully to Hamburg with the bills and brought me the sad news. Though he, peace unto him, did not want to tell me, he could not keep it from me.

At the time I was pregnant with my son Leib. I was beside myself—our feelings are easily imagined. Less than fourteen days before we had lost 1500 reichstaler through a bankruptcy in Prague, and 1000 with a merchant in Hamburg. Besides this, my son Nathan was engaged and was to marry within half a year, and this had to cost us more than 3000 reichstaler. We reckoned that in this year more than 11,000 reichstaler of our capital had passed out of our hands. We were still young people, had married off one child and had a houseful of children, God protect them. It hurt us sorely. To keep our honest name clear, we had to keep everything secret. I fell very ill because of my grief, but to the world at large I put down my condition to my pregnancy. But a fire burnt within me. My husband comforted me and I comforted him, as best each could.

This happened about the time of the Frankfurt Fair, which my husband always attended. He returned on Thursday morning and on Friday he left for the Fair. I felt very dispirited. Before he left I begged Issachar to accompany him, for heaven's sake, because he was so downcast and I did not want him to travel alone. But Issachar showed us his wickedness then, as always, and refused to go with him unless my husband promised him two per cent of what he bought or sold. What could I do? As I did not want him to go alone, I agreed to this. My husband spoke to me and begged me, for God's sake, not to think any more of this sad affair—it was passed and could not be altered. I had to give him my hand on this and promise to

[1] At this time, Stettin belonged to Sweden.

H

forget all, and he promised me that he, too, would think no more about it. We held the bills of little value; we received payment for only one; he denied his signature on the others and this cost us a few more hundreds in expenses.

My husband arrived in Harburg on Friday and was there for the Sabbath, till the post left. From there he sent me a long letter full of cheer and comfort, that I should be contented for God would return our losses—as indeed happened. My husband reached Frankfurt and had such successful deals at the Fair as never before in all his days. He earned many thousands, for which we thanked the All Highest for His mercy and grace in healing our wound.

I thought then that there was no one in the whole world with more care and sorrow than I and forgot that the world is full of care, each has his share.

Once a philosopher walking in the street met a friend. He greeted him and asked how it went with him. 'Very badly,' answered the friend, 'I have more burdens and sorrows than anyone else in the world.' On this the philosopher replied, 'My dear friend, come on the roof with me and I will show you all the houses in town and tell you about the sufferings and misfortunes in each house. Then, if you desire, you can cast your cares among the other sorrows and pick another in its place. Perhaps you will find something to satisfy you.'

Together they went on to the roof. The philosopher pointed out to his friend *this* sorrow in *this* house, *that* trouble in *that* house, and so on. 'Do as I have told you,' he said.

Thereupon the friend answered, 'I can well see that there are so many troubles in each house, that perhaps there are greater sorrows and hardships than my own. I would fainer hold fast to my own.'

Such are our human thoughts: each thinks he suffers the most. Therefore, nothing is better than patience for, if the Almighty so wishes, He can take all cares from us.

My father about this time was very ill; he suffered from gout which led eventually to his death. His limbs swelled and he was bedridden for more than three months. We stayed with him till midnight every night, expecting the end at any moment. Once, when I was near confinement my husband, my mother and I sat together at night, and my mother persuaded us to go home. We had been in bed an hour when someone came from my father's house and knocked loudly; my husband was to go there immediately. As this had happened before we were not unduly alarmed. My husband would not allow me to go with him but persuaded me to remain where I was. If it was necessary—God forbid!—he would send for me. I allowed myself to be persuaded, remained in bed and fell asleep at once. As soon as my husband entered the house, about midnight, my father passed away. My husband would not allow anyone to awaken me, saying that there would be plenty of time for that in two or three hours. As I lay in deep sleep, I heard three heavy knocks on the door, enough to make the whole house fall in. I sprang from bed immediately and asked who knocked, but received no reply. Thereon I threw a robe over me and ran to my father's house and found what I have already related. My feelings may be easily imagined, as also my deep, sincere mourning over the loss of my beloved father. He died on the 24th of Tebet, in old age, leaving a good name behind him.

For a long while I was not comforted, till after the thirty days of mourning God sent me a son, through whom my father's name Leib was again born.

His birth was unusual. When he came into the world he lay groaning for twenty-four hours, so that the midwife and all the women thought he would not live. But it pleased the Lord that the child should improve day by day, and I comforted myself with the child that came to me in place of my dear father and I rejoiced over my son.

My dear mother was left with three orphans. My father left her 1600 reichstaler in her *Ketuba* and left each unmarried child about 1400 reichstaler. They would really have had more, but more than 1000 reichstaler was lost—of this I shall, perhaps, write later. My husband, and my brother-in-law, Reb Joseph Segal, desired no share in the inheritance, though they had 'half-male' portions. They left it all for my mother and her orphans. A year after my father's death they betrothed my brother Wolf to the daughter of Reb Jacob Lichtenstadt of Prague. He was known as an outstanding, upright man; until his death he was *parnass* of the whole land and was very wealthy. But he quarrelled with his stepson Abraham Lichtenstadt and towards the end his fortune grew less and less. My brother-in-law Joseph journeyed with Wolf to the betrothal. When Joseph

returned from this feast, he told of its wonders, how expensively
and in what a costly manner everything was prepared; at that
time Reb Jacob Lichtenstadt was still in a high position. At the
time of the next Leipzig Fair, my husband went to the wedding
with the bridegroom and accompanied by our servant, Issachar Cohen. Both my husband and Joseph travelled at their
own cost and did not charge my mother a pfennig for expenses.
The wedding passed all description. My husband on his return
home left my brother together with his young wife, and there
they remained a while longer.

My father's whole fortune at the time of his death was in
jewellery. My husband and Joseph made a sale, sold everything by auction, so that my mother should have cash to marry
off her daughters, in case a good match presented itself. Not
long after this my sister Mattie was betrothed to the son of the
wealthy and learned Dayan Model.[1] The wedding was celebrated in Hamburg. It is known what an exceptional, well-
respected man Dayan Model was, and also his wife, the pious
Pesselé; she had no equal in the world with the exception of
our Mothers—Sarah, Rebekah, Rachel and Leah. There was
no woman like her for piety and benevolence. Particularly, she
was a 'woman of virtues'. She carried on the business and saw
to her husband and children in a handsome way, as well in
Vienna as in Berlin, where they lived later. Her husband was
bedridden and so could do little business. Still, he was an exceptionally clever man of whom the whole world spoke and
was well liked by the Duke of Brandenburg, who once said, 'If
this man's feet were as sound as his head, he would have no
equal.' He and she died in Berlin in wealth and honour. She
left a wonderful will. I cannot write of it, but anyone who
wishes to read it can still find it with her children; they would
surely not have thrown it away.

Well, my youngest sister Rebekah, poor thing, was still un-
wed at the time, though later she was well married to the son
of my brother-in-law Reb Leib Bonn, an honest man, for many
years a *parnass* and possessed of much riches. He came here with
his son Samuel when the marriage was celebrated. All was joy

[1] Model Ries, formerly of the Vienna Rabbinate, settled in Berlin after
the expulsion of 1670 by the special permission of the Great Elector. He
was the founder of the old Berlin cemetery (1672).

and happiness. It could not be seen that my beloved, pious mother was a widow; it was all done in such fine style as though my father of blessed memory was still alive. Not one of the prominent members of the community was absent; they all came to do her honour. After the wedding my brother-in-law Leib returned home and scarce six months later, in wealth and with a good name, he died. Later, my sister and her husband Samuel Bonn moved to Bonn to take over the inheritance. He did much good and was made *parnass* in his father's place.

A few years later, however, there was war between the King of France and Holland and the Emperor. The French marched on Bonn and captured the town. The house which Samuel had inherited from his father was plundered and burnt. He could stay there no longer, so moved to Hamburg. There is too much to write of how he grew rich again, and then lost all his money once more; but here is not the place. He is an honest, God-fearing man. May God help him and all Jews out of their troubles, also his children, who were born and brought up in riches, and married well, and are now, unfortunately, poor. May God in His graciousness have mercy on them all.

Concerning this, it is said, no one can call himself fortunate until the day of his death, as the following tale will show.

There was once a great king at whose court there dwelt a philosopher, Solon by name, of whom the king thought highly, for Solon was, in truth, a very wise man.

It happened once that King Croesus clothed himself in his finest royal raiment, displaying his jewels and treasures. He summoned all his courtiers to appear before him likewise arrayed in their grandest garments. He also ordered Solon's presence.

When Solon came before Croesus, he bowed before him as is customary. The king said to him, 'My dear Solon, have you observed our riches and great honour? Have you ever seen a more lucky person than I am?'

The philosopher answered, 'My gracious king, I have observed everything well, but I cannot count you as lucky as a certain citizen of Athens who had ten children whom he brought up well. He was a rich man and gave his children to important people. They all served their country faithfully and did much service. He was not only held in high renown, but also saw how greatly esteemed were his children. Thus he died fortunate.

'The same I count more fortunate than you, in your kingly state. There is no king as rich as you, but your majesty is still young—and one cannot tell what may happen. Perhaps another monarch will conquer you and drive you from your lands and people.'

King Croesus asked, 'You prefer a private person rather than your king?'

'Your majesty,' answered Solon, 'the other died happy. No one should boast before he knows his own end. It may be, and is, indeed, to be desired, that the king's fortune should last till his end; but it may be, also, as I have said.'

Thereupon the king grew angry, seized his golden sceptre and pushed Solon from him, at the same time ordering him nevermore to appear in his court.

So the good Solon went on his way.

Many years passed. King Croesus lived in great riches and was much honoured. He forgot his philosopher completely.

But later, Croesus had a quarrel about some frontiers and before very long it led to bloodshed. War lasted some years—and Croesus lost the war. His opponent took Croesus back as prisoner to his own land. There he held council with his ministers and asked in what manner he should be killed.

With one voice they all declared he should be burnt and arrangements were made to carry this out.

A large number of spectators assembled to see the sight. A great pyre was built; and there was much oil and balsam such as are used for embalming, as well as sweet-smelling perfumes for the burning of Croesus.

The other king stood at his window to watch Croesus led to the stake. As he was being led Croesus suddenly remembered the philosopher who had declared that a person should not deem himself fortunate before he knew his end. He began to weep, and cried aloud, 'O Solon, how truly you spoke!'

The king at the window heard his cries and what he said, and sent messengers to bring Croesus before him. When he came into his presence, Croesus fell on his knees. The king bade him rise as he wished to speak with him. 'My Croesus,' he said to him, 'what did you say while you were being led forth to your death agony, when you cried so bitterly?'

So he told him of Solon. 'And now in my tribulation, I thought of him and of what he said.'

The king heard him out and thought, 'Croesus was also once a great king, and God gave him into my hands. Who knows? Perhaps this thing will happen to me.'

So he freed Croesus and returned to him his land and throne.

Therefore, when things go well with us, do not boast or be proud, for we know not what our end may be—as this tale proves.

My mother married off her daughters well and honourably. She was about forty-four years old when my father died, and though she had many matches offered her, so that she could have married again and been quite wealthy, the dear, devout woman preferred to remain a widow. She supported herself on what was left her, in a fine, respectable way and lived in her little house alone with her maid, quietly and well. The good God grant that every woman who is left—God forbid!—a widow, and is of the same mind as my mother—to remain in widowhood—be no worse off. Much could be written of her, the contentment, the good she does with her little, and her patience. Her joy of her children and grandchildren is indescribable. The Lord grant her good health until her hundredth year.

Later, we betrothed our daughter Hannah to Samuel, the son of my brother-in-law Abraham Segal. Whether we were pleased or not with this match is unimportant, for it was fated from God, and my blessed brother-in-law insisted on it. It was about the time of the Frankfurt Fair, to which my husband travelled in company with Jochanan, Mendel and Leib Goslar. From there they had to go direct to Leipzig. When they reached Fulda Jochanan fell ill and after four or five days died. The other three wished to remain with him, but the gallant Jochanan would not allow this. So they went on to Leipzig, while his son Aaron, who had accompanied them, remained with his father. Before they reached Leipzig the tragic news of his death reached them. The fear that fell upon them may easily be imagined. In Leipzig, immediately after, Mendel, the son of the learned Reb Michael Speyer of Frankfurt, fell ill and within eight days he, too, died. The terror and woe in Leipzig cannot be lightly recalled. We, in Hamburg, too, heard the tragic news. Not enough that they had to witness the tragic death of such a fine young man, not yet twenty-four years of age, so woefully snatched from life, but his father-in-law Moses the son of Nathan, who was also in Leipzig, did not know how to give him Jewish burial, for conditions were difficult and dangerous in Leipzig then. In short, after much trouble, through influence and much money, they managed to take the corpse from there to Dessau, the nearest Jewish community, about six miles distant. This cost more than 1000 reichstaler. Nevertheless, they thanked God that they had been able to take the body out of Leipzig.

Meanwhile my husband and Leib Goslar fell seriously ill, and in the middle of the Fair were taken to Halberstadt. Moses Schnauthan and Issachar Cohen were with my husband, who upon his arrival in Halberstadt became so ill that all hope was given up. Issachar wrote comforting me that he was not dangerously ill and that I should not be alarmed; and worried my husband till he was forced to put his signature to the letter. But this signature should have been seen! It was impossible to recognize a single letter. My children's feelings and mine can easily be imagined. I received this letter on the first day of Pentecost. On the eve of the festival all the merchants arrived home, save only my husband, and each, before he went to his own home, came and comforted me that everything was for the best. They did all in their power to appease and allay my fears. But how could this help? Our festival may easily be left to the imagination; indeed, because of it I could do nothing. But immediately after *Yom Tov* I sent my son Reb Mordecai Segal and Jacob the son of Chaim Pollock and Eva to Halberstadt, to see how my husband was and whether he was still alive. May God remember it for good. I prayed and fasted all day, arranged for people to learn Talmud, did much charity and everything else in my power. God—blessed be He—had mercy and helped my husband, so that he recovered a little and was able to hire a wagon. He had stayed with Israel Kirchahn, who arranged a bed for him on the wagon, and besides this hired another vehicle for his attendants. In the first wagon there was but one person who attended him. Thus, weak and ill my husband arrived home. But we praised God fervently that 'He had given him to us and not to earth'. The Lord prolonged his life six years and allowed him to marry off two more children, as will follow.

But I have forgotten to write of the death of my saintly father-in-law, which I should have described much before this, for he died three years before my husband fell ill in Leipzig. When his father was in his last illness, they wrote to my husband, 'Behold, thy father is ill.' He left everything and set off immediately for Hanover and there remained three weeks. My father-in-law, a man of eighty, was very weak. He thought that as soon as he saw my husband, his youngest and best-loved child, he would die. But when he saw, at the end of three weeks, that God had not taken him to Himself, he said, 'My son, I called you to me that you should be here at my end. You are doing big business, and have already been here three weeks. You have done your duty. I put my trust in the Lord. Return in His Name to your house.' Though my husband hesitated, and wished to remain, his father insisted that he should return home; the other children, too, returned to their homes.

Before my husband reached home, the following had happened. Opposite our bed stood a small one in which the children lay. At that time my daughter Hannah and Mattie, a child of about eleven, slept in it. I rose early one morning and went to the synagogue for first prayers. My daughter Hannah ran out of the room to the synagogue, and out of sheer fright could not utter a word. People asked, 'Hannah, what has happened? Why are you so terrified?' The child replied, 'Ach, God! I woke up and wanted to see if Mumma was still in bed, and I saw an old man with a long white beard lying there. I was so frightened that I jumped out of bed and ran down the stairs, and when I turned to look back, the old man lifted his head and stared after me.'

When I returned home from synagogue there was much whispering and gossip in my household. I asked what was the matter, but no one would tell me. Two days later my husband returned and he was here scarce a week when the news of his father's, the pious Reb Joseph's, death came.

It is impossible to tell of my husband's grief and tears. Immediately after the seven days of mourning he hired ten rabbis and set aside a room in our house in which nothing was done by day and night other than Talmud learning by the *minyan*.[1] My husband during the whole year did not journey from home, so that he might not miss *Kaddish*.[2] Twelve weeks after this death, my brother-in-law Isaac Hameln was in Wesel to attend the marriage of his son Reb Samuel. From thence he went to Hanover, where all the brothers met. He wrote to my husband

[1] A quorum of ten men, the minimum number requisite for religious services.   [2] Prayer for the repose of the dead—recited by sons.

that he, too, should come to Hanover. Early the following morning he rose and went to Harburg. There were several people, enough to make a *minyan*, so that he did not miss one *Kaddish*, even though it cost him much money.

When he reached Hanover the will was read. It was a wonder to read the will, so wisely and piously was it made. They told how my father-in-law, of blessed memory, had died in his full senses, 'with a kiss',[1] as did all his children. What he left was shared in accordance with his will; there were no differences or unseemly words between the brothers. My husband was only eight days in Hanover and comforted his dear mother as best he could. Though he tried his utmost to persuade her to go back with him to Hamburg, she refused, for the devout woman would not be parted from her saintly husband in life or in death. Two years later she, too, died, and was buried beside her husband. She was eighty-two years old. They were a loving, God-fearing pair, whose like cannot be found. May God reward us for their merits. If only my husband and I had lived together to such fine old age. But God willed otherwise.

After this my husband went to Amsterdam, where a match was proposed for our daughter with Moses Krumbach.[2] My husband decided and agreed to the match too soon, as will follow. After the betrothal, when the dowry was deposited, he wrote to inform me of the event. The money was deposited with Reb Elia Cleve in Cleve, father of my son-in-law Kossman Gompertz, who was authorized to receive it by Abraham Krumbach. But before I received his letter informing us that Esther was betrothed, I received letters from all over the place cautioning us against this match, as the young man had many faults. And the very next day I got the letter to tell me that the dowry had been deposited and that my husband was leaving for home. One may imagine how I felt and with what joy I regarded the match. But I could do nothing until his return.

A week later my husband arrived home, expecting me to await him overjoyed because of the match. But he found the opposite! In place of joy I met him with heavy spirits and could

---

[1] The death of the pious, as Moses, who died, according to the Midrash, with the kiss of God on his lips.

[2] Moses Krumbach-Schwab was the son of the Abraham Krumbah-Schwab and Jachet, daughter of Elia Gompertz of Cleve.

scarcely open my lips. He saw very well that something was amiss. He understood, but not wishing to disturb our reunion for the first few days, did not mention a word of the match. Meanwhile, he too received letters from some very good friends who wrote that they had heard that we desired this match and begging us not to do anything, at least till we had first seen the young man. My husband was very upset over this and said to me, 'Glückelchen, you must know something of this. I have noticed your low spirits.' Upon which I showed him the letters I had received before his return home. He was alarmed and sad, for only the young man's virtues and not his faults had been made known to him. We did not know what to do, for the match was already agreed to. I wrote to the young man's mother, Mistress Jachet. I can still remember the very words I used. I first, as is customary, wished her a hearty *mazal tov* and then continued: as we had received several letters informing us that the young man had many faults, which we assumed to be lies, we begged her to send the bridegroom to the betrothal feast to meet the bride; and if we saw that what these denouncers, these retailers of lies, these mischief-makers, as we hoped, had said was false, we would receive him with much joy and give him precious gifts, and he would lack no honour. If, however—God forbid!—what they said was true, we begged her not to send him, for our child must not be so cruelly deceived. If she intended, all the same, to send her son, thinking that, as we were already closely related by birth and marriage, we would disregard any faults because the first stage of the betrothal was completed, she must not do so. In the latter event—God forbid!—the betrothal must be cancelled and forgotten on both sides, and so on.

The effect of this letter on Mistress Jachet may easily be imagined, and how it put her nose out of joint! She sent an angry reply: she had intended sending her son to his bride, but since receiving our letter she would inform us that if we wished to see her son, we could come ourselves or send someone to Metz! Much time passed in vain, angry correspondence and we drew no nearer an agreement, especially as a great war between France and Germany[1] had broken out and neither could go to the other.

[1] The predatory war of Louis XIV began in 1688. At that time Metz was already under French suzerainty.

Meanwhile, we celebrated the marriage of my daughter Hannah, with much joy. I have forgotten to mention that the marriage of my son Nathan with the orphan Miriam, daughter of Reb Elia Ballin, was celebrated long before this. My son-in-law Kossman and daughter Zipporah came to the wedding and we returned them their expenses and gave them presents besides. Jacob Hanover[1] and his wife Süssa were also present, apart from many distinguished strangers, so that it was a very grand affair. In that year we spent more than 10,000 reichstaler banco. Praised be the Lord who has given and taken, the true God who replaced all that we had spent! Had God but left me the crown of my head, there would not have been a happier, more fortunate pair in the whole world. Because of our sins He took him to the Eternal World, and left us in this transient, wearisome universe. We must pray to the Creator that when our end comes, He will bring us to the Garden of Eden. Amen.

My husband returned from Hanover, as you have already heard, where his father's legacy was shared, about twelve weeks after the death. At the time I was pregnant with my son Joseph and during the whole period of my carrying my husband hoped that I would bear a son so that the name of his saintly father would be renewed in his child. This, God be thanked, came to pass.

Here, my dear children, I will write of an incident that is true. If young, pregnant women at any time, anywhere, see fruit or anything tasty which they fancy, they should not go away but should first sample it, and not listen to their own silly heads which say, 'Ay, it cannot harm you!' and go away. For it can, God forbid, be a matter of life and death to them, as well as to the unborn child, as I found to my cost. I used always to laugh and make merry when I heard that a pregnant woman had longings after anything and suffered any harm by not indulging in her fancy. I would not believe it. On the contrary, many times when I was pregnant and went to the market and saw some nice fruit which I fancied, if it was too dear I would not buy. And in truth, I never suffered any ill effects. But not all times are the same: this I

[1] Jacob, son of Lipman Cohen (Leffman Behrens) Glückel's brother-in-law. His wife Süssa was a daughter of Elia Gompertz of Cleve.

discovered when I was in the ninth month with my son Joseph.

My mother had some business to transact with an advocate who lived in the Horse Market. She asked me to go with her. Although it was far from my house, and the time for evening prayers was approaching, it was the beginning of the month of Kislev,[1] I could not refuse her. I was in fine health then. We went together to the gentile quarter. Opposite the advocate's house there lived a woman who sold medlars. I was always very fond of medlars and ate them with relish. I said to my mother, 'Mumma, do not forget, when we come back, I want to buy some medlars.' We went to the advocate and there accomplished our business. It was very late when we were finished and nearly night. We walked homewards and both of us forgot the medlars; I remembered them only when I got indoors. I felt sorry that I had not bought any and gave no further thought to them, just as one thinks of food one likes, but which is not immediately to hand. I went to sleep, feeling as well as usual, but after midnight, my pains commenced. The midwives were summoned and my son was born.

The news was immediately conveyed to my husband, who was overjoyed that he now had his father's name. But I noticed that the women who were with me put their heads together and whispered among themselves. I wanted to know what was the matter and insisted that they must tell me. At length they informed me that the baby had brown spots over his head and body. They had to bring a candle to the bed so that I could see for myself. I saw that not only was he covered with spots but that he lay like a lump of clay, not moving an arm or leg, just as though, God forbid, his soul had departed. He would not suckle or open his mouth. My husband, too, saw this and was very much upset. This was on Wednesday night and the circumcision was to be celebrated on Thursday week.

There was no improvement during the week, and he grew weaker day by day. Sabbath came, we celebrated *Shalom Zochor*.[2] But still there was no improvement in the child. At the

---

[1] Either the end of November or the beginning of December.

[2] A feast on the first Sabbath evening after the birth of a son, in celebration of the event.

close of Sabbath, while my husband was reciting the *Hab-dalah*,[1] I said to my mother who was with me, 'I beg you, send the *shabbos-goya*[2] to me. I want to send her somewhere.' My mother enquired where to? I answered, 'I have been puzzling all the time why the baby should have these spots, and why he has grown so much weaker. I wonder whether the cause is that on the night I was brought to bed I had a longing for those medlars and did not have any? I want to send the woman to get me a few schilling's worth. I will squeeze a little into the baby's mouth. Perhaps God in His mercy will help, so that the child will get better.'

My mother was very cross with me and cried, 'You've always got such nonsense in your head! The weather is as bad as if heaven and earth were joining, and the woman won't want to go out in it. It is all a lot of foolishness.' But I persisted, 'My dear mother, do me but this favour. Send the woman. I will give her as much as she wants, as long as I get the medlars; otherwise my heart will not be at rest.' So we called the woman and sent her to get the medlars. It was a long distance. She ran all the way. It was wretched weather, not fit to send a dog out in. The time passed very slowly until her return, as is natural when one waits impatiently for anything. Each second seemed as long as an hour. At length the woman returned with the medlars. Everyone knows that medlars, being sourish, are not food for such a young child. I called the nurse to unbind the baby and seat herself with him in front of the oven and squeeze a little of a medlar into his mouth. Although everyone laughed at what they called my foolishness, I insisted on this, and it had to be done. When she squeezed a little of the medlar between the baby's lips, he opened his little mouth so eagerly, as though he wanted to swallow it whole, and sucked away all the soft part. Before this he had not opened his mouth wide enough to take a drop of milk or sugar-pap such as one gives to babies. The nurse handed the child to me in bed, to see if he would suck. As soon as he felt the breast, he began to suck with the strength of a three-month babe, and from then till the day of his circumcision there remained no spot on his face or body,

[1] A prayer recited at the close of the Sabbath.
[2] A gentile woman employed in Jewish homes on the Sabbath to perform small duties forbidden by Jewish law.

save one on his side, as large as a broad lentil. The child was fine grown and hale at the time of his circumcision. The ceremony was performed, praised be God, at the right time. There was a great celebration on his initiation into the Jewish covenant, the like of which Hamburg had not seen for a long time. Though we lost 1000 marks banco the same day through the bankruptcy of a Portuguese Jew Isaac Vas, my husband did not take it to heart because of the joy he had in his son. So you see, dear children, women's longings are not all folly and should not be despised.

After this I was again with child and very ill. When I was in the seventh month I fell into an unnatural fever. In the morning I was cold for four hours; after this I had four hours of heat and—pardon me—sweated profusely, which was worse than either the cold or the heat. This exhausted me. I could not eat a bite, though the choicest dishes were put before me. Once, on a beautiful summer's day, my husband asked me to take a little walk with him along the bank which was not far from the house, to refresh myself a little, perhaps I would fancy some food later. I said to him, 'You know I have no strength for walking.' To which my dear husband made reply, 'I and the nurse will support you.' I allowed myself to be persuaded and was led to the bank where I seated myself on the green grass. My husband meanwhile had ordered Todros, the cook of Texeira,[1] to prepare a meal fit for the royal table while we were out, and to call us home when all was ready. My husband thought that when I returned and saw such a beautifully

[1] Texeira, a member of the Portuguese Jewish community in Hamburg, was financial adviser to Queen Christina of Sweden in Hamburg. He founded the Hamburg *Bet Hamidrash*, Jewish house of study.

In his interesting autobiography (trans. by Bernard Miall and published by Unwin and Co., 1928) Johann Dietz, surgeon-barber, writes of the above-named cook: 'There was a rich Portuguese Jew in Hamburg, by name Texeira, who visited my master almost daily . . . he often dined with my master.

'One day, when the cook had prepared a tench, with a yellow cream sauce, as the Jew had enjoyed it exceedingly, he spoke to his own cook: "You never give me anything as good as that." The cook came to see our cook and asked him how to prepare the dish in question, and informed his master on returning that the fish was a tench. The Jew began to execrate himself and to spit, for the Jews may not eat any fish without scales; however, the thing was done, and he was never again so trusting.'

dressed table, prepared so unexpectedly and without my knowledge, and such fine foods, my appetite would return. But, my
God and master! When I got indoors and into the dining-
room I was nauseated as soon as I smelt the food and begged
that either I or the food should be taken out of the room.

Thus I suffered for two whole months. I lost all my strength
and often thought, 'Dear Lord, when my time comes and my
child is born, I shall have neither strength nor power to help
myself.' But when the time arrived, the trusty God helped me
so graciously that I brought forth the child without any pain.
It was a fine, beautiful baby, but, unfortunately, had the same
fever from which I suffered. Though we had doctors and all
earthly aid, nothing availed. The baby lived fourteen days and
then God took it to Himself, and left us our portion of affliction. I had another two or three attacks of fever, though I
eventually left childbed hale and well.

After this I was brought to bed with my daughter Hendel-
chen, two years later with my son Zanwill, and after with my
son Reb Moses, then my daughters Freudchen, Miriam—the
two youngest did not know their father well.

What shall I write of the much that happened between these
times? Every two years I had a child, and suffered much, as is
natural, when there is a household of small children God protect them. I often thought that no one had such a heavy burden
as I, and suffered as much as I through offspring. But I, foolish
one, did not know how well things were with me when my
children were like olive branches about my table.

But what can I do? I mention my omissions.

My heart-beloved children, the history of your father, Reb
Chaim Hameln Segal, of blessed memory, is before you. Good
and pleasant would it have been if the Holy One had left him
to us so that together we had led all our children under the
marriage canopy. But what shall I say and how shall I speak?
My sins caused this; I a sinner did not merit anything else.

My son Mordecai grew up, a fine talented young man, in
every way gifted. God reward him for the honour in which he
held his parents. He was in Leipzig with my husband when he
fell ill with colic. All who were there could not cease from
relating of all he did for his father. He sat up with him all night
and neither slept, ate, nor drank. Though it was his duty to do

Die Zwei Häuser der alten und Neuen Juden Schulen in Fürth, wie je von außen her an Gebäun
sambt ihrer Hochzeiten Versammlungen

24. *The Old and New Synagogues at Fürth with Wedding Procession.* Engraving, 1705

Die Inwendige d. d. alten

25. *The Interior of the Old Synagogue at Fürth with the Women's Gallery on the right.*
Etching, 1705

26. *Memorial-Stone of the Burial Fraternity of Altona.* 17th–18th Century

this, still, he was very young. God aided him so that in health and peace they returned home together.

Unfortunately my pious husband was not a strong man. That was why he hastened to marry off all the children, and feared the day which was to fall on us. Mordecai was betrothed to the daughter of the *Parnass* Moses, son of Nathan. My husband gave him 2000 reichstaler in Danish kronen and Moses gave his daughter 3000 reichstaler in the same currency. They shared the expenses of the wedding equally. We gave them two years' *Kest* and they lived with us. But scarce half a year later, most unfortunately alas, my husband's time came and because of our sins God took from us my devout husband, the crown of my head. In the year 5449 [1689] God's wrath fell on us and He tore my dearest from me. I was left with eight orphaned children, and the four already married still had need of their faithful father. What can I say? I lost such a lovable husband and my children so exceptional a father. We were left like sheep without a shepherd. I had always thought I would be the fortunate one, that God would take me to Him first, for I was always ailing during my husband's lifetime. When anything was not well with us, the pious man wished that he might be the first of us two to die. He always said, 'What could I do then with the dear children?' whom he loved with all his heart. It may clearly be seen what great piety was his, for God took him first from the world. He, peace unto him, died in wealth and honour and saw no evil. His married children, too, were also wealthy and highly honoured. He was a distinguished man and left behind him an unimpeachable name, and an example for his children to follow. One may, indeed, say of him that he died happy, in the way Solon shows in the tale I have related.

But I was left in great loneliness. Every morning came new sorrows, of which I shall write in my fifth book, which is, unhappily, a book of lamentation, a book of bitter woe. Though my husband left money and wealth enough, this was nothing against the great loss.

Here I will end my fourth book. The Lord make us rejoice even as He has afflicted us. And may He have mercy on my orphans. Amen, and Amen!

I

BOOK V

My heart-loved children, I shall now begin my fifth book by telling of my great sorrow, from the beginning of the illness of your beloved father until his death.

On the evening of Tebet 19, 5449 [January 11, 1689] your dear father went to the gentile quarter to meet a merchant with whom he had an appointment about some business. As he neared the merchant's house he fell over a sharp stone and hurt himself so badly that we have need still to weep over it. He came home quite miserable. I happened to be in my mother's house and was called home. On entering the house, I saw my husband standing near the oven, groaning. I was alarmed and asked what ailed him. He answered, 'I fell down and fear it is something serious.' He could not move, and I had to take everything from his pockets, for when he left the house he had put jewellery into all his pockets. We did not then understand the injury. He had been ruptured many years before and stumbling, fell on the ruptured part, and his intestines became twisted. We always had a bed prepared in the room, but he refused to use it and we had to take him up to his own bed.

The weather was then as cold as though heaven and earth were freezing together. We sat up all night with him and did all we could, but did not remain there longer, for it was too cold, and, also, this was dangerous for him. At length he saw that it was not good for him to remain there and we brought him down. It was then past midnight: we did what we could, but there was no sign of improvement. I saw my sad plight before me and begged him for heaven's sake to let me send for a doctor and call in some people. He said, 'I would sooner die than reveal this rupture to people.' I stood before him weeping aloud and asked, 'What are you saying? Why should people not know? You have not had it from any sin or disgrace.' But my words had no effect: he had persuaded himself that this would harm his children in some way and that people would say it was hereditary: he loved his children so deeply. We did our utmost for him all night, trying all sorts of remedies. But he grew visibly worse. When it was day, I said to him, 'Praise be to God that it is day! I will send for a doctor and a surgeon.' He would not allow this but asked instead that we should send for Abraham Lopez, who was a Sephardi, a barber-surgeon as well as a physician. I sent for him immediately. When he saw the injury he said, 'Do not worry. I will put something on and it will soon improve. I have had several hundred such cases and cured them all.'

This was early Wednesday morning. Lopez applied several things, thinking this would relieve him. But—may God have mercy—about midday Lopez said, 'I see that my cure will not help him. I will call in a special rupture-cutter.' The cutter came and applied ointments all day to soften the wound. But the longer it lasted the worse it got. On Thursday I called in another rupture-cutter and two more physicians, one of whom was Dr. Fonesca.[1]

When I spoke to him and told him all the facts, he said, 'This is a special case: his intestines, unfortunately, are all twisted so his bowels cannot act in the ordinary way.' What should have passed through the lower extremity, he brought up and vomited through his mouth. Nothing we did was of any avail; still he would have no strangers about him and begged us to keep it secret. I understood my misfortune only too well and foresaw the terrible sorrow about to befall me.

In great pain and with much fear Thursday, day and night also, passed. On Friday Lopez brought a physician from Berlin, who had been the medical adviser of the Elector for several years. He gave my husband something to swallow and applied a plaster: they were of no help. On Sabbath morning, my brother-in-law Reb Joseph Segal, with whom he was not on friendly terms, heard of this. He came to the house and begged to be allowed into the room. I went to my husband and said, 'Joseph is outside and wishes to come in.' He said, 'Let him enter.' When he entered and saw the condition my husband was in, Joseph knocked his head against the wall, and pulled out handfuls of hair, and with bitter tears streaming down his face, cried out: 'Woe is me that I should lose such a brother-in-law!' He threw himself on the bed, and with hot tears begged for pardon. With a full heart my husband answered: 'My dear brother-in-law, I forgive you and everyone; I ask

[1] Member of a distinguished family of Portuguese Jewish physicians.

pardon of you.' This quieted Joseph, and he sought to comfort him telling him to be patient, God would help him. And my husband, of blessed memory, said he would be content with all that God did.

But to me he did not reveal half the seriousness of his illness. My son Leib, of blessed memory, was a youth of sixteen years at the time, and he remained with him. When I went out of the room, he called him to him and exhorted the youth so that he wept. But as soon as my husband saw me enter the room, he said to him, 'Be quiet, for God's sweet mercy. Mother is coming in; do not let her see you crying.' He was already in his death-throes, yet he still thought of me.

On Sabbath, after dinner, my mother went to him, and fell on him kissing him, and crying with tears: 'My son, will you leave us thus? Have you nothing that you desire to ask of us?' And he answered: 'My dearest mother-in-law, you know I have loved you as though you were my own mother. I have nothing to ask of you; only comfort my Glückelchen.' These were his last words to my mother. After this more physicians and surgeons came, but it was all in vain. At the close of Sabbath there was no one but I and Abraham Lopez; he wanted no one else. At midnight the surgeon was again sent for; Lopez thought that the wound was now ready for cutting. But when the surgeon came he saw immediately that there was no hope, and went away again. Then I said to him: 'My heart, may I make you more comfortable?' (for it meant touching him, and I was then unclean).[1] He answered: 'God forbid, my child; it won't be so long now before you will have bathed.' But he did not live till then.

I stood there a while longer talking with Abraham Lopez. He advised me to send for Feibusch Levi, who was able with sick people. I called up the children's teacher also. It was 2 o'clock, Sunday morning. Feibusch went straight to my husband and asked: 'Reb Chaim, have you anything to ask?' He answered: 'I have nothing to will; my wife knows about everything; let her do as she has done up to now.' He then asked

[1] At certain times, according to Biblical and Talmudic teaching, a woman is ritually unclean until she bathes. At a time when cleanliness was a virtue observed in its breach every Jewish community had its *mikveh* —ritual communal bath.

Feibusch to hand him the learned Rabbi Isaiah Horowitz's work.[1] This he studied for half an hour, then said to the children's teacher and Feibusch, handing back the book, 'Do you not see my condition? Take my wife and children out; it is high time.' We were forcibly pushed out; our parting may be imagined. After this Reb Feibusch wished to talk to him, but he answered him no more, and spoke to himself; only his lips moving. This lasted about half an hour, and then Reb Feibusch said to Abraham Lopez: 'Lay your ear close to Reb Chaim's mouth, to try to hear what he says.' Lopez did so, and heard after a little while: '*Shema Yisroel Adonai Alohenu Adonai Achad.*'[2] Then his breath was hushed, and his soul escaped in holiness and purity. From his end it was clear what sort of a man he was.

What shall I write, my dear children, of our great loss? To lose such a husband! I who had been held so precious by him, was left with eight orphaned children, of whom my daughter Esther was a bride. May God have mercy and be father to my orphans, for He is the only father of the fatherless. But though I silence my weeping and lamentation, I shall have to mourn my friend all the days of my life. He died on Sunday, Tebeth 24, 5449 [January 16, 1689], and was buried the same day. The whole community mourned and lamented him: the unexpected blow had fallen so suddenly. Surrounded by my children, I sat the seven days of mourning, a pitiful sight, I and my twelve children thus seated. I immediately ordered men for prayers and Talmud study for the whole year, to study day and night in the house. My children recited Kaddish untiringly. All our friends and acquaintances, men and women, came every day of the week of mourning, to console us. My children, brothers, sisters and friends comforted me as well as they could. But each one went home with a loved one, while I remained in my house in sorrow with my orphans.

I was thrown from heaven to earth. I had had my husband thirty years and had enjoyed through him all the good that any woman could wish for. He was always thoughtful for me,

---

[1] This was 'The Two Tablets of the Covenant', a cabbalistic work highly esteemed for its holiness.

[2] 'Hear, O Israel, the Lord our God, the Lord is one.' This affirmation of God's unity is the last conscious utterance of every believing Jew.

even after his death, so that I could remain in a comfortable position and of good repute. But what help is that?

My heart-beloved children, our trusty friend died as a saint. He lay ill only four days and was fully conscious until his soul departed. May my end be as was his. May his merits rank for me and his sons and daughters. When his soul fled away, my riches and fortune departed from me. It was his good fortune to depart from this sinful world in riches and honour, and suffer no trials through his children. As the proverb says, because of sinners, the saint dies. But I was left desolate in sorrow and tears, with my married and unmarried children, and toil and troubles increased every day. My friends and relatives stood afar off. What shall I say and to whom shall I cry? Yes; this is because of my sins and I shall always mourn. I shall not forget him all the days of my life. He is engraved in my heart.

My dear mother, sisters and brothers comforted me, but their comfort only increased my sorrow and poured more oil on the fire, so that the flames grew ever higher. These talkings and comfortings lasted two or three weeks; after that no one knew me. Those to whom we had shown kindness, repaid us with evil, as is the way of the world. At least, that is how it appeared to me, for the mood of a widow who so suddenly loses such a kingdom is such that she easily imagines that everyone wrongs her. May God forgive me this. My dearly loved children, the day that my beloved comrade lay dead before me was not so depressing as those that followed. Day by day it grew worse and my sorrow heavier. But God Almighty had pity on me and my orphans and taught me, a weak woman, patience.

After the first thirty days of mourning, no brother, no sister, no relative came to ask: 'How are you? and how are things?' When they had been here before the end of the thirty days their talk was insincere and of little help to me and the children.

My husband would not appoint trustees: I have already mentioned what he said to Reb Feibusch. After the thirty days of mourning I went over the books. I found that we owed 20,000 reichstaler. I knew this already: it gave me no anxiety, for I knew that the debts could be easily met and I would have as much again for my children's wants. Still, it was no easy matter for an afflicted widow to owe so much and not have 100 reichstaler in cash in the house. My sons Nathan and Mordecai, like loyal children, came to my aid, but they were still very young. I collected everything, made my balance, and decided to have a sale—as came to pass.

Dear children, you have read how your saintly father departed this sinful world. He was your shepherd and friend. Look after yourselves, dear children, for you have no one, no friends, on whom to depend, and even if you have many friends, when you need them you cannot depend on them. But when you are not in need of them, everyone will willingly be friendly. When they are wanted they cannot be found—as the following story shows:

There was once a king who sent his son to far-off lands to learn all manner of wisdom. After he had been away thirteen years the king wrote, recalling him home. He obeyed the order, and returned. The king sent many people to welcome him and they met him with much joy, as did also the king, who prepared a great feast. Everything was full of jollity.

'Dear son,' said the king after the feasting was over, 'did you have many friends in the city where you studied?'

'Lord king and father,' he answered, 'the whole town were my friends.'

'How were they all your friends?' the king asked.

And his son replied, 'I gave parties every day and they were good drink-brothers, for I gave them fine wines.'

The king sighed when he heard these words and shook his head, saying, 'I thought you had gone to learn wisdom; but what I have just heard is not wisdom—that you hold your boon companions to be your good friends. That is not right, for drink-brothers are drunkards and no trust or faith can be put in them. So long as there is drink, there are no better friends on earth—as if they were born of the same mother. But when the feast is over, they go from you, wipe their mouths, thinking: "If you invite me again, I am ready to come." If you don't, or if they get other friends they pay no further heed to you and forget your comradeship.'

'Tell me, then,' asked the prince, 'who is a friend I can rely on?'

And the king answered, 'You should hold no one to be your friend until you have proved his worth.'

'How shall I try him?' asked the prince, 'so that I may know his thoughts and be able to rely on his friendship?'

Thereon the king answered, 'Take a calf and kill it secretly so that no one knows. Place it in a sack and at night carry it across to the residence of your equerry, your valet, and your secretary, and tell them this tale: Alas! What has befallen me! I have been drinking all day,—till now,—and lost my temper with my father's royal Chamberlain when he contradicted me. I could not control myself when he admonished me and took my dagger and struck him dead. I am afraid lest my father hears of this, for he is an angry man and perhaps in quick fury will revenge himself. I have the corpse in this sack and so beg of you to help me bury it now! Then,' ended the king, 'you will see what sort of friends you have.'

The prince did as he was told. And, the calf in the sack, he went that night to the house of his equerry and knocked at the door. The courtier looked down from his window and asked, 'Who knocks so late at night?'

'It is I, your master, the prince,' he answered.

The lord-in-waiting ran quickly downstairs and flinging wide the door cried, 'Oh! What brings my master so late at night?'

As instructed, the prince told him, ending, 'You are my trusty retainer. Help me to bury the dead man before day breaks.'

As soon as the equerry heard this he cried, 'Turn away from me with such things!' The prince begged that he should help him, but he declared angrily, 'I will have nothing to do with an idle drunkard and murderer. And if you do not wish to retain me in your service, you may find others,' and shut the door in his face, leaving him in the cold.

The prince then went to the house of his secretary, who answered him as had his equerry. From there he went to the groom-of-the-chamber, his valet, told him the same tale and begged for his help. 'True I have to serve you, for you are my master,' he said, 'but I did not enter service as a grave-digger. I would do it for you, but I am afraid of your father's hasty temper. If he finds out he will kill me and you. You bury the corpse yourself, in the cemetery which is near here. I will keep guard to see if anyone comes.'

They did so. The prince buried the calf, then each went his way. The next day the three met. The equerry told of the prince's evil deed and how he had wanted him to bury the corpse. The other two related how he had also been to see them, but neither had wanted to have a share in the evil affair, and that he had himself buried the corpse in the cemetery. They held counsel together and decided to inform the king: they reasoned that when he heard all this, he would slay his son and hold them to be trustworthy servants.

This they did. They informed the king who spoke thus: 'By my crown, if my son has done this thing, I will slay him.'

He called his son and repeated what the informers had said. The prince denied the charge. But they persisted, 'You did this! And you put him in a sack which you buried in the cemetery.'

Then said the king, 'I will send my servants—and you go with them and point out where the sack was buried.'

And thus it came to pass and they brought the sack sealed with the prince's seal. Whereupon the king demanded of his son, 'What have you to say to this?'

He answered, 'Dear master and father, I killed a calf for a sacrifice, and slaughtered it in an incorrect manner. So it is *treifa* [ritually unclean] as a sacrifice; and as it is disrespectful to throw it in the street, being intended for a religious purpose, I buried it in the sack.'

The king demanded that the sack be opened and emptied—and lo, the dead calf fell out! The three servitors were shamed before the prince. He ordered them to be thrown into prison and this was done.

After these happenings the king called his son and said to him, 'See now, can you take any one to be your friend until he has been proved?'

On which the prince answered, 'I have really learnt my lesson now more than in my thirteen years abroad. I found only half a friend—the valet who stood guard for me. My dear father, advise me what I should do with my servants.'

The king replied, 'I know of no other advice but that you should put your servants to death. For the sake of the valet who was half faithful so that he should not take them as an example the other two must be slain.'

'Because of one, must the other two be slain?' asked the prince. 'How can I do this thing?'

'If a wise man is taken prisoner together with a thousand fools,' declared the king, 'and there is no way to separate him from them, I advise that the thousand be slain for the sake of saving the one wise man. Therefore it is better to slay the two, for the sake of turning the half into a whole friend.'

This was done and the valet was his friend all his life.

And thus, the son admitted, a friend cannot be known until he has been proved.

So, my dear children, there is no friend to rely on save the Holy One, blessed be He. May He be a standby and our help. Though you have lost your father, the heavenly Father lives for ever and ever and He will not forsake you if you serve Him faithfully. But if, God forbid, punishment comes, *you* are to blame because of your actions.

But what more shall I write? I will begin anew from where I left off. You have seen how your father died in holiness and purity and I have written how I made up my accounts, then went to my brother-in-law Reb Joseph that he should go over everything to see whether I had priced the things too cheaply or too dearly. He examined them and said to me: 'You have priced everything too low. If I sold my goods so cheaply, I should—God forbid—be bankrupt.' I replied, 'I think it is better for me to price them low and sell them dear, than that I should price them high and have to sell cheaply. I have made my accounts so that even if I sell at the cheap prices, there will be a handsome capital for my orphans.'

So I made full arrangements for the auction and got handsome prices. Everything sold well. If the creditors had not pressed me but had given me six months' grace, I would have obtained even better prices. Still, everything went off well, and God be praised, I suffered no losses. As soon as the money came in, I paid out what was owing, and within a year all the debts were paid off. Further, the rest of the ready money I loaned out at interest.

As I have already mentioned, my daughter Esther had been for some time betrothed, and the affair was neither here nor there. After the thirty days of mourning I wrote to Mistress Jachet in Metz and informed her of my sorrowful position, that as I was now a widow and the bride an orphan, the matter could be no longer delayed; the bridegroom must come forthwith to see the bride and himself be seen. But she answered that because I had written so much about her son, and people had slandered my daughter, which slander she believed, she would not send her son! If I thought that the slanderers had spoken the truth concerning her son, I should send a good friend to Metz to see and report on the bridegroom. Besides this, war was then raging between France and Germany and it was too dangerous to send him. A year passed in this contrary correspondence.

In the meantime my son Leib grew up, a fine young man. Many handsome matches were proposed. My brother-in-law Reb Joseph Segal spoke privately to me and told me he wished to give him his daughter and asked what dowry was desired. But my son had no inclination for this match, and desired a match in Berlin, the cause of my and all our misfortunes. But I blame no one. All our sins were ordained by God, who took my pious husband, peace unto him, from this world that he might witness no ill of his children.

My son Leib was still young and was led into all sorts of foolishness by wicked people. I thought to myself: If I marry him into a Hamburg family the temptation to go astray would be the same. I was a widow and the people here were mostly men in a large way of business who would have little time to look after my son well. My brother-in-law Reb Elia Ries suggested a match with his brother Hirschel's[1] daughter. This I rather fancied, thinking to myself: The man has few children and carries on his business in his own house, and being a strict man would certainly take good care of my child. So I betrothed my son to his daughter, and thought I had done well. When the time of the wedding approached I went with the bridegroom to Berlin and was accompanied by my son Zanvil, my brother-in-law Reb Elia and Issachar Cohen. I was there the guest of Reb Benjamin Mirels.[2] How shall I write of the high honour paid me by Hirschel, his uncle Reb Benjamin and other well-known Berlin people? I cannot describe it, especially how I was honoured by the distinguished and wealthy Reb Judah Berlin[3] and his wife. Although Reb Judah was in opposition to the Vienna community, he sent me Sabbath gifts, the finest that could be had, and besides, made a great feast in my own honour. In short, I received more honour than I deserved.

The wedding was held amid great joy, gladness and honour. A few days later we returned happy to Hamburg. Before I left, I spoke with Reb Hirschel and begged him to look well after my son for he was still very young and understood little of business; that the reason I had wedded him to his daughter was that he should find a father in him. He answered that I need have no worry, and that I should wish I might have as little concern about my other children as I need have for this one. But, my God and Master, that the page should have been so unhappily turned!

[1] Son of Dayan Model Ries.
[2] Benjamin Mirels, brother of Pessel Ries, who was the mother of Hirschel Ries and wife of Dayan Model.
[3] Jost Liebmann, the Court Jew.

In the betrothal contract, Reb Hirschel had agreed to give three years' board to the bridal pair, and to put aside for them 400 reichstaler each year. But he adhered to this as little as he did to other things.

Now I will leave my son in Berlin and write of my daughter Esther. After the useless exchange of many letters, as I have mentioned, it was decided that as Mistress Jachet would not come to Hamburg with her son, and I would not go to Metz with my daughter, we should meet in Amsterdam, that Abraham Krumbach should go there with his son, and I would take my daughter. If, after seeing one another, they liked each other, they should marry there. To this I agreed—what else should I have done? I arrived in Amsterdam at the appointed time with the bride and my son Nathan. We had very good company and a most enjoyable journey. We were the guests of my son-in-law Kossman. The bridegroom, who had arrived a few days earlier, was the guest of Reb Moses Emmerich. Towards night, after evening prayers, the bridegroom called on us. I conversed with him and was overjoyed: he satisfied me in every way. Of the faults with which people had charged him, I saw nothing. We were together two or three hours, and I thanked God in my heart and was well pleased. My son Nathan and I traded in precious stones while we were in Amsterdam.

We had been there a week when Miriam, the wife of Reb Elia Cleve, wrote that I and the bridal pair should honour her by paying a visit to Cleve; she had been the matchmaker and had had so much unpleasantness as a result, that now we really must give her the pleasure of visiting her. Although our business did not allow us to go, I could not refuse her request and so together we went to Cleve.

At first glance, on meeting, we wept, for we both saw one another for the first time in our widowhood.[1] But after the first sadness, everything passed in delight and gladness, and we were very happy together.

My daughter Zipporah was also with us. Miriam Gompertz wished to have the wedding celebrated in Amersfoort,[2] but

[1] Elia Gompertz had died in Cleve, in 1689, the same year as Chaim Hameln.
[2] A small town near Utrecht.

this place was not convenient as we had to be again in Amsterdam.

We spent five joyful days in Cleve, after which we returned to Amsterdam. Immediately on our arrival the marriage was celebrated, and instead of thirty or forty guests we had more than four hundred. We had a fine wedding, the like of which Amsterdam had not seen for a hundred years. It cost us more than 400 reichstaler each.

I remained for some weeks after the wedding in order to complete some business. I asked my son-in-law Moses to travel as far as Hamburg with me, at my expense, but he did not wish to. So we left for home and arrived to find the children and all our good friends well.

I received letters by every post from my son Leib, peace unto him, telling me that he was doing good business and that everyone praised him for being such a fine businessman. He had a big shop in Berlin, and bought goods in Leipzig. My children (in Hamburg) did business with him. I wrote several times to his father-in-law Reb Hirschel asking whether he watched over my son, reminding him of his youth and inexperience, for he had only been to *Yeshivah*.[1] He always answered, reassuringly, that I need have no worry. I had to be satisfied with this, and thought all was well.

My daughter Hendelé, peace unto her, was then a fine young woman. She had no equal for beauty and refinement. Yossell, the matchmaker, proposed a match for her, another unfortunate one, in Berlin. The widow of the rich and well-known Baruch[2] was left with two sons and two daughters. Yossell suggested the elder son, telling me that the young man was respectable, knew Talmud well, had 5000 reichstaler ready cash apart from half a house which was worth 1500 reichstaler, besides silver ornaments on a Scroll of Law, other sacred objects, besides other things. His mother wished to have him longer with her and promised two years' board, for she still carried on business. I told the matchmaker that I did not object to this match, but before agreeing I would consider it and then give him an answer. I then asked my brother-in-law Joseph and

[1] Rabbinic College for study of the Talmud.

[2] Baruch, known as Benedictus Veit, was the representative of the Viennese Jews in Berlin.

other good friends and they all advised in favour of the match and said: 'You have a son living in Berlin: he can tell you everything.'

So I wrote to Leib, asking him for the truth. He answered, advising the match and saying that the matchmaker had spoken truly of the 5000 reichstaler and other things. So I sent him permission to conclude the betrothal by proxy and to deposit the dowry in Berlin—to my great sorrow. The wedding was arranged for eighteen months later.

I had done this for the best, thinking that as I had already one child in Berlin who was getting on quite well, I would marry another child into the same town so that they could enjoy each other's company. Unfortunately it happened otherwise. As mentioned, my son Leib was still young and inexperienced in business. His father-in-law, instead of giving him his personal attention, neglected him entirely and left him to go his own way, like a sheep without a shepherd. My son started a big business in Berlin and had a large shop full of all sorts of wares. His father-in-law, Reb Hirschel, married his son Model to the daughter of my brother-in-law Reb Joseph. This same Model was also young and not well brought up. His dowry of 4000 reichstaler Reb Hirschel put into my son's business. Model was always in the shop, he was supposed to look after the business. But, may God be merciful! how he looked after the shop! The men and women assistants stole everything; every swindler that lived round about in Berlin pretended to deal with him and helped in the stealing, even to the white of his eye. He trusted thousands to Poles and all the money was lost. I and my children knew nothing of this; we thought they did big business and made fine profits. That was how it was we gave him big credit. I had at the time a factory of Hamburger stockings, of which I had many thousand talers' worth made up. My unfortunate son wrote that I should send him 1000 reichstaler's worth of stockings, and I did so.

At the Brunswick Fair I met Amsterdam merchants who had bills for about 800 reichstaler on my son. Leib wrote to me, in Brunswick, to meet the bills and he would remit the money to me in Hamburg. As everything I did was always for my children, I decided that I would not allow his bills to be dishonoured and him to be disgraced, so I paid them. On my return I expected to find a bill from Leib. Nothing arrived, and when I wrote to him, he sent me all sorts of excuses. Though this did not please me, what was I to do? I had to content myself with them.

Fourteen days later, a good friend came to me and said, 'I can't keep it from you, but must tell you that your son's business does not look well to me. He is heavily in debt. He owes his brother-in-law Model 4000 reichstaler, and he is in Leib's shop, which he is supposed to look after; but he is a child and not competent. All day he eats dainties and gobbles food and drink. Every assistant is master in the shop. Your son is too good and pious and lets everyone govern and rule. Besides, the Berliners suck him dry with interest. He has two wolves over him—one is Reb Wolf the son of Rabbi Zalman Mirels,[1] the rabbi of Hamburg, and the other is the brother-in-law of Reb Benjamin Mirels. The latter goes into the shop every day and takes away what Leib sees and does not see. Besides this, he does business with the Poles; as far as I know he has lost over 4000 reichstaler with them.' This and similar things the man said to me. My soul flew from me. I fainted on the spot, powerless. When this friend saw how upset I was, he began to comfort me and told me that we still had time to save him. I repeated all this to my sons Nathan and Reb Mordecai Segal. They, too, were alarmed and told me that he owed them also several thousand. God above knows how I felt over this unwelcome news. Leib owed me more than 3000 reichstaler, but this did not upset me so much as that his two brothers were so deeply involved. What were we sorrowful folks to do? We dared not even mention anything about it to anyone.

We talked it over together and decided that I and my son Mordecai should go to the Leipzig Fair to see how things were, for Leib attended every fair, taking with him a large stock of goods. He had arrived before us. I spoke to him, saying: 'Thus and thus runs the rumour. Bethink yourself of God and your pious, honest father, that you do not bring yourself and us to

[1] Rabbi Zalman Mirels was one of the first members of the Viennese community in Berlin. From 1680 till his death in 1706 he was chief rabbi of the three communities, Hamburg, Altona and Wandsbeck. His son Wolf, son-in-law of Benedictus Veit, was a publisher and printer of Hebrew works.

shame.' He answered, 'None of you need worry about me. Not
four weeks ago my father-in-law Reb Hirschel and his brother-
in-law Reb Wolf of Prague, who was staying with him, took
stock and found that I, thank God, am in a good position.'
I said to him, 'Show me your accounts.' He answered, 'I have
nothing with me here. Do me the favour and come back to
Berlin with me. I will show you everything and you will be
happy, I know.' 'In any case,' I warned him, 'do not buy any
goods at all now.' But Isaac and Shiman the son of Rabbi
Mann of Hamburg sold him goods on trust for more than 1400
reichstaler, behind my back. When I found this out I went to
them and begged them, for God's sake, to release him from the
deal; it would be my son's ruin and he would be forced out of
business. But nothing I said helped and they made him take the
goods.

After the Leipzig Fair, I, my son Mordecai, Reb Hirschel
and other Berlin merchants went to Berlin. The first evening in
my son's house passed quietly, for I was very tired after the
journey. Still we spoke together and he said to me, 'I am short
of nothing; the only thing is that I am overstocked.' I said to
him, 'You owe me more than 3000 reichstaler. I will take goods
from your stock to that value, from what you have paid off.'
He answered, 'Dear mother, if you will do so, I shall be
released from my trouble and no one will suffer through me.'

The following morning I went to his shop with him. There
was really a great stock of goods in it. He gave me goods to the
value of 3000 reichstaler of the money he owed me, at the price
that he had paid. One can imagine the face I made and how it
pleased me to have to take goods instead of money, but I only
wanted to help my child. We packed the goods in bales to send
to Hamburg. The two bales that Leib had bought from Isaac
and Shiman stood in the shop, still unpacked. I said to him,
'Send back the two bales to those men. I will undertake that
they take the goods back, even if it costs me money out of my
own pocket. I have my own,' and added, 'but how will Nathan
and Mordecai get back what you owe them?' He handed over
Polish bills to the value of 12,000 reichstaler to Mordecai;
from these he was to be paid. We spent the whole of the day
in the shop and afterwards went home together. The supper
did not taste good to me.

סדר
תקוני שבת
מחיים הללהי קדרום
יאמר לו כוכינתקדריסת
נהורית עתימ'שרי מוהרר
יצחקלוריא
אשכנזי זל

תלח לפח

כשנת

יגי הכותב יעקב סופר
כמהורר יהודת ליב זנל
מברלין לעלט סופר פה
המבורג

27. *A Page from a Sabbath Prayer Book.* Hamburg, 1728

29. *The Saying of Grace after Meal. From a Manuscript Book of occasional Prayers. Amsterdam,* 1734

28. *Saying of Night Prayers. From a Prayer Book with Miniatures. Amsterdam,* 1734

Early next morning Leib came to my room and told me that
his father-in-law had declared that he would not allow the
goods to be taken out of Berlin for he, Leib, owed his son Model
4000 reichstaler. If I paid him that amount I could send the
goods where I liked. This is what Leib told me with streaming
eyes. A trembling and anxiety as though of death came on me!
I could not arise from my bed, and so long as I was in unlucky
Berlin, I was unable to leave my bed. I sent to Reb Hirschel
and asked what he did—did he wish to slay my son and me
at the same time? What shall I write more? Ten sheets of paper
would not suffice. I had to give Reb Hirschel a bill for 2500
reichstaler to be met within fourteen days of my return to
Hamburg. Reb Hirschel said also, 'I hope no one will be short
through this, for he has much stock in his shop. Besides, he has
goods in Frankfurt-on-Oder for about 2000 reichstaler, and
your son Mordecai has several bills of his in hand, from which
you will be paid.' We had to be satisfied with this arrangement.
I signed the bill and then sent on my goods to Hamburg. I
went with Reb Hirschel to the shop, pointed out the two
bales of Shiman and Isaac, telling him to see that these were
returned straightway and so relieve my son of his undertaking. The bills which Mordecai had were of little use to us
—we gave them to Reb Hirschel Ries. He gave us his hand,
promising to collect the money, for it was easier to collect in
Poland from Berlin, and remit to Hamburg. My son owed
Leib Beschere and Leib Goslar about 2000 reichstaler; he sent
these bills with me. I could have retained these bills in payment
for what was owing to us, but thought that if I did so, my son
would really be bankrupt, so I gave them the bills. Sad and
disheartened, we returned home. My soul had almost departed
from me. My beloved, devout child Reb Mordecai sought to
soothe me and lighten my heavy heart, but God knows that he
suffered more than I, as was later shown.

The fair at Frankfurt-on-Oder was near. On this we placed
our hopes of retrieving our fortunes. But Hirschel Ries fell on
my son's shop, took everything he found for himself, not only
all the goods, but even bills, and the two bales of goods. He left
nothing, even to the value of a farthing, for any of us. Worse
still, my son owed a merchant 1000 reichstaler and was going
to give him a bill on Hamburg; but the merchant found out

K

how things were with him and would not leave him alone and threatened to have him arrested in Berlin. What was my son to do? His father-in-law would sooner see him rotted and wasted in prison than help him with a hundred, not to mention a thousand reichstaler. My son spoke thus to the merchant: 'You can see quite well that there is nothing to take here. I will go to Hamburg with you. My mother and brother will not forsake me. You can have me arrested just as easily there.' He wrote to me forthwith: 'I will be with you on Friday. I cannot give you the reason in writing, but will tell you when I see you.'

I received this letter a day before his arrival, and as may be quite easily imagined, I expected no good. I knew that his father-in-law had taken everything from him and that he was heavily in debt in Hamburg and had no means of payment. I was soon rid of any doubts I may have had. Early Friday morning I received a message informing me that Leib was in the merchant's house, and I or one of the children should go to him. The message alarmed me very much and I could not move a step. Mordecai went and returned to me with the bitter, sad news. I held counsel with my brothers-in-law Reb Joseph and Reb Elia Segal: what was to be done? If the other creditors got to know of this, he was indeed lost. At length we decided that 1000 reichstaler should be taken away from the money left by my husband and put aside for the children, to free him from the merchant. He was to remain with the latter till evening and then be with me till Sunday. Then I was to send him to my brother-in-law Samuel Bonn, in Hameln. He was to remain there some time. We would then decide what he could start doing. Thus it was and again it cost me much money. On his way to Hameln he had to pass through Hanover where my wealthy relative Jacob Hanover[1] lived. He gave him pity and sympathy—it was all he did give him—but no help. They wrote from Hanover sympathizing with me and I was comforted. I answered as was fitting and thanked them for their sympathy. But nothing more than this was done to help bring my son to his feet again: he was still young and God would help him. I received a reply from Reb Jacob Hanover: if my sons Nathan and Mordecai would be securities, he would assist him with

[1] Jacob Cohen, son of Lipman Cohen (Leffman Behrens) and Jenta Hameln, of Hanover, Glückel's nephew.

500 reichstaler. From this we can see again that we should hold no one to be a true friend till he has been proved. I believed that Reb Jacob was a close friend of my family who, for the honour of my saintly husband, his uncle, would have done much more and offered thousands. But it was as I have related.

My son Leib was six months in Hameln, when the Elector of Brandenburg visited Hanover. I got to know of this and immediately wrote to my brother-in-law Reb Lipman (Behrens) that he should go to him and obtain a safe-conduct for Leib so that he could return to Berlin, collect his debts and come to some settlement with his creditors. He was well liked by Jews and gentiles and everyone knew that he had been robbed by swindlers and evil-doers—may their names be blotted out! He was too good and trusted everyone.

My son returned to Berlin. There were still a few debts to be collected, and he thought that God would have mercy and he would return again to his former position. He began business anew. He stopped up one hole and made another, as is usual with such people, and always expected to better himself.

As I have already related, thinking that my son was in a fine position in Berlin, I had betrothed my dear, devout daughter to a Berliner; but after the unfortunate mishap with my son, the town was very distasteful to me. Besides this, Leib informed me that the young man did not possess as much money as his letters had stated. He was already in trouble—his parents had lent him some money, which helped to ruin him, and he wrote as they wished. I held counsel with my friends, for the time of the tragic wedding was at hand. They wrote from Berlin that the bridegroom had no more than 3500 reichstaler and his half-house. I did not desire the match, as the conditions of the bridal contract had not been fulfilled. The writing backwards and forwards lasted more than a year till I, God pity me, was dragged by the hair into it and went with my daughter to Berlin to celebrate the marriage. Her dowry remained on interest in Hamburg, while the bridegroom's was on interest in Berlin. Because of my son's circumstances, I went with little joy to the sad wedding, for it was entirely against my taste, as will later be revealed.

I and my daughter, peace unto her, went to Berlin together for the wedding and were the guests of my son Reb Leib.

Though I had little joy of him, I hid my feelings for I did not wish to distress my child. Should I write of my son's circumstances? His state was such that God pity it. He did his utmost. Though my heart burst with sorrow within me, I would not show him my heavy spirits.

The marriage was celebrated with joy and happiness and much honour. The wealthy Reb Judah Berlin, his wife and family did us the honour of being present. Everyone wondered at this, for they never attended a 'Vienna' wedding. He gave the bride a handsome present and after the wedding invited us and the bridal pair to a princely meal.

When it was over, we prepared to go home. Because of Leib's unfortunate state, I was still downhearted but comforted myself with the hope that God would once again help. We went back to Hamburg and I left my dear daughter in Berlin, whom I was never more to see. The sorrow we both felt at our parting is indescribable, as though we knew we were not to meet again in this world. This was our eternal farewell.

By every post I received pleasant letters from my daughter. Although Leib's condition caused her grief, the pious, clever child would not write of this but buried her sorrows deep in her heart, for she did not wish to grieve us. Day by day the news of him got worse. At length he could remain no longer in Berlin and went to Altona, which was under the protection of the President.[1] May the pain and heartache I suffered because of this and his creditors atone for our sins! Daily it cost much money. Leib fell dangerously ill. I sent two doctors from Hamburg every day besides a nurse and other necessaries; this again cost me much money till at length he was restored to health.

After this my daughter Hendelé fell ill in Berlin, and, unfortunately, alas, had to pay with her young life's blood, to the deep heartache of all who knew her. Oh, my God! it was a heavy blow! Such a fine, lovable child, slender as a fig-tree; tender love and piety were hers; virtues such as were found in our Matriarchs. Her mother-in-law and everyone in Berlin loved her so—their sorrows cannot be described. But does this comfort my bereaved, maternal heart? She died only seventeen weeks after the wedding. But I shall not tear open my wounds afresh.

[1] Altona, under Danish rule, was administered by a President.

After the week of mourning my son Leib sent for me. When I arrived at the Allon-Bacuth[1] we both wept sore. He comforted me as well as he could and said to me, 'Dear mother, what will be the outcome of my tragic state? I am a young man going about idle. My dear sister died and left no child; her husband must return her dowry and this belongs to her brothers. If only my brothers will have pity and help me with this money, so that I can come to terms with my creditors and return to Hamburg again so that, with God's help, I can stand on my own again.'

My sorrowful heart was heavy and full, and because of my bitter tears I could not at first answer him. Then I said to him, 'This is vile of you! You know how ruined your brothers are because of you, and cannot afford the losses caused by you. And now when this sad bit of money has come to them, against their will, you want to tear it out of them in their hour of bitter grief.' Then we both wept and lamented for an hour, and could not say a word to one another. Then I quietly wrapped my raincoat[2] about me and in tears arrived back in Hamburg. I told not a word of what had passed to my children; but my son Leib would not let the matter drop. He sent letters to the others and begged them so hard that out of pity they promised to help him. After a short while this was done, he settled with his creditors and came to me in town. When his father-in-law learnt of this, he sent his daughter, Leib's wife, and child, also to me, and sent her 2 reichstaler every week as pocket-money. What was I to do? I had to be content with things as they were.

At that time I was still quite energetic in business, so that every month I sold goods to the value of 5000 or 6000 reichstaler. Besides this, I went twice a year to the Brunswick Fair and at every fair sold goods for several thousands, so that I could have recovered the loss I suffered through Leib, if I had had peace. I did good business, received wares from Holland, bought much goods in Hamburg and sold them in my own shop.

I did not spare myself but travelled summer and winter and all day rushed about the town. Besides this, I had a fine

[1] Oak of weeping (Genesis 35: 8).
[2] Made of *Berkan*, a cloth woven of camel- and goats' hair.

business in seed pearls. I bought from all the Jews, picked and sorted the pearls and sold them to the places where I knew they were wanted. I had large credits. When the Börse was open and I wanted 20,000 reichstaler, cash, I could get it. Yet all this availed me nothing, for I saw my son Leib, a pious young man, well versed in Talmud, doing nothing! I said to him, one day, 'Listen to me: I see no prospect for you. I am doing big business and it is beginning to be too much for me. I want you to help me and I will give you two per cent of everything I sell.' He accepted this offer with great joy. He was very industrious and had a chance of re-establishing himself if only his goodness of heart had not been his undoing. Through my introductions he became well-known among the merchants, enjoyed big credits and everything of mine was under his care.

My son Joseph was fourteen, a fine lad who studied well,[1] and I wanted to send him to study away from home, but did not know where to send him. There was a fine young man from Lissa, Isaac Polack's house-teacher, a great Talmudist. He came to me and suggested that, as he had heard that I wanted to send my son to study, I should send him with him. He asked nothing beforehand for food and teaching, but I should pay him at the end of two years, when he had taught Joseph *Halacha* and *Tosafat*,[2] so that he knew both perfectly. I made enquiries about him and everyone advised me to it. I made an agreement with him, and sent Joseph in God's name to Lissa. He wrote every week telling me first of his happy arrival, and then to say how pleased he was with his teacher and how earnestly he studied. More than this I did not desire. Fourteen days later Joseph wrote, earnestly requesting me to send his teacher board and teaching money for half-a-year. Everything was very expensive in Lissa, his teacher had to worry as to where he was to get his money, which must hinder him in teaching. If he was relieved of this worry he could apply himself more industriously to his work. He had other Hamburg children with him whose parents had sent him money. Though I was not bound to do this, I could not hold back from doing the same. Besides, it made little difference whether I sent it earlier or later. Everything was well and people travelling

---

[1] This would, of course, refer only to Talmud study.

[2] Special divisions of the Talmud dealing with Law and Commentary.

through Lissa brought me good news, that my son was studying well.

But one Friday afternoon, towards the end of the first six months, when it was time to go to synagogue, I received a letter from my son Reb Joseph, written as follows: 'My dear mother, you know quite well that I have always been a faithful child and never did anything against your wish. Do not now with-hold from me your true, maternal love and do not allow me to be given over into the hands of gentiles. For, my dear mother, you must know that the community owes much money to the powers-that-be and cannot pay them either the money or interest. As the heads of the community cannot help them-selves they have to give the German children who study there as security for the debt and the German parents must ransom their children. This is what the head of the community secretly told the teachers of the German children and this is what a good friend of mine told me in great secrecy. I am not writing this myself but through this friend, for my teacher pays every atten-tion to me and reads all my letters. Therefore, my dear mother, for God's sake, write to Tockel's son-in-law that he should give me 50 or 60 reichstaler, so that I can arrange with my teacher that he should send me away secretly, and so escape their hands—I beg you, for God's sake, not to delay, for if you neglect to do this, I shall, God forbid, fall into their hands. It is Poland and if this befalls me, it will cost ten times as much. So, dear, beloved mother, do not forsake your child because of a little money and see that I am not delivered into their hands, for from them it will be hard to be freed.'

When I read this letter I fainted. I sent for my son Mor-decai and gave him the letter. He too was greatly alarmed. As it was already Sabbath, we could do nothing. We decided that immediately after Sabbath he should leave for Lissa and fetch Joseph home. So Mordecai went first to Berlin and from there to Frankfurt-on-Oder. As he was about to ride out of the Frankfurt gates, my son Joseph, in a little Polish wagon, came riding in! They came face to face in the gateway! Mordecai told him to alight and asked what had brought him there, so unexpectedly and, what about the letter he had written home? He showed him the letter. Joesph read it and said, 'I know nothing at all about this. It must be from my teacher, may his name be blotted out! He must have wanted to get a heap of money through me. He has already had more than was due to him. He has taken everything from me and even cut off the silver buttons from my coat and pledged them. When I wanted my things back, he falsely accused me of pilfering sweetmeats and gorging all the food, and, above all, said he had pawned the things for me! I saw that no good would come of it, so I begged Tockel's son-in-law to come to terms with him. He gave him 30 reichstaler, took me away from him and sent me here. I thank God that I was rescued from that wicked man. In any case, he taught me nothing.'

Mordecai was delighted to have met him thus, and they straightway returned in the same carriage to Hamburg. I was overjoyed to see them and immediately engaged an honest teacher to teach the lad at home.

About this time [1687] a wonderful incident occurred. There lived in Altona a man, Abraham Metz by name, may God avenge his blood! He was married to my kinswoman Sarah, daughter of Elijah Cohen.[1] Before he moved to Hamburg he had lived in Herford and was married to the daughter of Leib Herford. She died two years after the marriage, and he then moved to Hamburg and married Sarah. He brought with him a fortune of 3000 reichstaler. But he was a stranger here and knew nothing of the manners and the business ways of the Hamburgers and within a few years had lost his entire fortune. He was a money-changer and lived at that time in Altona.

One morning his wife came into town and asked all her friends whether her husband had stayed the night at any of their houses; but after innumerable enquiries found no one with whom he had stayed. She was greatly alarmed. Many said she had quarrelled with him and he had run away from her. It was three years to the time of the incident of which I am now writing, and nothing more was heard of this Abraham Metz. Everyone had his own opinion and said just what he liked. Many spoke evil of him, which I do not care to repeat, or mention in connection with such a martyr—God avenge his blood! But unfortunately, human weakness is such that we speak with our mouths of what our eyes have not seen. For three

[1] Elijah Cohen, died 1653, was married to Glückel's aunt, her mother's sister.

years this poor Sarah was a 'living widow'[1] alone with her sad orphans and had to allow people to talk as they would and say what they liked of her husband.

There was in the Hamburg community an honest man who, although he was not rich, supported his wife and four children quite comfortably. He was a money-changer. Every money-changer rushes around all day for his living, and towards evening, at the time of afternoon prayers, goes home and thence to synagogue. Each one belongs to a *chevra*[2] and with the other members studies, and after studying returns home. It was very late on this particular night when the wife waited for her husband's return from the *chevra* so that they could have their supper together. Her waiting was in vain. She ran to all their friends' houses, but could not find him. He was, through our sins, sad to tell, lost.

The next day there were rumours flying about the town. One said he had seen him here, the other that he had seen him somewhere else. At midday they spoke of it on the Börse. Zanvil the son of Reb Meyer Hekscher related, 'Yesterday a woman came up to me and asked whether I had 600 or 700 reichstaler with me; if I had I should go with her—a distinguished stranger was in her house and had much gold and precious stones to sell. But I had no cash and so did not go with her.' As he finished saying this a man named Lipman who stood near asked him what sort of a person she was and what she wore. Zanvil answered, 'She wore this and that.' Upon which Lipman said, 'I know the woman! and also know whom she serves. I do not trust her master. Good cannot come of it.' And with such talk they left the Börse, everyone going to his own house.

When Lipman reached home, he said to his wife, 'Do you know what I am going to tell you? The woman who is a servant of the son of the owner of the Mariners' Tavern went to Zanvil Hekscher and would have taken him with her if he had had 600 or 700 reichstaler on him. I am sore afraid that the man who is missing went with her and has been murdered.' Upon

[1] A woman whose husband is missing and his fate unknown.
[2] A small group meeting for the purpose of study; each *chevra* studying a different subject, but all dealing with the Bible and Talmud. A *chevra* is known by the name of the subject studied.

this his wife beat her hands on her head, and cried, 'Through
our sins! I've just remembered: the same person was also here
and wanted you or me to go with her. You know very well
what an evil man her master is; he is a murderer; it is certain
that the upright, pious man was killed in her house.' The
woman, who was very capable, continued, 'I will not rest or
be still until I bring the whole thing to light.'

'Mad woman!' cried her husband. 'If it is true, what are
we to do? We are in Hamburg and dare not utter a word.'[1] So,
things remained as they were for some days. However, with
beat of the drum the town council proclaimed that anyone
who knew anything of the missing Jew, dead or alive, should
come forward and say what he knew: he would receive 100
ducats reward and his name would be kept secret. But no one
came forward and the matter was soon forgotten, in the usual
way. However worthy, if nothing follows, it is forgotten. But
the 'living widow' and her orphans remained bereaved.

It happened that one early Sabbath morning in the summer
Lipman's wife could not sleep, just as once happened to the
King of Spain. He once asked a Jewish scholar, 'What is the
meaning of the verse, *Hineh lo yonum v'lo yishon shomer Yisroël?*'
The scholar translated, 'The guardian of Israel neither slum-
bers nor sleeps.' The King answered 'That is not what it means.
The real meaning is that God is the guardian Who does not
let others sleep or slumber. Had I slept as usual this night
you would all have been lost as a result of a blood-libel.
But the Lord who is your guardian made me unable to sleep
and I saw how a child was thrown into a Jewish house. Had
I not been witness of this, all Jews would have been put to
death.'

In the same way Lipman's wife was unable to sleep. Early
in the morning she stood at her window. She lived in the
Ellern Steinway,[2] a passageway through which everyone going
in or out of Altona had to pass.

It was on Friday night that she could not sleep and drove
everyone mad. Her husband reproached her, asking what sort
of a game this was; she would really become crazy. But she
answered that nothing would help her as long as the murder

[1] As Jews with no residential rights they lived in Hamburg on sufferance.
[2] Old Stoneway.

was unavenged, for she knew quite well, her heart told her, that *that* man was the murderer.

Day dawned and she still stood at the window looking out on to the street. And there she saw the man whom she took to be the murderer, his wife and a servant, carrying a large box, go by. When she saw this, she cried out, 'O God, stand now by me! This is the beginning of my satisfaction!' She rushed and straightway snatched up her apron and rain-cloak and ran out of the room. Her husband sprang from his bed to restrain her, but could do nothing. She ran after those people, followed them to Altona, to the river Elbe, and saw them place the box upon the bank. Rebekah, for this was her name, decided that the corpse of the murdered man was in this box.

She ran to the people of Altona and begged them, for God's sake, to help her; she knew for certain who was the murderer. But they were unwilling and said, 'It is easy to begin anything, but one cannot foretell the end.' But she insisted that they should go to the President with her and at length two house-holders went with her. They appeared before the President and told him everything. He said to them: 'If you cannot prove your accusation I will confiscate your goods and chattels.' Rebekah would not allow herself to be turned aside by this, but answered, that she not only risked her property but her blood as well. 'I beg you, for God's sake, Herr President, send for the murderer and take him with all that he has with him.'

Upon this watchmen and soldiers were sent to the Elbe. But they arrived just in time to see them go on board ship for Harburg, an hour's journey from Altona. If they reached Harburg they would be free, for Harburg was under other jurisdiction. But the soldiers arrived in time and took the murderer together with his wife and box and brought them before the President, who ordered the box to be opened. Naught but the clothes of the murderer and his wife were found!

The fear and anxiety that fell on the poor Jews can be imagined! The man was closely examined and questioned but would confess nothing. On the contrary, he used threats and terror fell on every Jew, for he came of a large, well-known family in Hamburg. All fled in fear, but Rebekah kept saying, 'I beg you, dear folk, do not despair; you will see how God will help us.' In her great anxiety she ran from Altona to town. As she came into the field between Altona and Hamburg, she came face to face with the woman who was in the murderer's service. Rebekah recognized her; she was the one who had gone to the sons of Israel asking which one had about 700 reichstaler and taken him to her master's house. Rebekah went up to her and said, 'It is lucky for you and your master and his wife that you have met me. They are both imprisoned in Altona for the murder they have committed. They have confessed everything, only your confession is missing. When you have confessed there is a ship waiting for you and your master and mistress to sail away in. For we Jews are only eager to know that Abraham is dead, so that his wife can marry again. We want nothing else of you.'

She spoke more to the woman, for Rebekah was very clever and persuasive. Because of her words, the woman too began to talk and told her everything: how she had met Abraham on the Börse after she had called on Rebekah's husband Reb Lipman and other Jews. But no one else was so unlucky as Reb Abraham when, to his undoing, he had a full purse on him. She had shown him a small gold chain and told him that an officer in her master's house had much gold and diamonds to sell. 'So Abraham came with me and when he entered the house, his slaughter-bench was ready. My master led him down to his room and together we took his life. We buried him under the threshold.' Then the woman added, 'Rebekah, I am telling you all this in confidence. Do not betray me.' Rebekah answered her, 'Are you a fool? Don't you know my honest heart? Everything I do is for your master and mistress, so that they may be soon released and out of Altona. As soon as you tell all this before our people, everything will be all right.'

So the servant went to the house of the President with Rebekah. He heard out the former, and though now she stammered, repenting what she had said, still, everything was out. Most important of all, she had already revealed the burial place of the murdered man. In the end, she confessed everything to the President as she had to Rebekah. After this he again examined the master and mistress, separately, but they denied everything and said, 'All that the maid has told, the hussy has herself invented.' Fear again fell on us. The President said to us, 'I can help you no further. Shall I torture these two on the bare word of their servant? And if he does not confess on the rack, what then? You must see to your rights in Hamburg and as soon as possible you must get permission from the Council there to search the house for the corpse. If you find it, as the maid says, you can leave the rest to me.'

The *parnassim* immediately got busy and tried to get hold of twenty soldiers to dig the place that the maid had mentioned. They obtained permission to bury the corpse, if it was found, in the Jewish cemetery in Altona. At the same time they were told: 'Take care: if the corpse is not found, you will be in great danger. You know the Hamburg mob! It will be impossible for us to restrain them.'

We were all in great danger, but Rebekah was all over the place, and told us not to despair; she knew for certain that the corpse would be found, for the maid had sworn on her own life and had given her full particulars. Ten trusted men and several sailors who were known for their trustworthiness went, in God's name, into the murderer's house which was not far from Alten Schragen—the old shambles.

Meanwhile the news had spread in the town, and all sorts of workmen and canaille in countless numbers gathered before the door of the murderer's house. The mob had decided, 'If the Jews find the murdered man, it will be well for them. If not, there will not remain a Jewish claw.' But the Holy One, blessed be He, did not leave us long in doubt. As soon as our people entered the house and dug up the threshold they found what they sought. Tears filled their eyes while joy filled their hearts. They wept that such a fine pious young man, only twenty-four years old, was found in such tragic circumstances and on the other hand rejoiced that the Community was out of danger and that vengeance was near. The whole town council was summoned and the corpse shown them and also the place where it had been found, all according to the maid's statement. The Council registered and attested this. The corpse was then placed on a wagon and brought to Altona. A multitude of sailors and apprentices was present. The sight was indescribable; perhaps there were a hundred thousand people present but not one bad word was uttered. Though they are a rough people and in quiet times we suffer much harm and distress through them, still this

time everything passed off quietly and each person went his
way peacefully.

The day after the *parnassim* brought the attestation to the
President of Altona, who had the murderer within his jurisdiction. The Jews preferred that judgement should be given in
Altona. Again he had the murderer brought before him and
informed him of what had occurred. On this he made a full confession. The widow received a part of the money of her murdered husband, which was still there. The murderer, poor
thing, was in prison till the time of his trial.

Meanwhile Sarah was still a 'living widow'. No news of her
husband was to be had, and, as already related, there were
many rumours. After this new murder, when everyone knew
the murderer so well, it was remembered that before he moved
into the house near the Alten Schragen, he lived with his father
who owned the Mariners' Tavern, the best known inn in the
whole of Hamburg. It is quite near the Börse and Jewish as
well as gentile merchants who had business, or a reckoning
with one another, went there and they used to drink there out
of silver dishes. The son was therefore well known to Jews.
When it became known that this very son was a murderer, and
remembered that Sarah's husband was a money-changer, it
was also remembered that the changers used to meet in that
inn and do their business there, counting out money, for the
place was well known for its security. Sarah knew also that her
husband had been quite friendly with this son. She therefore
went to her friends and said, 'You know that my husband was
lost a few years ago. The murder of Abraham has come to light.
My husband went often in and out of that house. I believe that
the same man killed my husband. Help me, perhaps we may
find that my husband lost his life by the same hand.'

What need have I to dwell long on this? They went to the
President and put this before him. He spoke to the murderers
with good and bad words, threatened them with torture, to
confess that he had killed Abraham Metz. For long he would
not confess and only agreed that he had known him well. But
the President spoke so long to him until he confessed that he
had killed Abraham Metz in the Mariners' Tavern. He had
buried him in a deep hole in the room kept only for cheeses
and filled it up with lime before closing it up.

As soon as this was known, the *parnassim* went to the Hamburg Council and as before asked permission to make a search. Again Jews were in dire peril, worse than before, that such a well-esteemed and distinguished house should be turned into a den of murderers. It was dangerous in case the corpse should not be found. Luckily for us it was found; he still wore his red underwaistcoat with silver buttons and *arbakanfos*.[1] He also was given Jewish burial.

There was great mourning in our community, as though they had been killed that day. The friends of my kinswoman Sarah, before they allowed the burial, examined the corpse well, for Sarah told of certain marks on his body that it might be known for certain that he was indeed her dead husband and that she was really widowed. These were found and she had permission to marry again. After this the result of the trial was made known: the murderer was to be broken at the wheel and his body, bound round with iron bands, placed on a stake, that he should be an example for a long time. His wife and servant were freed, but had to leave the country. On the day of the trial and sentence there was a great tumult in Hamburg; for more than a hundred years no trial had caused such a sensation. Jews were in dire peril, for hatred for them was roused, but God in His great mercy did not forget us that day. So this too passed without harm to Jews.

Now I will begin where I left off. Many matches were proposed for my son Joseph, none of which, however, was fated except the one with the daughter of Reb Meyer Stadthagen of Copenhagen. The betrothal was celebrated in Hamburg and the marriage arranged for a year later. When the time of the wedding, which was to take place in Copenhagen, approached, I got ready to attend it, together with my son Nathan.

At that time my son did big business with the wealthy Reb Samuel Oppenheimer and his son Mendel, in Vienna. He had accepted several of their bills, to the value of 20,000 reichstaler, which were nearly due. He had, however, received no remittances from them in the usual way, nor even a letter to tell him what had happened. Because of this he could not accompany me to the wedding: he had to see to his own and his

[1] A four-cornered garment which every Jew, according to Biblical command, must wear.

correspondents' honour. Our grief and worry may be imagined.

I journeyed together with Joseph to the wedding. God knows with what anxiety and bitterness of heart I rode forth, for I did not know how things stood with the Oppenheimers in Vienna. I left Hamburg together with the bridegroom and Moses the son of Meyer Stadthagen, the son-in-law of Reb Chaim Cleve. We arrived quite safely in Copenhagen and there I expected to find letters from Nathan telling me that he had received news and remittances from Vienna. There was one letter in which he wrote me, as a dutiful son, that though he had not yet received news from Vienna, I should not worry but be happy and be of good cheer because of the wedding. Though this was not good news, I left everything to God and did not worry any more. As the marriage was to take place the following week, we both handed over the dowries. Meanwhile I hoped, from one post to the next, to receive good news from Nathan and this, God be praised, arrived the day before the wedding. He wrote that the wealthy Reb Mendel had sent good remittances and several thousands more than he owed, excusing himself that he had not been at home, otherwise he would have sent the money sooner. So the wedding was celebrated with joy and good spirits and to the satisfaction of both sides.

I wanted to leave soon after the marriage, to be home the sooner, but had no other companion than Moses, the son of Meyer Stadthagen. He was not eager to leave his parents' house so soon and because of this, against my will, I had to wait fourteen days longer. Although I had the finest treatment and all possible honour paid me, I was not at my ease and would sooner have been at home with my children. At length I pressed Moses until he was forced to accompany me to Hamburg. We journeyed together and arrived home in good health. I took stock of the goods I had left with my son Leib and was well satisfied with the account he rendered me.

I had four orphans still at home: my sons Zanvil, peace unto him, and Moses, and my daughters Freudchen and Miriam. Although many fine matches were proposed for me myself so that I could have again attained honour and riches, I thought it would be against my children's interests and wishes and to my misfortune, and, as will later be related, I refused them all.

My son Zanvil, meanwhile, grew older, and as he would not

30. *A Jewish Merchant from Lorraine.* Engraving by Sebastian Le Clerc.
Metz, 1664

31. *View of the 'Judengassen' in Augsburg.* Engraving, *ca.* 1700

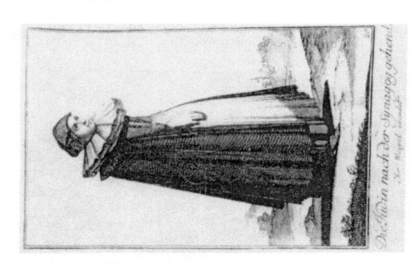

32–33. *A Jewess and a Jew on the way to the Synagogue.* Engravings, *ca.* 1700

study I took him sometimes with me to the Brunswick Fair so that he might learn to become a merchant. Moses, on the other hand, studied well and I sent him to Frankfurt to study in the Klaus. At the same time I sent Zanvil there with goods.

While Zanvil was in Frankfurt, my brother-in-law Joseph received a letter from Moses Bamberg, his faithful friend, asking his advice concerning a proposed betrothal in Hamburg for his daughter. He received this letter on a Sabbath and sent for me at once. He was strolling in the garden with my sister Elkele when I arrived. He said to me, 'Mazal tov! Your son Zanvil is betrothed.' I laughed and answered, 'If he is betrothed, I ought to know something about it.' On this he showed me Reb Moses Bamberg's letter; he was then in Vienna and the learned chief Rabbi Samson Wertheimer had also written in the same letter asking for his frank opinion of this match.[1] I read the letters and then said to Joseph, 'I do not see from these that Zanvil is betrothed.' He answered me, 'I can assure you that when I write to Vienna, he will become betrothed to Moses Bamberg's daughter.' This same Reb Moses was the brother-in-law of Rabbi Samson Wertheimer of Vienna.

Joseph sent a letter about my son and through two letters the match was arranged. Rabbi Samson wrote that Zanvil should be sent to him forthwith. He would remain with him until the time of the marriage, which was fixed for two years later. He made many promises and wrote to me that Zanvil and his brothers would fare well through him.

After this I received many friendly letters from Rabbi Samson. Zanvil was then at the Frankfurt-on-Main Fair. I wrote, informing him of his betrothal, and told him that after the fair he was to go to Vienna and remain there till the time of his marriage.

Zanvil journeyed to Vienna and arrived there safely. Rabbi Samson received him with great respect and wrote to me that he was well pleased with him and had engaged a teacher for him. But Zanvil was still very young and did many childish things. Rabbi Samson did not look after him carefully and during the two years he wasted much money. Zanvil wrote and told me everything, begging me that his marriage should be

[1] Samson Wertheimer, of Vienna, was the renowned court factor and land rabbi.

L

celebrated as he did not wish to remain longer in Vienna. But the bride was still very young and small and his betrothal lasted three years.

Some time after Reb Moses was in Vienna and in reply to my many letters to him on the subject agreed to celebrate the marriage in Bamberg on Tammuz 1st.[1] Zanvil wrote he and his father-in-law would leave Vienna together and I should arrange to be in Bamberg on the date mentioned. I intended going there straight from the Leipzig Fair. But Samson Wertheimer wrote to me that as great hatred for the Jews ruled in Bamberg, I should go to Vienna immediately after the wedding and stay at his house: he would give up his two best rooms for my own use and allow me freedom for any business I wished. And to this end I received a safe-conduct from the great Emperor. I arranged everything and had no other plan in mind than to go to Vienna after the wedding. At that time I had jewellery to the value of 50,000 reichstaler which I wished to take with me to Vienna. Man may plan, but God's will prevails.

Accompanied by my sons Nathan and Moses, still a young bachelor, I went to Leipzig. On arrival Nathan received a letter from Hamburg informing him that he must return immediately after the fair: special business awaited him. So nothing came of my journey to Vienna, for I would not go without Nathan. I kept a few thousands' worth of jewellery and gave the rest to Nathan, to take back to Hamburg with him. Together with Moses I journeyed from the fair to Bamberg. I underwent much hardship on the way, for it was a bad road; I was the only woman and Moses was young, a youth of fifteen. Still, if one has money, all ways can be put to rights; this journey was very expensive.

We arrived in Bamberg about midnight. The following morning the bride's parents and the bride received me. I thought that the wedding was to be celebrated on New Moon's day, Tammuz, but a great disturbance came to prevent this: my brother-in-law Joseph had, without my knowledge, written my son's dowry in the betrothal contract as 5000 reichstaler, while he had no more than 4000. It was in Hamburg that we got to know of this and I had written immediately to Rabbi Samson

[1] About July.

Wertheimer about this mistake. He had answered that it made
no difference; the betrothal contract should remain as it was—
5000 looked better than 4000 and at the wedding there would
be no difficulty about it. Yet now Reb Moses spoke quite
differently: he cared for nothing but stuck to his contract. We
had heated arguments about it and as a result the wedding
could not take place on the first day of Tammuz. Reb Moses
wrote to Vienna and Rabbi Samson answered and could only
tell him the truth. Meanwhile, before this letter arrived, Reb
Moses thought he would be able to squeeze more money from
me, but when he saw that there was nothing more to be
squeezed and that the letter from Vienna gave me right, the
wedding was celebrated in the middle of Tammuz, with all
honour and splendour, as finely as we Jews can. Many distinguished Jews came to the wedding, amongst whom were the
two married sons of Samson Baiersdorf.[1] They came with a
matchmaker. Already in Hamburg a match with the daughter
of Samson Baiersdorf had been suggested for my son Moses. I
had arranged with the matchmaker that as Baiersdorf was only
three miles distant from Bamberg, where I had in any case to be
for my son's wedding, that I would take Moses with me—to see
and to be seen. The two married sons of Samson Baiersdorf
spoke with me and told me what dowry their father was giving.
I answered that the reason I had brought Moses with me was
that he should be seen. After the wedding we would take a
pleasure trip to Fürth, which was two miles from Baiersdorf and
there we would settle the matter. A match in Bamberg and yet
another in Fürth had been also suggested for my son. I held
council with Reb Moses Bamberg and we decided to take the
trip to Fürth together. We had seen the principal[2] in Bamberg;
still, I wished to see those in Fürth and Baiersdorf and make my
choice.

So Reb Moses and his wife, my son and I took the pleasure
trip. We arrived in Baiersdorf and saw Reb Samson's daughter.
He saw my son. The matter was near settlement but could not
be concluded because of 1000 marks. So, we left for Fürth and
stayed there overnight. I cannot describe the honour that was

[1] Samson Baiersdorf was Court Jew of Margrave Christian Ernst of
Bayreuth.
[2] Pun here intended. Principal is the bride, while dowry is the interest.

extended to us there. The most distinguished men of the Community and their wives came to our inn and wanted to take us by force to their houses. In the end we could not refuse my cousin Mordecai Cohen's son, and we went with him. We were well regaled that night. Next morning we rode away again as we had nothing to accomplish there except the match. So we were again in Bamberg and at once got ready to return home with my son Moses.

Now the matchmaker who had proposed the match in Baiersdorf lived in Fürth, had remained the whole time in Bamberg and was very anxious to bring about the match. But I gave him my terms: 'Thus and thus it must be!' and at length the matchmaker said, 'Well, I can see that you have made up your mind and are ready to leave. I beg you do me this favour and remain here till midday, two o'clock. I have written everything to Baiersdorf and know for certain that before 2 o'clock I shall receive an answer that everything is in order. If no reply has arrived by that time I will keep you no longer.'

I was satisfied with this and in the meantime continued with my preparations to go. My son Zanvil and his father-in-law wished to accompany me part of the way. Meanwhile a feast was held, like the feast of King Solomon in his time. I cannot tell what an upright, fine, clever man Reb Moses Bamberg is and what respect he paid everyone.

After we had eaten and drunk well, it was three o'clock. Nothing had been heard and nothing seen of anyone from Baiersdorf. About five o'clock we and our company rode out of Bamberg. Reb Moses pressed me to stay overnight as it was nearly night and leave early in the morning, but I wanted no one's advice and in the name of the Lord rode forth. We were scarcely a quarter of an hour from the town when the matchmaker, poor thing, came riding after us on horseback and begged us, for God's sake, to return to Bamberg, for Samson Baiersdorf's sons were there to settle about the match. But I would not do this, and refused to return. So Reb Moses Bamberg said, 'See, here lies a pretty village and a respectable inn. It is now nearly night and we cannot ride on. We will therefore remain in the inn overnight and if Reb Samson's sons wish to come to us, they may do so!'

I was satisfied with this and the matchmaker was happy that

he had brought us to a standstill. He rode back immediately to Bamberg.

In less than an hour there came to us in the inn Rabbi Mendel Rothschild[1] of Bamberg, Reb Samson Baiersdorf's sons, as well as Leib Biber and his brother Wolf, refined, upstanding, wealthy people. In short—we had no lengthy arguments and the dowries were deposited. Both sons were proxies for their father and signed for him. The night passed in joy and gladness. Reb Samson Baiersdorf was not at home, but in Bayreuth with His Highness the Margrave, whose Court Jew he was, as everyone knows. His sons begged us to do them the favour of going to Bayreuth with them out of respect for their father. That seemed impossible to me for we had hired our driver to take us to Halberstadt. But we asked him and arranged that we would give him two reichstaler more if he would take us to Bayreuth and from there to Naumberg, where a fair was being held. Seckel Weiner was with us and advised me to do this. Moses Bamberg said that, if it was pleasing to me, he also would journey with us to Bayreuth. Although I declined these offers with polite compliments, and did not desire to put him to such trouble, it was settled that I and the whole company rode to Bayreuth, where we met the wealthy Samson Baiersdorf, who was delighted to see us.

It was then the beginning of the month of Ab, when we must diminish pleasures.[2] That was why we had only a light meal on the first evening; especially as on these days of mourning there was little to be bought. But the following day Samson Wertheimer sent for all sorts of excellent fish and other 'milk' foods, which could be quickly prepared, for I would be delayed no longer. My new relative promised not to keep me an hour after the meal. We bade each other farewell after the meal, and I, my betrothed son, and Seckel Weiner took our seats and, with tears in our eyes, parted from Moses Bamberg. I had to tear myself away from this fortunate gathering.

We reached Hamburg safely; there I found my children and

[1] Rabbi Mendel Rothschild, land rabbi of Bamberg and also of Bayreuth and Baiersdorf, was later Rabbi of Worms. He was a grandson of Isaac Rothschild of Frankfurt-on-Main, progenitor of the Rothschild family.

[2] A day of mourning and fasting as, according to tradition, both Temples in Jerusalem were destroyed on the 9th day of Ab.

the whole family well. I had been parted from them for twelve weeks, all told.

Some time after this, God visited my kinswoman Beila, peace unto her, the wife of Rabbi Baer Cohen, with an uncommon malady—she could not pass water. This lasted for four weeks. Although the rich Rabbi Baer Cohen took every care, called in many physicians, sparing no money and seeking every possible cure for his wife, there was no remedy, for her death was already decided upon by the Lord. When Beila saw that she grew worse day by day, and that nothing relieved her, she sent for my brother-in-law Joseph and Rabbi Samuel Orgel[1] to be witnesses, then summoned her husband Rabbi Baer. She spoke to him movingly of the orphan girl Glückelchen, whom they had brought up and who was then about eleven or twelve years of age. They were both passionately fond of the child. She begged her husband to give her this assurance: and give her his hand on it, and promise that if she died he would marry no one else but Glückelchen, who was the daughter of Feibusch Cohen, Baer's uncle. With streaming eyes he promised and gave his hand to my brother-in-law Joseph and Rabbi Samuel Orgel, thus pledging himself to keep his word. Thereon Beila was pacified and said she could now die, for she knew that her Glückelchen was provided for. But, my God! things never happen as people expect.

They wrote to Reb Selig in Hanover, a brother of the orphan girl whom they had also brought up and whom they had married to the daughter of the rich Hirsch Hanover. They asked him to come to his aunt Beila, who longed to see him before she died. Meanwhile the remedies had begun to work and several buckets of water were taken from her. We thought that this would lead to her recovery, but the contrary was the case: it hastened her end. When her nephew Selig arrived he found her seemingly better. But he was not a day with her, when God took her to Him—to her husband's great sorrow, ours and whole Community's. For she was—God be gracious to her—an honest, clever woman who knew how to rule the heart of her husband. But what did all this help her? All the money, all the good and everything that her husband did for her sake—nothing helped. He had many men to 'study' for her, he dis-

[1] Renowned Talmud scholar and commentator.

tributed much in alms, but her time was up; on New Year's day, when it is decreed who shall die and who shall live, her death was decided. So, with a good name, in all honour, she died and was carried to the grave. Her husband and all her friends mourned her deeply, especially my kinsman Amschel and his wife Mattie, who was her niece, and Reb Reuben, Mattie's brother who had also been brought up by Rabbi Baer Cohen. Mattie Wimpfen was the aunt, and her brother Reuben the uncle of Glückelchen.

After the seven days of mourning they comforted themselves with the thought that Baer Cohen's house would still be open to them and they could come in again to their cousin Glückelchen. After some time her relatives pressed him to declare that he would marry her, so that he would be free of the pesterings of the matchmakers. In truth he had no rest from them, for whoever had a daughter, was eager to ally himself with Baer Cohen, even if he was ruined by it. But Baer Cohen put Beila's kin off from time to time and pleaded that it was too early. But at length the truth came out: it was impossible, he declared, for him to marry the orphan, for he had brought her up as his own child and it was impossible for him to take such a child to wife. Besides, he was childless and was no longer young: how could he wait a few years till she was of an age and growth to bear children? Even if he was willing to wait a few years, until she was marriageable, who knew how long a person would live? If he waited any longer, he would not be fulfilling his religious duty.

At these words his friends were sorely alarmed. They reminded him that he had promised his wife on her death-bed, had given her his hand on it and pledged himself to marry Glückelchen. Baer Cohen replied, 'Yes, it is true, but I only did it to pacify my wife. Besides which, I was so troubled that I did not know what I was doing. I beg of you, let Glückelchen release me from my promise. I will give her a fine dowry so that she can obtain a better man than me for her husband. But if you fear that I will be estranged from you, if you have a marriageable girl among your kin, I will marry her, and do to Glückelchen as I have said.'

But Amschel and his wife Mattie and her brother Reuben Rothschild would hear of no one else. Perhaps they were afraid that if he married anyone else, even from their own family, they would no longer be welcome in the house of Baer Cohen. They were, in fact, held in high respect by him and he in general actually took their advice in the management of his affairs.

At that time my daughter Freudchen was twelve years old, but she was well grown for her age, a beauty without an equal. My brother Wolf came to me and said, 'Why do you sit so still? Baer Cohen will not marry Glückelchen; I want to propose your daughter to him.' I laughed at him and scolded him and said, 'What are you saying? That I should injure the chances of the orphan child Glückelchen!'

My brother swore to me that he knew for certain that Rabbi Baer would not take Glückelchen in any circumstances, and if it were not my daughter, it would only be someone else, and the whole house would be estranged from us. Well, who would not willingly be allied in marriage with Baer Cohen, who possessed every advantage in the world to recommend him? So my brother went to propose the match. He answered him that he did not know my daughter, but still they should mention it to Reb Amschel, his wife Mattie and Reb Reuben Rothschild. If it could induce Glückelchen to release him from his promise he would be content. But when my brother spoke with the relatives, they were full of rage, and Mattie Rothschild went so far as to say that she would prefer Reb Baer to marry an absolute stranger rather than my daughter. When I heard this, I let the matter rest.

Meanwhile Baer Cohen spoke with Glückelchen herself and begged her to release him; he would provide her with a splendid dowry and a fine bridegroom. But she would not agree to do this. At length Reb Baer communicated with several rabbis, and after relating the whole affair asked them to cancel his vow and grant him permission to marry another woman. The learned rabbi of the Altona *Klaus* would not release him, but he received permission from the other rabbis. Then Amschel clearly saw that he would not marry Glückelchen. It appears that he had long set his heart on marrying the daughter of Tewele Schiff.[1] He married her and before the end of a year a son was born to them. Reb Baer's joy may be imagined! Shortly before this Amschel died suddenly; he went to bed quite

[1] Later rabbi of the German community in London.

well, and had lain scarce an hour when he died. He was mourned by the whole Community, for he was an upright, pious man.

About eighteen months after Reb Baer's second marriage, while I was at the Leipzig Fair, letters arrived informing us that his wife was very ill, and by the next post news came to say that she was dead. Not long after, Baer married his wife's sister.

These matches had been arranged by Rabbi Samuel Orgel, who was held in high respect by Reb Baer. Not long after, in synagogue one Friday evening, Rabbi Samuel fell dead on the spot. Great terror fell on the Community, that in so short a time Amschel Wimpfen, Rabbi Samuel Orgel and Baer's wife had all died. Whether or no the cause of this was that my relative Beila would not cancel her husband's oath given before others—God knows! I and others are too humanly frail to think on it. We must pray that God may turn His wrath away from us and all Jews.

After this Baer Cohen married his niece Glückelchen to the son of the rich Reb Judah Berlin. He did much for her brothers and sisters, as everyone knows. I have written this in my book, for it strikes me as unusual and from it we may learn how human fortune changes. Beila, my kinswoman, before her death, thought that she was on the highest rung that human fortune may reach. Baer Cohen was her husband: he was a great Talmudist, a Cohen,[1] very rich, of good family, a good-natured man who did much good to poor and rich alike. They lived happily together, and though they had no children of their own, they brought up Feibusch Cohen's children as though they were their own flesh and blood. Beila's sole care was for their well-being. She lived to see Selig betrothed to Hirsch Hanover's daughter. I heard from her own mouth that this cost more than 15,000 reichstaler—which shows Reb Baer's good heart, to spend so much on a nephew. As the young man's betrothal was according to her own joy and wishes, she expected to spend as much on Glückelchen. Beila, peace unto her, was held in higher esteem than any other Jewish woman in all Germany. But, for our sins, where the pull is strongest, there the rope breaks. In her best years she was forced to leave

[1] Literally priest, a descendant of the Biblical priests, the name being handed down from father to son.

all. When, on her death-bed, she wanted the satisfaction of making her husband take oath so that she could feel sure that her desire that he should marry Glückelchen would be carried out, even this was not fulfilled. How did all her wealth and honour help her? Nothing was of use. Her great humility and the good that she did, will stand her in good stead; that is all that remains to her of her great wealth. She was about fifty-one years old. When first they married, they had less than 900 reichstaler between them, but the Lord blessed them, as is known, and granted Baer great riches, enough for his posterity. May God never take them from him and enlarge his boundaries. For he has a generous heart and his equal is hard to find.[1]

But to return: after a time I betrothed my daughter Freudchen to the son of Reb Moses, son of Rabbi Leib.[2] We were delivered from a blow which the Holy One graciously turned aside. I have already mentioned that my son Nathan had business dealings with Reb Samuel Oppenheimer and his son Mendel of Vienna. At the time of which I write he had several bills of theirs, some of which had already fallen due. Before these fell due, the Oppenheimers would send money to my son so that he could meet the bills. But on this occasion he received neither letter nor cash. At length the sad news reached us: Samuel Oppenheimer and his son were imprisoned. As soon as this intelligence reached Hamburg, all my son's credit was withdrawn from him, and everyone who had bills in hand, whether Oppenheimer's or another's, pressed him for payment. He met all the bills; he did not allow any to be dishonoured. This was just before the time of the Leipzig Fair, which he had to attend. He paid all he could, pawned all his gold and silver vessels and left for the fair with a heavy heart. He parted from me with these words, 'Dear mother, I am leaving you now. God knows in what state we shall meet again; I still owe a few thousand. I beg you to help me as much as you can. I know that the Oppenheimers will not desert us.'

[1] Here follow lengthy moralizings from the work *Yesh Nochalin*, Ethical Will of Abraham Horowitz of Prague.

[2] Mordecai Hamburger, known also as Marcus Moses, settled in London where he founded the Hambro' Synagogue. He was a dealer in gems and traded in the East Indies, where he amassed a large fortune.

On Sunday Nathan and a company left for Leipzig. On Monday my trouble meeting the bills began. I did what was possible. I pawned all my things and was buried up to my neck so that I could do no more. On Friday I had only 500 reichstaler more to pay, but could get no cash. I had good bills from well-known Hamburg houses which I wanted to sell on the Börse. With a heavy heart I went myself all round the Börse, and then gave them to the brokers to sell for me. But they returned the bills after the Börse: no one wanted to buy them. I was sad at heart. At length God helped me and I paid the 500 reichstaler. On Sabbath I made up my mind to leave on Sunday for Leipzig, and if I found that the Oppenheimers had sent the money on there, I would return home: but if no money had come, I would go on to Vienna, to Rabbi Samson Wertheimer, who was a true friend of ours, and would help us to our rights. I asked my brother Wolf to accompany me. On Sunday we left in a hired coach.

We halted at one of the small villages just outside Leipzig. I sent a messenger to my children in the city and asked them to come to me. They came with the news that the Oppenheimers had been released, and had sent money to honour their bills. As soon as I heard this, I and my brother took our seats on the coach, turned, rode back and were again in Hamburg on Friday, in good time for Sabbath. So within six days I journeyed to Leipzig and back. Shall I write of the joy of my children, especially Nathan's wife Miriam, that, when we were in such a terrible plight from which there seemed no escape, God in an instant helped us? Though the Oppenheimers paid all the expenses we had incurred, in all their lives they cannot repay us for the frights and anxiety we suffered through them. May God have mercy on us and supply us with our daily bread, from His hand and with all dignity. So thanks to God this also passed happily.

After this my daughter Freudchen's marriage to the son of Moses, son of Rabbi Leib Altona, was celebrated. The wedding in Altona was a splendid affair, full of joyousness.

The time of my son Moses's marriage drew near. I wrote to Reb Samson Baiersdorf that I was ready to travel to the wedding. But he replied that it was impossible for him to prepare for the wedding in the agreed time. As God had given him the merit that he should live to marry off his youngest child, he could not have the wedding in his old house. He had already begun to build a new one, and when it was finished he would write to me so that we could all celebrate the marriage in splendour and honour.

The building of the house was not really the only reason for the delay. The Margrave had taken a new counsellor who was a Haman against Samson Baiersdorf and wished to destroy him. In truth he was in a critical position; all his possessions were in the Margrave's hands, and he did not know which way to turn. This was the reason that he did not celebrate the marriage within the agreed time. But the Holy One saw the great good that came from his house, the hospitality to rich and poor alike, all he did for the Jews of the whole land—he supported the whole dukedom—and the good that he would do in the future. So God turned the evil of this Haman to good, so that the evil one fell lower and Samson Baiersdorf from day to day rose higher and higher. It is impossible to describe in what honour and trust he, a Jew, is held by the Margrave. May God grant that this exalted position remain his till the coming of the Messiah.

Nevertheless a whole year passed before the marriage could be celebrated. And here I will end my fifth book.

BOOK VI

HERE I begin my sixth book in which I will write of the change in my state which I had avoided for fourteen years.

Matches with the most distinguished men in the whole of Germany had been broached to me, but as long as I could support myself on what my husband, peace unto him, had left me, it did not enter my head to marry again. God, who saw my many sins, did not will that I should agree to one of the proposed matches through which I and my children would have been truly fortunate and that I in dreary old age should have comfort. Such did not suit the Lord and for my sins I was induced to the match of which I shall now tell. Yet, despite all, I thank my Creator, who has shown me mercy in my heavy punishment, more than I, a sinner, deserve. In truth I must be grateful, even though I cannot pay for my sins with fasts and other penances, as I should do, because of my troubles and sojourn in a strange land, though to God I know this is no excuse. Therefore I write this with a trembling hand and hot, bitter tears for it is written *Thou shalt serve God with all thy heart and with all thy soul*. I beg Almighty God to strengthen me that I may serve Him only—and that I may not appear before Him in soiled garments, for, as is said in the 'Ethics of the Fathers': *Repent one day before your death*. As we do not know the day of death, we must repent every day. This I must do, even though I have a feeble excuse for myself: I had thought that after first settling my fatherless children I would go to the Holy Land.

This I could have done, especially as my son Moses was betrothed, and I had only my young daughter Miriam to provide for. So I, a sinner, should not have married again but should first have seen Miriam wedded, and then done what was seemly for a good, pious Jewish woman. I should have forsaken the vanity of this world and with the little left, gone to the Holy Land and lived there, a true daughter of Israel. There all the sorrows and cares of my children and friends, and the vanity of the world, would not have troubled me and I would have served God with all my heart. But the Lord led me to other thoughts and to a decision less worthy than this.

Well, to continue. A year passed before I could attend Moses's wedding. All sorts of trouble and misfortune befell me through my children meanwhile, and it always cost me much money. But it is not necessary to write of it: they are my own dear children and I forgive them, those that have cost me much as well as those who cost me nothing. Through them my fortune grew less and less. My business was large, for I had extensive credit with Jews and non-Jews. I afflicted myself: in the heat of summer and in the snow of winter I went to fairs and stood there in my shop all day; and though I possessed less than others thought, I wished to be always held in honour and not, God forbid, dependent on my children, sitting at another's table. It would be worse to be with my children than with strangers, in case, God forbid, through me, they sinned. This would be worse than death to me.

I began to find that I could no longer stand the strain of long journeys and going about the town. I was fearful lest any bales of goods or outstanding debts were lost and I, God forbid, became bankrupt; so that those who trusted me should be losers through me, thus disgracing me, my children and my sainted husband, who lay under the sod. I then began to regret that I had let pass so many good matches and the chances of living respected and rich in my old age, and, perhaps, of helping my children at the same time. But regret does not help me now: it is too late. God did not wish it and bad luck thrust something else in my mind, as will now follow.

It was in the year 5459 [1698–9], at the time of the delay over the marriage of my son Moses, which I have already explained, that I received a letter from my son-in-law Moses Krumbach of Metz, Sivan 5459 [June 1699], in which he mentioned that Reb Hirsch Levy[1] had become a widower. He extolled him as a fine, upstanding Jew, very learned in Talmud, possessed of great wealth and a magnificent household. In short, he praised him highly and according to all accounts what he wrote was true. But man sees with his eyes; God looks into the heart.

This letter reached me as I meditated my woes. I was then fifty-four years of age and had endured many cares because of my children. If the circumstances were as my son-in-law related, I could in my old age join a devout community, as

---

[1] Hirsch Levy was the foremost financier of Lorraine.

Metz then had the name for being, and there pass the rest of my life in peace and see to the good of my soul. I trusted, too, that my children would not advise anything that was not for my good. I therefore wrote thus in answer to my son-in-law: 'I have been a widow for eleven years and had no intention of marrying again. It is generally known that I could have made one of the greatest and most distinguished marriages in the whole of Germany, had I so desired. Notwithstanding, I will agree to this match, because you urge me to it so earnestly, if my daughter Esther advises the same.' On this she wrote me as much as she, poor thing, knew and had seen. There was not much argument about the dowry. I was to give my husband as much as I could and he agreed that if I died first, my heirs would receive back my dowry; if he died first, he would leave me 500 reichstaler, besides returning my dowry of 1500 reichstaler. My daughter Miriam was then a child of eleven and he bound himself to support her until her marriage. If I had more money I would have given it to him as well, for I thought that my money would be safer nowhere than with this man. I meant this also as a benefit for my daughter Miriam; she would not need to spend any of her money, all of which was lent out on interest. Furthermore, this man had a fine reputation in business: who knew what great benefit my children could derive in business as a result? But many thoughts are in the heart of man and He Who reigns in heaven laughs.

Unfortunately, God laughed at my thoughts and plans, and had already long decided on my doom to repay me for my sins in relying on people. I should not have thought of marrying again, for I could not hope to meet another Chaim Hameln. I should have remained with my children, for good or ill, and taken all as God willed; first married off my fatherless Miriam and then later, as I had decided, spent my last days in the Holy Land.

Still, all that has happened has passed and so cannot be changed. I have now only to beg of the Lord to hear and see only good of my children. With reference to myself, I receive everything from Him with love. May God the Just give me patience as heretofore, and let all atone for my sins. I accept everything as medicine from a doctor, as I stated in my first book.

The betrothal took place and the dowry was deposited with great secrecy. I did not want it to become known, for if the Town Council got to know of it, I would have to pay several hundreds on leaving Hamburg for good. I was very well known throughout the town and all the merchants who had business dealings with me thought that I was worth thousands and thousands. Meanwhile, I realized cash for my stock and paid all my debts. I thank and praise the Lord that I left Hamburg owing not a single taler to Jew or gentile. I thank Him again and again that He granted me this.

My children, long may they live, and my brothers and sisters and friends all knew of the marriage beforehand, as I had taken counsel with them and they had all advised me to it. Still, it was a misfortune, as will follow, for that which I feared came to pass. I entered into this marriage, for I feared that if I remained single longer, I might lose everything and be disgraced so that—God forbid—I would harm other people, Jews and gentiles, and then be dependent on my children. But nothing helped me, and I had to fall into the hands of a man and live the shame against which I had hoped to protect myself. Though not through me, yet still through my husband, because of whom I had thought to live in honour and wealth, I now find myself in such a position that I do not know if in old age I shall have a place to rest overnight, or a slice of bread to eat. I worry in case, God forbid, I shall have to come to my children for help. I hoped to benefit my children by marrying such a well-known businessman, but it did not come to pass. On the contrary, he owes to my son Nathan, several hundreds who through him was half ruined. His bills were not met, and I see clearly that, if God had not helped and protected him, Nathan would have been ruined. I had thought to do well for my orphan Miriam, that her money might be saved, but I brought her also into this blunder, which the Holy One averted from her, as I shall relate later.

My heart-beloved children, as can be seen, I thought everything over well and did all for the best, but the result was bad. I can only conclude that my sins are the cause. Therefore, my loved, trusty children, what more shall I say? There is nothing new under the sun. I am not the only one on whom misfortune has fallen. Others, more pious, more God-fearing than I, in

The Effigies of the highe borne Prince
Maurice sone of the Prince Palatine of Rhein
borne in Cistrine in Niew ? Brandenburch

Sould in ... ... Streat by ... ...

34. *Prince Maurice of Nassau as a Youth.* Contemporary Print.

36. *Sabbatai Enthroned.* From a Prayer Book, Amsterdam, 1666

35. *Sabbatai Zevi* (1626–1676), *the False Messiah, at the age of 40.* Contemporary Engraving

whose footsteps I am unworthy to tread, have suffered, as the following story, which I know for certain is true and really happened, will show. May it happen to me as it did to this pious and devout king. If you are wise and consider it, you must agree that the story is true. I have translated this tale from the Holy tongue [Hebrew] into German in order to show what eminent, devout people also have to suffer. Yet the Holy One, blessed be He, also helped them. May He help us and all Jews so as to make us rejoice even as He has afflicted us. Amen and Amen!

The story is of a king who lived in the land of the Arabs. A mighty king, Jedidiah by name, who had many wives as is usual in eastern lands. He had also many children, all of whom he loved, princes and princesses, who were all brought up as befitted their station. Among them was a son, the most beautiful of all his offspring, whom the king loved most. He let him have his own way and from this much evil resulted as will be shown later. The name of this son was Avadon. He had a sister who was also most beautiful. She was known as the lovely Danella. There was another son, Amoris by name, who fell in love with Danella. He could not have her for himself and dare not entrust anyone with his secret desire for fear of the king's anger, though he knew that the king loved and honoured him.

Time passed. Amoris suffered the pangs of love and grew thin and dispirited. One of his companions, a good friend, noticing this, said to him, 'My lord and good friend, I have noticed that for some time your jollity has vanished. You go in solitary places and your body has grown thin. What is amiss with the royal prince Amoris, who has riches and honour enough? I beg my friend to tell me what lies so heavy on his heart. Perhaps his burden will then be lifted, for I may be able to help him.'

And Amoris answered his friend, 'You have spoken in truth and with understanding, but no one can lighten my suffering. Only death can relieve me! I dare not disclose it to anyone but you, my dear friend. Before my death I will tell you, though you cannot help me: I have sucked the poison of Danella's beauty. This is my danger and my sickness. I have done everything to cure myself of this disorder, but God have mercy, the more I try to estrange myself, the more I suffer for love of her. Well, my trusted friend, if you cannot help me and advise me, I am altogether lost!'

Thereupon his friend answered, 'Not if you will follow my trusty advice. Do as I say and you will soon be well: Go to bed and declare

M

that you are ill, as indeed your face confirms. Your doctor must announce that you are gravely ill. Without doubt the king will then come to see what ails you. Whereon, my dear Amoris, you must declare that you are sore stricken and in a weak voice that you cannot sleep nor partake of food. But you have just bethought you that there is just one thing that may restore you—if the king will grant it—if he will graciously request Danella to come to your chamber and prepare a special dish. Perchance God will then be gracious and this food save your life. I know that the king will not refuse your request and will send Danella to you. When she enters ask all present to withdraw as you will then better partake of the food. And thus, my friend, by coaxing or by force you will gain what you desire. Thereafter, whatever happens cannot be altered and your mother, who holds in her hands the king's heart, will soften his wrath.'

'My dear friend,' answered Amoris, 'you advise me well. I already feel stronger—and shall do as you advise, even if I die as a result.'

Thus Amoris retired to his chamber and lay in his bed as one sore stricken. His own trusted doctor reported his illness to the king who soon came himself to enquire of the invalid. Amoris in a weak voice spoke as his friend had advised.

The king said to him, 'Be comforted, for you will be refused nothing. I shall send your sister so that her dishes may restore your former health and strength.'

He parted fondly from Amoris and sent a message to his daughter that she should go forthwith to her sick brother, and prepare a special dish for him to sample.

The fair Danella did as her father bade her. She went to her brother's apartment and there obtained from the servants everything necessary for preparing a tempting dish. As soon as Amoris saw that the food was ready he ordered everyone out of the room, saying as soon as he was alone with Danella, 'My dear sister, bring the food to me in bed so that you may feed me. It will then certainly taste better.'

As she brought the food to him he seized hold of her, declaring, 'My sweet sister, you must lie with me or I shall die.'

At this Danella was very frightened and said, 'My dear brother, do not commit such knavery. Approach the king concerning me. I am certain he will not gainsay you.'

But neither talk nor pleas helped Danella. Amoris pulled her to him and forced her to lie with him.

After he had had his evil will of her, Amoris's former love was turned to hate. He pushed her from him and bade her be gone.

Danella wept bitterly, 'Not enough that you have brought me to this shame,' she wailed, 'but now you spurn me.' Lamenting loudly as she went forth she met her brother Avadon. Hearing her cries and seeing her royal garments so rent, he said, 'My sister, a calamity befell you in Amoris's apartment. Say naught but remain in my chamber until I have avenged you.'

So Danella, having with shame told her brother all, went. The king heard of the matter and was very enraged; but the queen, because of the great love he bore her, softened his heart towards her son. But Avadon nourished hate in his heart.

Some time after there was a great chase at which all the king's sons were present, Amoris among them. As they all sat round the board of costly viands, eating and drinking of the best, Avadon signed to his retainers. They fell on Amoris and slew him. Alarmed, all the royal princes took to horse and fled.

A messenger ran to the king and informed him that Avadon had slain all his offspring. The king set up a loud lament. Near him stood the friend and evil adviser of Amoris. 'My lord king,' he said, 'weep not so sore. Only Amoris of the royal princes is no more. Your son Avadon has taken vengeance because of his sister.'

Just then the princes came riding up. The king's rage was great against Avadon and he ordered him nevermore to come before him and declared another son his heir. Avadon could not suffer to live under this banishment and disinheritance, for he had expected to succeed to the throne on his father's death.

Following this, by means of fair words and promises, he attached many persons to him and began plotting against his father who, however, had followers who remained loyal. Avadon moved against his father, captured the capital city and had much wanton sport with the king's wives. The king and his faithful men had in order to protect themselves fled from the city. Some who had formerly served him, and now followed Avadon, threw missiles after him cursing him as they put him to flight. Whereupon his trusty servers could not bear to witness how they treated him like a dead hound, and cried, 'Let us attack them, even if we are annihilated.'

But the pious king would not allow this, saying to his trusty men, 'This is from my own son, flesh of my flesh, who threatens my life. It is because of my sins. Why then should others suffer?'

Then the battle raged sore against the king and his men, who took refuge in a walled city. The king asked his loyal men to deal moderately with his son Avadon, for if he took the city they were all lost. They hearkened to him; and when he wished to march into battle at the head of his men they would not allow him, saying, 'The king knows that the whole struggle is because of him. If Avadon slays the king he will obtain the kingdom. Let the king remain here and pray to God that he delivers our enemy into our hands.' To which he replied, 'Go in peace and God be with you.'

So they marched forth from the city. The king begged the generals and officers to take heed for the life of Avadon. The soldiers went gladly, putting their trust in God and their own just cause. Though they were half as strong as Avadon and his army, they caused a panic, defeated them and put them to flight.

Though Avadon fled he was captured and slain by the king's men. Thus ended the fight. But no one dared tell the king of his death. When he asked, 'Does Avadon live?', no one had the courage to answer, as though the battle had been lost.

One of the king's generals saw this and spoke for the faithful men who had been willing to lay down their lives for the king and his dynasty. 'Behold,' said he, 'if Avadon were alive we would all be slain and the king would not show much concern. We beseech him to stand in the gate and address his people so that they may receive him back and do for him more than they have ever done.'

So the king went and spoke to his people in the gate. His enemies came to him and he pardoned them the wrong they had done him— and friend and enemy alike led him with much rejoicing again to his kingdom. The pious king proclaimed throughout his land: that all who had left the country and feared his anger should return—they would be received with clemency. He added, 'It is as though I am made king today: everyone shall receive of my grace.'

Thus the king reigned in peace and honour. And before his death saw his son Friedlieb anointed and crowned king in his place.

From all this you see that God's punishment is slow but sure. Amoris, who had such evil inclination to his sister, lost his life by the hand of his brother Avadon. The king, against whom Avadon had done so much wrong, was compelled to flee and suffer much hardship. If he had not had so wonderful a heart who knows what further wrong might have been done?—and in the end he might himself have been slain. Avadon, who had wrought so much evil, who had even threatened to kill his own father and had raped his father's harem, suffered indeed a miserable end.

Let all take this lesson to heart and know that God is a righteous judge repaying wrong and goodness. We do not know when God will punish or when He will do good. He slays and He heals. May His Name be praised now and evermore.

But to return. Our betrothal was in Metz, Sivan 5459 [June 1699] and was arranged by my son-in-law Moses and his parents. What can I write of these people? They surely did this for the best, for the sake of a meritorious deed and what they thought was for my good. The marriage date was fixed for *Lag b'Omer*[1] [Friday, May 17, 1700]. It was kept secret for the reason I have already given. Meanwhile I realized as much cash as I could, settled all my debts and sent a money-draft to the wealthy Gabriel Levy in Fürth, the father-in-law of Reb Moses Brandeis, to accept and hold until our arrival. I also, in the meantime, exchanged letters with my husband. In all his, which I and others read, there was pleasure and best assurances so that no one could foresee any of the evil that was to befall. About the month of Tebet 5460, when I was to attend the marriage of my son Moses, intending to go on to Metz, the Lord visited me—not unto us!—with an illness that kept me confined to my bed for six weeks. My betrothed heard of this through a merchant. The comforting letters he wrote me, and the concern with which he wrote to my brother-in-law Joseph, impressing upon him the need for my care—it is indescribable. But God knows what his intentions were. I do not know if it was for the little money I had.

When I was restored to full health, I left Hamburg with my son Reb Moses and my daughter Miriam and went to Brunswick, where a fair was being held and sold the remainder of my goods there. After the fair, together with a goodly company, we went to Baiersdorf, expecting to celebrate Moses's wedding on New Moon's day, Nissan (March–April). I remained in Bamberg for Purim, and immediately after went with my son Zanvil to Baiersdorf. There we stayed in an inn, opposite Samson Baiersdorf, for his new house was not yet finished and there was no room in the old one. We were invited to have our meals, three times daily, with him and received princely attention there. But all this did not please me. I therefore said to Samson Baiersdorf and his wife, 'I have no cause to hurry from here, but I have a reason that I would have my son's marriage celebrated on New Moon's day, Nissan. You know of my betrothal; I must be in Metz for *Lag b'Omer*. Besides, the man has my money already in hand'—as was the case.

[1] During the seven-week period of the counting of the Omer, between Passover and the Feast of Weeks (Pentecost), no marriages may be performed except on *Lag b'Omer*—the 33rd day.

There was a good deal of talk and much advice. At length Samson Baiersdorf said I could do as I liked: it was impossible for him to arrange for the wedding before the Feast of Weeks. In the meantime I could take my children with me and go to Metz for my own wedding, he would give me 100 ducats for my expenses. This I would not do, for it was not seemly.

So, I decided to have patience with that which could not be altered. The differences that we had concerning the dowry were put aside till after the wedding, when they were settled quite amicably.

I remained ten weeks in Baiersdorf, from Purim to the Feast of Weeks, 1700. The marriage was celebrated in Sivan with all the splendour in the world. There were many distinguished guests on both sides and the wedding passed most agreeably. May God bless them and give them fortune that they may pass their lives in wealth and honour[1] until the Redeemer comes; that their offspring may be excellent and that they may study God's Law. In their days, in our days, may God help us and send our Messiah. Amen.

After the wedding I prepared for my journey to Metz. I hired a man in Baiersdorf, Koppel by name, the synagogue beadle, to accompany me to Frankfurt, where, my husband had written to me, he would send someone to accompany me to Metz. I went with my daughter Miriam and Koppel to Bamberg. Moses, my son, wished to accompany me as far, but I would not allow this as it was still his wedding-week. We took sorrowful leave of one another, weeping bitterly, though in truth I was full of joy that I had led my son honourably under the canopy and had, God be praised, brought him fine connections: in truth, the eye wept while the heart rejoiced—this is nature's way.

I arrived in Bamberg, where I stayed overnight. Next morning the coach which I had ordered a long while before, took the road to Frankfurt. I could not prevent my son Zanvil, peace unto him, accompanying me to Würzburg. There we took eternal farewell of one another, as though the thought lay in both our sad hearts, that we would never meet again in this world.

[1] Moses Hameln was later rabbi of Baiersdorf and was held in high esteem.

I continued on my way. On Friday, Sivan 20, 5460 [June 11, 1700] we reached Frankfurt-on-Main quite safely. There I found a man from Metz, by name of Lezer, and a letter from my husband. He sent us gingerbread and other comfits for the journey and wrote so politely that I could not dream of my misfortune. In Frankfurt I received all the honour a woman could possibly desire, as well as on the whole journey—more, indeed, than of which I was worthy. Especially in Fürth, which is only three miles from Baiersdorf. There my son Nathan had sent me a draft on the wealthy Gabriel Levy, the dowry of Moses and the little money I still had over, but this was only a small amount. Shall I write of the honour accorded me by his whole household? I could not write enough of it. Not sufficient that these trusty people took so much trouble with me to obtain cash for the bill, but they gave me part of it, and part they sent to other places, according to my order. Moses's money, up till the time of his marriage, I had loaned on interest to different people. Zanvil's father-in-law, Reb Moses of Bamberg, did me the favour of taking 1000 reichstaler on interest; Rabbi Mendel Rothschild also took 1000 taler, as did Leib Biber of Bamberg, and the rest we had loaned out in Baiersdorf on interest. After this, I went over the accounts with Gabriel Levy and wanted to pay him commission, as is customary. But he refused to take even a pfennig, and said it was not money from business; it was an obligation and a meritorious duty. I gave him many good reasons for accepting the commission, but without any fuss he refused to take even the cost of the postage. May God reward him as he merits.

To return again to our journey. On Monday, accompanied by Lezer, we left Frankfurt, where I had met Lieberman of Halberstadt. He was going to Metz to visit his old father Abraham Speyer and also Doctor Hirsch. They kept us company till Metz and we had a pleasant journey.

Two miles from Metz we were met by my husband's clerk on horseback. He rode beside the carriage until we reached the inn. He had all sorts of food and drink with him—as much as his horse could carry. This clerk, Lemle Wimpfen, had welcomed me in my husband's place. After we had food and drink, we journeyed on again another two or three hours. The messenger Lemle remained part of the evening with us. Before we went to our rest he took his leave, for he had to be in Metz in good time. The place we stayed at overnight was not five hours distant from Metz. Though everything was good and fine, showing every appearance of wealth, and though my husband's letters were full of respect and delight, still, God knows, I was depressed. Was it that my troubled heart foretold the unhappy end? Or was it that I was sad at taking another husband? But the reflection had come much too late; I had to hide my dejection and control my sorrowful heart.

When, on Friday, the 22nd of Sivan, we were an hour from Metz, Lemle Wimpfen came riding to meet us, and another person was with him. They rode close to a coach in which three finely-dressed women sat. They were the wife of the Rabbi of Metz, the wife of Rabbi Aaron of Worms, and the wealthy Mistress Jachet, mother of my son-in-law. They received me then and there pleasantly and with much honour. I had to go into their coach. In this way we rode together into Metz. It was indeed a great honour that three such grand ladies should come to meet such an ordinary woman as me, but later this welcome was too salted for me. When not far off Metz, my dear daughter Esther who was then near the end of her pregnancy, came, borne in a sedan-chair, to meet me.

· I stayed with my daughter, who then lived in Beila Krumbach's house. My son-in-law Moses was not then at home, but in Paris. The ladies who had ridden out to meet me went home again, parting from me with polite excuses, as Sabbath was nearly in. I thanked them for the honour paid to me, and the trouble they had taken, as well as I could in the frank German way I had been taught. My daughter made me some soup that I might eat something, but my heart was heavy and I did not know what ailed me. I put it down to the fatigue of the journey.

An hour later came my bridegroom accompanied by the wealthy *parnass* Reb Abraham Krumbach. They welcomed me, stayed a short while, then left. As I live, I did not know at first which was the bridegroom, for I had not seen either before, until my son-in-law's father said, jestingly, I should not make the mistake of thinking he was the bridegroom—which I answered with silence. The time passed and it was holy Sabbath. I did not go to synagogue, though Esther went, for, as everyone knows, she never missed going when she was able. Her good name cannot be described. She was all my joy and comfort in Metz. During the time of prayers my stepchildren came and greeted me, but I did not know who they were and no one was present to tell me. So I said to them, 'I do not know who honours me, for I am a stranger here and know no one.' Hendelé answered, 'Don't you know us? You are going to be our mother.' Thereon I said to them, 'If I am to be your mother, you shall be my children.' After a few more words, for people were returning from synagogue, they left me.

When my daughter returned we seated ourselves at the table. Isaiah Krumbach was then staying with her. As we ate, the servant boy Solomon, who was a sort of valet to my husband, and the maid, entered with two large gilt dishes. In one were the best and finest confects, in the other beautiful foreign fruits, such as lemons and oranges, and the best native fruits. On it lay a golden chain with one piece of gold and two very large gilt goblets full of wine. This was my Sabbath gift; it was very costly. I thought in my deepmost heart, 'God grant that the end may be as fine as the beginning.' But, my Lord and Master! the golden chain, unfortunately, became rope and iron fetters!

About an hour later my bridegroom and Mistress Jachet called. They remained about half-an-hour with us, then each left for home again. Everything was splendid and done in magnificent style, and I should have been happy and not given way to my heavy, troubled thoughts. Everybody envied me, and all said with a full mouth that I must have done many good deeds that I was now so fortunate and had received such a fine, good husband, and so much wealth. My sad heart was not at rest, and the end proved me right. To what shall I ascribe this, if not to my sins?

On Sabbath morning my daughter Miriam was invited by my stepdaughter Frummet, who presented her with a golden chain as a Sabbath gift. All the letters which my son-in-law sent from Paris were full of reminders to my daughter to wait on me well, and were full of love and affection, which is as it should have been. But the love lasted 'Until the day breaks and the shadows flee away,'[1] as will follow in its place. My son-in-law thought that his was a good deed and that I was making a good marriage.

[1] Song of Songs, 2: 17.

So the week passed and nothing out of the ordinary happened. The following week, on Thursday, New Moon's day, Tammuz, the marriage was celebrated. In the morning I was led from my daughter's house to the neighbouring house of my husband. There I remained till midday when he plighted his troth with a valuable gold wedding ring weighing an ounce. The Rebbit-zin[1] Breinelé and wealthy Mistress Jachet were my attendants under the marriage canopy, which was set up in the court-yard of the summerhouse. After the ceremony I was led into the drawing-room, which was handsomely furnished; there food and a wedding cake was brought to us, as is the fashion in Germany. I had eaten nothing the whole day.[2] My heart was still overcharged with tears; when Esther and I parted we both wept bitterly, in tune with our spirits. My husband led me to his study and showed me a large box full of all sorts of chains and rings; but from that time till now he did not give me the smallest ring, or even a silver or gold coin, so it was not through me that he went bankrupt. In the evening there was a magnificent repast and everything passed off in a grand manner. I found many men and maid servants, and wherever I looked, or whatever I asked, there was much abundance. His cabinet was full of gold and silver, so that what happened was the last thing expected. He was *parnass* of the community for a long while and people went in and out according to his wish. Everyone respected and feared him, Jews as well as gentiles. The week following our wedding all the most important people called to welcome me and wish me *mazal tov*. I wished for nothing but that I could talk French, to speak and answer everyone. As it was, my husband spoke for me.

A good while passed, really in great enjoyment. I was short of nothing. My husband gave me money for housekeeping, as much as was needed; but I found that the servant in the house was lord and master and had everything under her charge, all foods, whole sugar-loafs and other things so that she did not ask me what she should cook or make.

This did not suit me, for in my own house in Hamburg I had not been used to this, that a servant should be mistress. I spoke

[1] Wife of a rabbi.
[2] It is customary among Orthodox Jews for the bridal pair to fast on their wedding day until after the marriage ceremony.

about it to my stepchildren and my sister-in-law Freidel, but they told me that Blumchen, Hirsch Levy's first wife, had given her full charge over everything, and there was no doubt of her honesty. When I came into my new home, I found two men-servants, two maids, besides various labourers and running footmen. Although all this did not please me, I was talked out of my dislike for it, and was assured that all this was nothing compared with the time when my husband's first wife lived. My married stepchildren sighed over this and often hinted what good and pleasures they had received from their mother. Some of them she really supported outright. This I could not do and sent them only such foods as were rare or special. If I bought Sabbath fruit on Friday for a quarter-taler, or a livre, I was laughed at and told that more than a reichstaler's worth was always bought, and whole basketsful sent direct into the house of each child. After a while I became used to all this and even if it was 'a joy with trembling', thanked God, thinking that my long sad widowhood had not been in vain.

My husband was a good man and wealthy, as he represented himself to be. I saw more gold and silver in his house than I had seen in any wealthy man's in the whole of Germany. I also saw that he carried on big business and was honest in all his deal-ings, and that no one to whom he owed money had to come twice for it. He paid everyone straightway and with the great-est respect. He gave many people, Jews and gentiles, credit and, apart from his business, had large sums loaned out. Besides this, people held him to be such a trusty and reliable man that anyone who wished to be sure of his money, gave it to my husband for safe keeping. So, also, did my son-in-law Moses a few weeks before I arrived, when he had to go to Paris. He took all he had and, for the period of his absence, gave it into my husband's care, rather than into that of his own father. The name my husband had for honesty was so good, and he was possessed of such wealth that I had little cause to doubt that I had made a good match.

My husband groaned a good deal at night. Many times I asked what ailed him; he always answered that nothing ailed him, it was just his nature and habit. I asked the children and my sister-in-law Freidel what this meant. I thought at first, as everyone told me how happily he had lived with his first wife, that he could not forget her; but they all informed me that this was nothing new and that he used to do the same when his first wife was alive. So I was satisfied with this, though it still grieved me sometimes. I did not know to what sorrows his groans were due. His sleep and eating were also very restless. I had been here about eight weeks when, to my great joy, my daughter Esther was brought to bed with a son. She had no other child, for her beautiful children had all died. We all rejoiced over this beloved child, God protect him. My husband and I were the godparents. My husband gave him a costly gift, a bowl, gold inside and out, three ounces in weight. When Esther left child-bed, he sent her a doubloon[1] as a present. It was at the end of Ellul[2] that she arose hale and well and helped to provide and prepare for the circumcision. The third day after the circumcision she herself did the cooking, so that everyone marvelled. Her mother-in-law, Mistress Jachet, often spoke to me of her good cooking and fine household arrangements, saying, 'I must confess that Esther can cook better than I,' and in truth, if Mistress Jachet wanted something cooked extra well, she sent for my daughter to cook it for her.

What a name my daughter had among the rich and poor alike for piety, modesty and all the virtues! Though she was often sad over the loss of her children, she did not allow this to be seen in her household affairs. Though she was very economical and exact, everything was carried out in fine style. She always had a house rabbi and a Talmud student[3] at her table and did honour and paid respect to rich and poor alike, so that I had reason enough to rejoice. But may God have mercy on us and our fickle luck, which was the beginning of my misfortune in Metz. On *Yom Kippur* my grandchild Elia fell ill with heavy fits, which lasted eight days. The beloved child suffered so much pain that often I prayed in my heart that God should shorten his pains. No doctor or anyone else expected him to recover. But in a trice, God, blessed be His Name, cured him, from which it may be seen that when all human aid is in vain, then He, with His help, makes fools of doctors and wise men.

---

[1] An early Spanish coin.   [2] August or beginning of September.
[3] The Talmud student coming from another country or town to study in some well-known Talmudical school, would eat every day at a different Jewish house.

As it is written, 'I am the Lord that healeth thee.' May God spare him to his parents that they bring him up to Torah, to marriage and all good deeds. Amen.

My daughter's happiness, the alms that she gave openly and in secret for the ransom of her beloved child's life, may easily be imagined. But my son-in-law was like other people who are very keen on troublesome money, confirming what the Talmud says, 'There is a man whose money is dearer to him than his own body, and cannot be satisfied.'

Like the story of Alexander of Macedon. As is known he travelled the whole world and conquered it. Then he thought: 'I am a mighty person and have travelled so far that I cannot be far from the Garden of Eden,' for he was not far from the river Gihon, which is one of the four rivers flowing from there. He built great, stout ships and boarded them together with his men. Through his great wisdom he found the track to the Garden of Eden. When he was not far off a great fire consumed his ships and the men aboard, all save his ship and crew.

When he saw that his was the only ship that remained, Alexander prayed that he might yet enter the Garden of Eden so that he could tell its wonders to the whole world.

But a voice called to him bidding him to depart for he could not enter the Garden of Eden; for only righteous men could pass.

Thereupon he pleaded that if he might not enter, something should be thrown forth which he could show as proof to the world that he had been so near the Garden of Eden. So an eye was thrown to him.

When he saw this, he did not know what to do with it. He was then told to take all his gold and silver and precious things and put them in the scale of a balance and on the other scale the eye: this would outweigh all the rest.

King Alexander was indeed a wise man and philosopher, as is known. He learned much from his teacher Aristotle and wished to learn more of all manner of wisdom. He set out to discover why such a small thing as an eye should outweigh gold and silver. He took a strong, heavy pair of scales, placed the eye on one side, and on the other piled many hundreds of pounds of gold and silver. But as much as he put on, it was not enough—the eye outweighed all.

Alexander wondered greatly at this and begged hard that he should be told why so small an eye could weigh more than so much gold and silver—and with what this eye could be satisfied.

He was told that if a little earth was thrown on the eye, it would outweigh it.

This he did. He threw a small amount of earth on the eye—and this very small amount outweighed the eye.

When he saw this he was most astonished and begged to be told the meaning.

'Hearken you, Alexander,' he was told, 'know that as long as an eye is in a living person, it cannot be satisfied. The more a person has, the more he desires. Therefore the eye outweighs gold and silver. But as soon as a person dies and earth is thrown over him, he has enough. So with a little earth thrown on the eye, you overcome its power.

'You, Alexander, can see for yourself. Not satisfied with all the worlds you have conquered, you would even enter where are God's children and servants. While you live there is no contentment in you and you have no rest. I tell you that of a certainty you will shortly die in a foreign land. And when earth is scattered over you, you will be satisfied with four ells of earth —you, for whom the whole world was too small.

'And be warned, O Alexander. Ask no more and move no farther, for you will receive no other answer. Go speedily from hence lest what befell your other ships and men may not befall you.'

So the king sailed away in his ship to the land of India and not long after died a terrible death, for he was poisoned—as you may learn in the story of his life written by his teacher Aristotle.

There are many people who are very keen on making money and are never satisfied so that much evil comes of it. Yet it does not do to be too easy either, for a man should not spend his money on unnecessary things, for the groschen that is honestly earned is hard to come by. One must know that there is moderation in all things, and learn how to conduct oneself.

There is an ordinary proverb for this: 'Stinginess does not enrich; charity does not impoverish.' Every thing has its own time when to spend and when to save. The Hollander says,

'Chelt autzucheben in siner tid, dat makt profit' (Money spent in time brings profit). One finds gentile wise men who have written quite nicely on these things.

This then (*i.e.*, the child's illness) was the first storm that I suffered here. But—God have mercy—it did not stop at that! It went with me as with him who wished to run from the angel of death, to Lus, where people do not die. When in advanced old age he stood outside the gate, the angel of death said to him, 'You have come right into my hands, so that I can kill you: I have power over you only here.' That is how, unfortunately, things went with me. I came from Hamburg, my native town, away from children and friends, thinking that if I went so far from them I would see no evil of them. But, O God, you have shown me and show me still, that I could not fly from the measure of your wrath. Where shall I go and where shall I escape your face? I see well that I have come to a place where I shall have little joy and little satisfaction, but must bear much sorrow and hear unpleasantness of my dear children and myself. Despite all this, I acknowledge God as a righteous judge; and may He grant me patience that despite my sorrows and punishments I may still hold my own with people. God's punishment could have been worse, as the physician declared in my tale already mentioned.

Not long after I received the tragic news that my son, Reb Leib Segal, peace unto him, had died [1701]. He was a young man, not yet twenty-eight years of age. Though I had suffered so many troubles and such misery through him, his death was a heavy and bitter blow to me, as is natural with parents. One can learn this from pious King David's grief over the death of Absalom, who did evil and caused him such heartache. When he was going forth to battle against him, he begged his followers to spare Absalom. And when he learnt he had lost his life, he mourned deeply and cried seven times, 'Absalom, my son!' By this means he saved him from seven degrees of hell, and so brought him to the Garden of Eden.

I forgive my son everything from the bottom of my heart, all the foolish things he did. He was the best natured person in the whole world, but allowed himself to be led astray. He studied Talmud well and had a Jewish heart for the sufferings of the poor, so that his charity was renowned near and far.

Unfortunately he was too easy in business and wicked people saw this and brought about his ruin. I will let him rest and shall pray to God that he may enjoy the merits of his forefathers. What else can I do? I will go to him when God wills, but not he to me. It did not suit the Lord to take me before my devout, noble husband Chaim Hameln, who, at his age, should have lived many more years. But because of the evil to come, the righteous are taken. He, peace unto him, died in great riches and saw that all his children were comfortably secured. But what more to relate of this?

I have mentioned enough already. So I shall end my sixth book here. May God Almighty send no more troubles on all mine and on all Israel as are due to sinful people. May He in His mercy forgive us and lead us to the Holy Land, that our eyes may see again the rebuilding of the Temple and the atonement of all our sins. As it is written, 'And I will sprinkle upon you clean water.'[1]

[1] Ezek. 36: 25.

37. *Samuel Oppenheimer* (1635–1703), *Court Jew and Banker under Emperor Leopold I of Austria*. Engraving by Engelbrecht and Pfeffel, Vienna

38. *Silver Chanukah Lamp.* German, late 17th Century

39. *Betrothal Rings (Gold).* German, 16–17th Century

BOOK VII

HERE, with the help of the Lord, I will begin my seventh book, which will be partly of sorrow and partly of joy, as is the way of the world. May it be granted that no further sorrows befall my dear children and that in my old age I may only hear and see joy and their prosperity.

As I have already related, I had taken an everlasting farewell of my son Reb Zanvil. God have mercy, that such a young man should have to chew the black earth! I had not been in Metz two years when the tragic news of his death reached me. The deep sorrow and heartache this was to me, only God knows. To lose so beloved a son, of such tender years. Can there be greater grief? Not long after his death his wife gave birth to a daughter, who, God be praised, is a beautiful, healthy child. May we live to see joy of her on every side. She is now about thirteen years of age[1] and is said to be an excellent child. She is with her grandfather, Reb Moses Bamberg. Zanvil's wife married again, but she did not have her second husband long, for he, too, died. So the good, young woman lived miserably from her youth till now. But 'Who shall say: What doest Thou?' I cannot relate more of this, for it grieves my heart too much.

I expected to live here in comfort, as indeed the first year promised. If my husband had been able to stand another two years his business would have been saved, for two years after he had given everything to his creditors, business was so good in France that the whole Community became wealthy. My husband was a very clever man and a great businessman, well liked by Jew and gentile. But God would not have it so, and his creditors pressed him sorely so that he, peace unto him, had to go out of business and leave everything to them. Although they did not get back half of what he owed them, yet they dealt kindly with him, for they could have had him imprisoned. Although according to my marriage settlement a sum was due to me, I saw that there was nothing to be had. He had my daughter Miriam's money in hand, but this I got back from him in bills on other sons of Israel. God knows how distasteful

[1] This last book was therefore begun in the year 1715 approximately.

N

and burdensome this was to me! He also owed a few thousand reichstaler to my son Nathan. I also saw that this amount, too, was recovered. Therefore I could not think of my own marriage settlement and so resigned myself to all that the Lord had sent and done, like the eagle who took his children on his wing, saying, 'It is better that I and not my children should be shot.' How great were my troubles! My husband went into hiding. When the creditors heard of this they sent three bailiffs to the house: they made an inventory of everything and wrote down even the nail on the wall. Everything was sealed so that I was not left with enough for one meal even. I and my maid lived in one room. The three bailiffs remained and were the masters; no one could go in or out. On one occasion when I wished to go out during the day they searched me to see if I had anything hidden on me. In this miserable state we lived three weeks.

At length my husband made a settlement with his creditors. They made a list of everything we had and left all with him so that he could put the lot up for public sale. There was not even a tin spoon in the house that was not noted down, so he could not hide anything. He himself did not want to hide anything, for he thanked God that he had come out of it with his life. When his creditors saw that he had given them everything he had, though this came to less than half he owed, they had pity on him. They remained on friendly terms and did not press him too much, though they could have had him imprisoned. He was a worthy man and in prosperity had been loved and respected by all. For thirty years he had been *parnass* and *shtadlan*[1] in Metz, and had done everything in lavish style and was universally loved. Unfortunately, when this befell us, everything went so ill with us that really we often had no bread in the house. When, a few years ago, there was a great scarcity here, sometimes I bought with the little money of my own which I still had what was necessary for the house. As soon as he got any money he returned me mine again.

My son-in-law Moses Krumbach did much for him, though he had lost 2000 reichstaler through him. The Lord rewarded

[1] Mediator on behalf of his fellow-Jews. A peculiar office, honorary and exacting, which entailed diplomacy and perseverance in approaches to governments and kings on behalf of Jewish subjects with the object of alleviating their hardships.

him so that he is the wealthiest man in the Community, an upright man. He received a new heart so that he does much good
to the family on both sides, his own and Esther's. His door is
wide open to the poor, and he is now *parnass* of the Community.
Distinguished strangers from the four corners of the earth stay
with him and he honours everyone, as also does my daughter,
his wife. In short, they both have kind hearts and much goodness flows from their house. God reward them and their children that they may live a hundred years in wealth, honour and
good health.

On New Moon's day, Sivan, 5472 (1712), my grandson Elia
was betrothed and the marriage was arranged for Sivan 5476
[1716]—may it be for good, for the bride and bridegroom are
still very young. God prolong their days and years. Together
with presents they will have jointly not more than 30,000
reichstaler. May they be granted luck and blessings.

And now to write again about my pious husband, the remembrance of the righteous for a blessing. He could not get
used to his miserable state, and his children were not then in a
position to help him much. Still, they did as much as they
could. His son, Rabbi Samuel, was a great Talmud scholar,
very clever and thoroughly capable in every way. He had
studied a good time in Poland where he had obtained the title
'Morenu'.[1] He returned a few years before I came to Metz and
I found him settled in his own house.

My husband, of blessed memory, and the rich, pious *parnass*
Reb Abraham Krumbach, his father-in-law, had supported
Rabbi Samuel so that he could continue his studies. They
helped him so far, it seems to me, that through both their
influence my stepson became Chief Rabbi of Alsace, which position he filled wisely and well. He was liked by all, but a handful cannot satisfy a lion: his salary was not enough for the needs
of his household. Both Rabbi Samuel and his wife, Rebbitzin
Genendel, came of wealthy families, households that lived in
very grand style and did much good. They wished to continue in the manner in which they had been brought up, but
the position of rabbi could not allow of this. So Rabbi Samuel
engaged himself to the Duke of Lorraine, who then held his
court in Lunéville, for there was war at that time between the

[1] See footnote on p. 18.

King of France and the Emperor and his allies. These I do not
need to name as everyone knows who they were.

At that time Rabbi Samuel took over the mint of the Duke
which needed a large capital to run—more than Samuel himself could supply. Six months before he took over the mint he
had opened a shop. This also demanded large capital, for the
Duke and his court bought everything from him, for he had
found grace in the eyes of the Duke and his advisers. He was
really the sort of person who finds grace in the sight of God and
man. As Rabbi Samuel alone could not conduct the shop in
the style that it had to be carried on, he took into business his
two brothers-in-law who lived in Metz. One was Reb Jesse
Willstadt, a distinguished member of the Community, who was
wed to Samuel's sister, and the other, Jacob Krumbach, the
brother of his wife and my son-in-law Moses, an upright man.

These three men left their fine houses in the *Judengasse* [Jews'
Quarter] and moved to Lunéville. There they went into partnership with Rabbi Samuel and had in their store big rolls of
material which sold well. They had other business also, so that
they did well there. It was after this that Rabbi Samuel
obtained the mint and though there was not so much profit to
be made out of it, still the turnover was large, so that there
were handsome returns. When they undertook to mint the
coinage Rabbi Samuel wrote to his father. But this business did
not appeal to my husband, for he, peace unto him, was a clever
man and knew from its nature that no good could come of the
undertaking, especially as the French king would not tolerate
such a thing. Metz lies close by Lunéville, not more than a
day's journey away, and the money had to be circulated here.
My husband considered the whole matter like an experienced
man of business, and advised him on every point: how much
capital the business needed and what the risks were. But the
three partners were young men and keen on business. They
signed a contract with the Duke to supply large quantities of
silver, the payment to be given in the different minted coins.
All went well for a time, but, as will follow, the result was not
a happy one, for some of the coins were not up to standard, and
this was the cause of Rabbi Samuel's downfall.

For six months the three partners conducted their business,
the shop, and besides dealt in bills, as is usual with Jews. At

that time there lived here a householder, Moses Rothschild by name; he was rich and had, for many years, done business in Lorraine, where he was well known to influential people and merchants. When he heard what good business Rabbi Samuel and his partners were doing, he and his son, who was son-in-law of Rabbi Samuel, moved to the same town. Moses Rothschild had obtained permission through the Duke's council and settled not far from Lunéville, for he too had influence with the Duke and his advisers. And soon this Moses Rothschild too engaged himself to supply the mint with silver. For a while they were all satisfied with their business. Rabbi Samuel did much good to his father, my husband, so that he was short of nothing. The money was sent on here; sometimes it was held back here before being returned; sometimes they did not receive it back. Meanwhile my husband was very worried, for he saw that thereby was much risk and danger. He often wrote to his son, warning him of this. But it was of no use, for what had passed could not be changed.

The war between the King of France and the Emperor raged more fiercely, and the former issued a prohibiting order: Lorraine money was not to be taken in or out of France. This order he sent through his great minister to Herr Latandy, to have read out aloud to the Jewish Community here. The order named the five partners who had moved from here to Lorraine and further stated: if they wished to remain in Lorraine, well and good, but in that event they must nevermore set foot on French soil under pain of heavy penalties. They had the choice of returning to Metz and taking up residence again or of remaining where they were. They were given a few months in which to make up their minds. When the partners learnt of this decree they were very much alarmed. They did not know what choice to make, for they each had valuable houses here and were not willing to give up their rights of residence. On the other hand, they were bound, under great fines for breach of contract, to the Duke and his mint. Things were bad for them. The King also ordered that, if the Sons of Israel remained in Lorraine, the Community must record it in their books that they had no rights of residence in Metz.

The time drew near in which they had to give their decision. Jesse Willstadt was the first who decided to return; Jacob

Krumbach followed him. I do not know how they settled with the Duke. The goods in the shop were shared out, and each came with wife, children, and all their possessions to his own house in Metz. But Rabbi Samuel, Moses Rothschild and his son decided to remain where they were. This hurt my husband, and he took it so very much to heart that he could no longer withstand his troubles and afflictions. Besides this, he was not very strong and suffered from gout, which, added to his other burdens, laid him low.

Although his son Rabbi Samuel allowed him to suffer no want, sending him everything he needed, and even giving orders to his agents in Metz that his father should be given whatever he wanted, nothing helped. Rabbi Samuel sent him a renowned physician to cure him; he remained several days, and tried many cures, but he said straightway that he was already a dead man, and this soon showed itself to be the case. For the Holy One took him to Himself and to Eternity, and of a certainty he is a son of the Future World. For many years he was head of the community for which he sacrificed his life. Much can be written of him, but I do not find it necessary. He is gone to his rest, leaving me in misery and woe. I received little money from my marriage settlement, not a third of what was due to me. Afterwards—what was I to do? I relied entirely upon the Lord.

At that time I lived in Reb Jesse Willstadt's house, which was formerly my husband's, and thought I could remain in it as long as I lived, for Reb Jesse had promised me this. But when my husband died, and Jesse returned here with his family and furniture, I had to leave my house, and did not know where I should go. I could not be with my son-in-law, Moses Krumbach, for he had not yet rebuilt his house[1] as he has now done. I was very much troubled. At length a man of the name of Jacob Marburg built a little room for me in which there was no oven or chimney. I made a condition that I could cook in his kitchen, and also come into his winter room. If I wished to go to my room at any time, or when I went to bed, I had to climb twenty-two steps, which meant a great effort to me, so that for most times I was ailing.

[1] There is a MS. in the Bodleian which deals with the lawsuit concerning the party wall, the cause of the delay in the rebuilding of the house.

On one occasion when I was ill, it was in Tebet 5475 [January 1715] my son-in-law Moses paid me a visit, and told me that I must move to his house; he would give me a room on the ground floor, so that I need no longer climb any high steps. I refused this for various reasons, as I never wished to live with any of my children, but at length I could no longer hold out against this. That year there was a great scarcity in the town, and as I had a maid with me, which cost more community expense,[1] I gave in to what I had long refused, and moved to my daughter's house. This was about the middle of the month of Iyar 5475 [May 1715], and I am writing this in the middle of Tammuz of the same year [about July]. My son-in-law and daughter, long may they live, and the children, God protect them, were very pleased to have me. Shall I write in what esteem I am held by them? I could not write enough of it. May God reward them for it! They pay me all the honour in the world; the best is first given to me from the dish, more than I desire or need. My only fear is that this will be reckoned off by the Lord from my rewards in the Future World. If I am not present at the midday meal—for the meal is punctually at 12 o'clock, and about this time psalms are chanted for an hour or so in the synagogue for the soul of my son-in-law's pious mother, the dead Mistress Jachet, an old custom which will perhaps last till the Messiah comes—when I return home I find my food, three or four different dishes, with all possible titbits, such as do not behove me at my age. I often say to my daughter, 'Leave just a little for me.' But she answers me, 'I do not cook any more or less because of you.' In truth, I have been in many communities, but I have never seen such housekeeping. Everything is given with a free hand to each of the family, as well as to billet-holders[2] and to invited guests. May the Almighty enable her to continue thus till her hundredth year—in joy and health, in wealth and honour.

Shall I write of what happens here, and if the Community follows pious paths? I cannot say more than that when I first came here there was already an admirable Community, very

---

[1] This was probably a communal tax on servants.

[2] These were poor Jews who, passing through the towns, and forced to remain until after the Sabbath or any festival, were given billets by the *parnassim* to different households where they were provided with meals.

devout, with a fine communal hall. The *parnassim* were up-right, worthy old men who lent lustre to the place. At that time there was not a *parnass* who wore a peruke, and it was unknown for a Jew to go to law outside the *Judengasse*, to the gentile courts. If there were sometimes quarrels, as is usual among Jews, they were all hushed up and settled in the Community by the *Dayanim*. People were not so haughty then as now, nor so used to such costly food. They had their children taught and had the foremost rabbis as leaders. In my time the renowned, learned Rabbi Gabriel Eskeles was head of the Talmud school: I do not need to write of his piety and honesty, for it is known to the whole world or even mention a half or tenth part of his great superiority. His son married the daughter of the eminent and rich Samson Wertheimer of Vienna. The dowry and presents amounted to more than 30,000 reichstaler. Rabbi Gabriel, his wife, his son Leib, and the bridegroom, Rabbi Berish, went to Vienna, where the marriage was celebrated with so much pomp that never before had there been such glory among Jews. More I cannot dwell on this, for I cannot write of it in full detail. It was world-renowned.

The learned Rabbi Gabriel had received permission to be away a year, though no one here believed he would be absent for so long. But the one year grew to nearly three. When the year was ended, the congregation wrote to him, with the ut-most respect and politeness, asking him to return and take on again the rabbinate here, for the Community was like sheep without a shepherd. They could not be without their rabbi, although there were among them highly respected and wise men well versed in Torah, especially the old Gaon Rabbi Aaron Worms, a very great scholar, who had been many years a rabbi in Mannheim and surrounding parts, and also in Alsace.

This Rabbi Aaron was related through marriage to the son-in-law of Rabbi Gabriel; his daughter married the son of Rabbi Aaron, who was then rabbi in Alsace. Thus he joined the side that held that Rabbi Gabriel would return. He was ex-ceedingly clever, in worldly as well as in heavenly things, and his words were listened to. The congregation allowed itself to be quietened for a while. But at length it became known that Rabbi Gabriel had been nominated rabbi in Nikolsburg. There is much to write of the quarrels that ensued. Rabbi Gabriel's son returned here and sought to persuade the leaders of the Community to wait a little longer. But when they learned that he had been nominated in Nikolsburg, the leaders, with the agreement of the majority of the members, decided to take another rabbi. Then ensued the most bitter disputes between the two parties, the followers of Rabbi Gabriel and Rabbi Aaron and those who wanted a new rabbi. At length the leaders of the Community with a majority of members agreed, under penalty of a great sum, to elect another rabbi, as their own rabbi had not returned. They sent a contract, drawn up in proper form by special messenger to the learned Chief Rabbi of Prague, Rabbi Abraham Broda. After a few points had been altered in the contract, to which the leaders agreed, he wrote that he would come. I do not know if the worthy Rabbi Gabriel got to hear of this, or if he desired to return to his congregation; but he came here, thinking to regain his position through his supporters. I dare not write of what went on here! The quarrels that ensued! May God forgive each his sins. It is not fitting that I, an ordinary, weak woman, interfere between two such lofty mountains. God pardon each, on either side. A book could be written of all that each party did to obtain its own end. May the piety and deeds of both learned men be merited to us. When Rabbi Gabriel saw after a time that he received no salary, and that the leaders did not intend to go back on the step they had taken, he went away again, much honoured. No one in the Community was an enemy to him. They were all his friends and loved him, but could not go back on the contract they had made with the Rabbi of Prague.

I will restrain my pen and only write that Rabbi Abraham arrived here in peace. I need not write with what honour he was met, for it is well known. A house was built for his use, a *cheder* and special *yeshiva* for his Talmud study, which has not, as far as I know, been done anywhere else. All lived in great harmony with him, even those who before his arrival had opposed him. His person, great learning and good deeds are well known. He had no other desire but to study day and night and to spread the Torah in Israel. Children who had never been taught before, he took and taught so well that they were really well educated. What more to write of this, for his knowledge of Torah is well known. Unfortunately our joy did not last long, for the great scholar was appointed rabbi to Frankfurt. Although the leaders pressed him very much to remain, and wanted to give him all that his heart desired, he would not agree to remain. Since the great scholar departed we have had very bad times in wealth and health. Many fine young wives, of whom no one had ever heard any evil, died, most unfortunately. There was much misery. May God be merciful and lift His anger from us and all Israel. Amen! and Amen!

I cannot refrain from mentioning what happened on the Sabbath of the Feast of Weeks in the year 5475 [1715], when we were in synagogue. The reader and cantor, Rabbi Jokel of Rzeszow in Poland, had begun to intone the morning prayer 'O Lord, creator of lights,' in his sweet voice. Before he had reached the blessing, many people heard the sound as of something breaking. The women in the upper gallery thought the arch of the roof would fall in on them. The rumbling sound grew louder, just as though stones were falling. The alarm was very great; the women in the upper gallery rushed to get out, each wanting to be the first to save her life. One shouted this, another that. Some thought that the noise came from the men's part, and grew frightened, thinking that gentiles were attacking the synagogue. Each rushed to save herself and her husband and with such force that the stairs were crammed with people who had fallen, and others, rushing down, began to stamp one another to death with the shoes they wore. Within half an hour six women were killed and thirty injured, some subsequently dying, while others had to be attended by the barber-surgeons.

If each had gone down quietly, one by one, nothing would have happened. An old blind woman who was also up in the gallery had remained seated because she could not run. Nothing happened to her and she returned home safely.

The terror of what happened cannot be described. The women who were saved came out of the crush with heads uncovered[1] and clothes torn from their bodies. Many women who had remained seated told me that they, too, had wished to rush out but it was impossible to get out. So they returned to their seats saying, 'If we must die, we would sooner remain and die in the synagogue than be squeezed to death on the stairs.'

[1] All married women wore head coverings.

More than fifty women lay on the stairs, wedged together as though stuck with pitch; living and dead lying under one another.

The men came running up together, each to save his own; but only with great labour, and slowly, were the women taken off one another. The men rendered great help; there were many citizens, gentiles came into the *Judengasse* with ladders and hooks to bring the women down from the top gallery, for no one knew what was happening there. The men had heard the noise of the rumbling at the same time as the women and had also thought that the roof-arch was falling in on them; that was why they had called to the women to hasten down, and why they pushed so, falling on one another.

You can imagine the lament that went up when the six dead women were dragged out from under the living. An hour before they had been hale and well. May the Lord be merciful and turn His wrath from us and all Israel.

The women in the lower gallery lay also in the crush. I, Mother, sat in my seat in the lower gallery, praying, when I heard the sound of running and asked what it meant. My neighbour thought that a woman near her time had been taken ill. I grew alarmed, for my daughter Esther, who sat eight seats from me, was near her time. I went to her in the crush, as she was trying to push her way out, and said to her, 'Where are you going?' She answered, 'The roof is falling in!' I held her before me and sought with my arms to push a way and get her out, but there were five or six steps to descend. When my daughter reached the bottom step I fell and knew nothing more. I could neither move nor call for help. The men who went to rescue the women of the top gallery had to pass the place where I lay. A second later, I would have been trampled to death, but the men saw me and lifted me up so that I was able to get out into the street. There I began to scream, demanding where was my daughter Esther? I was told that she was in her house. I sent someone to see if she was there, but the answer came that she was not. I rushed about like one who had taken leave of her senses. My daughter Miriam came running to me, relieved and happy to see me. I asked her, 'Where is my daughter Esther?' 'In the house of her brother-in-law Reuben,' she answered, 'not far from the synagogue.'

I ran quickly to the house of Reuben Krumbach and there found Esther sitting without frock or head-covering. Men and women stood about her, to revive her from her swoon. I thank God that He helped her and that no harm came to her child. May He turn His wrath from us and all Israel and protect us from such evil misfortune.

Later, people went up to the top gallery to see whether any part of the arch or the building had fallen in. Nothing was out of order and we do not know whence the evil fortune came. We can only put it down to our sins! Woe to us that such should have come to pass in our day, and that we should hear and be burdened with such heaviness of heart. The verse 'I will bring fear into your hearts' was confirmed. 'Therefore is our heart faint, for these things our eyes are dim,' because of this desecration of the Sabbath and holydays and the disturbance of prayer. As the Prophet says, 'Who hath required this at your hand, to trample My courts?' This holyday, when our Holy Law was given to us, and God chose us from among all peoples and tongues, if we had merited it, we would have rejoiced in the Giving of the Torah and the Holy Commandments. But now, 'we are a reproach to our neighbours, a mockery to those around us,' just as if the Temple was destroyed in our own days.

Most of the poor women killed were young and one was pregnant. They went to their everlasting rest leaving grief, heartache and sighing our portion. The day after the festival the members of the *Chevra Kadisha*[1] went to the House of Life[2] early in the morning. The six women were buried in a row, close to one another. Now it rests with each of us to examine his sins according to his deeds. God is righteous and will show mercy and forgive us sinners. He will not blot us out; He will not waken His wrath, but will say to the Angel of Destruction, 'Draw back your hand!' Grant our request, O owner of mercy. Guard our going out and our coming in now and evermore. Let there be no more breach or lamenting in our street or among our brethren in Israel. Amen.

Much has already been said about this misfortune, but who

---

[1] An association of pious members of the community who attend to all the rites and the last offices connected with laying out the corpse and burial.

[2] Euphemistic term for a cemetery.

can write or believe everything? Yet I, Mother, will write what Esther, wife of Jacob our present teacher told me. This woman and her child, a boy of five, sat on the highest step of the women's gallery, when all this began. She saw six very tall women with short head-veils; they pushed her down the steps. She shouted, 'Do you want to kill me and my child?' They set the child in a corner and went on their way. It was at this very moment that the noise and confusion began and the women came rushing down from the top gallery. But she and her child were saved.

My son-in-law, the *parnass*, called to the women who remained and asked why they did not come down? The poor things shouted back that they were afraid that the stairs would break under them. The steps were quite sound; their fear made them imagine this. Esther and her child were rescued after much trouble. She was more dead than alive, and as a result miscarried and had so many injuries that she was attended by the barber-surgeon more than three months.

I, Mother, have just spoken with this woman. She swore to me that it happened just as she related. Her husband and parents confirmed all that she said. Many distinguished people and scholars called on her and she told them this on oath. She, her husband and parents are honest folk of whom no one has heard falsehood or any evil.

Further, one night shortly before all this happened, the wife of the rich Jacob Krumbach, whose house is close by the synagogue, heard a noise in the synagogue as though thieves had broken in, and were taking everything out, and the candelabra were falling down. She woke her husband and said, 'Don't you hear a noise in the synagogue? There must be thieves inside taking everything away!' They sent for the beadle, who unlocked the synagogue, but there was 'no voice and no answer'. Not a single object was moved from its place. No one knows whence this misfortune came.

The tumult was great. The women thought that the men's section was falling, while the men, in turn, thought that it was the women's gallery. That was why they shouted to them to get out. Most of them heard the noise as of a thunder-clap, as though a gun was fired. Others, on the other hand, amongst whom I was, heard nothing. The cantor, Reb Jokel, went home in the middle of the prayer, and another cantor took his place, but sang little or nothing at all.

A number of devout women together hired ten Talmud scholars to go to synagogue every morning at 9 to recite psalms and study Talmud for the sake of the orphans who had to say Kaddish. May the souls of those killed be received with grace and may their lives, so sadly lost, be an atonement for all their sins, and their souls be bound in life and the Garden of Eden. May they forgive those who, by trampling on them, were partly guilty of their deaths.

I would not have written of this in my book, only it was an occurrence that had never happened before, and, I hope, never will again. I would that everyone, man, woman, youth and girl, might take this to heart and pray to God that such a punishment should not again be visited on any Jewish child. May He redeem us from this long exile. Amen! and Amen!

I cannot, unfortunately, put it down to anything else but the disgraceful happenings on the Rejoicing of the Law festival in 5475 [1715]. As usual, all the Scrolls of the Law had been taken from the Holy Ark and seven placed on the desk when a brawl began among the women. In the fray they tore one another's head-coverings from their heads so that they stood bare-headed in the synagogue! Then the men began to quarrel and fight one another. Though the great Rabbi Abraham Broda in a loud voice threatened them with excommunication, to make them keep their peace and not desecrate the festival, it was of no use. The rabbi and the *parnass* left the synagogue quickly to arrange what each one's fines should be.

In Nissan 5479 [March 1719] a woman was on the bank of the Moselle, scouring dishes. About 10 o'clock at night it began to grow light as day and she looked into the sky which was open like a . . . [1] and sparks leaped from it and afterwards the heavens came together again as though a curtain had been drawn across and it was again dark. May God grant that this is a sign for good. Amen!

THE END

[1] A word is illegible here in the original manuscript. A note by Glückel's grandson Chaim, son of Joseph Hameln, physician in Frankfurt-on-Main, written Kislev 13, 5560 (December 1800), states that the word was rubbed away, and so indecipherable.

INDEX

INDEX OF PLACES

INDEX

The names of Glückel and her husband Chaim Segal of Hameln, so continuously mentioned, particularly in the earlier books, are not listed. For fairs, towns and other places see Index of Places.

o

CPSIA information can be obtained
at www.ICGtesting.com
Printed in the USA
LVHW041804250220
648170LV00006B/776